A note from the publisher of **DRY GUILLOTINE**

René Belbenoit was sent to Devil's Island off the coast of French Guiana in 1921, when he was twenty-one years old. Sixteen years later, he emerged from the jungle after one of the most harrowing and dramatic escapes ever attempted. At thirty-eight, he was mortally ema-ciated, almost blind, toothless, scurvy eaten and fever wrecked as a result of the inhuman treatment he had received and time spent hacking through vicious virgin jungles. He had one possession with him when he made his way to the United States in 1937—an oilskin-wrapped manuscript describing his incredible escape through Central and South America and the years spent in hell on Devil's Island, the Iles Royale, Saint Joseph and Cayenne.

This manuscript became the classic indictment of man's inhumanity to man, the all-time bestselling true adven-ture story, **DRY GUILLOTINE.**

Another prisoner of Devil's Island has made his escape now, and turned it into literature—the notorious "Pa-pillon," whose recently published book has prompted the reissue of René Belbenoit's classic at this time. **DRY GUILLOTINE,** the first documented story of such an es-cape—one man's lone victory over brutality and oppres-sion—will live as long as men cry out for justice.

D1603323

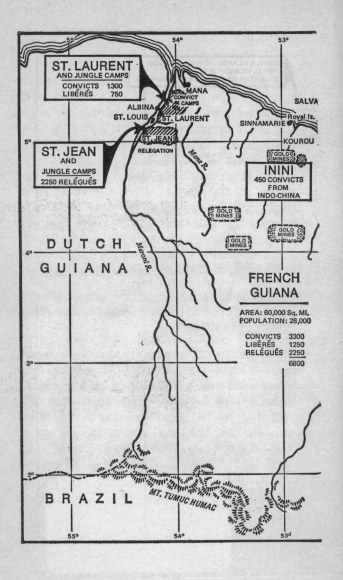

ST. LAURENT
AND JUNGLE CAMPS

CONVICTS 1300
LIBÉRÉS 750

ST. JEAN
AND
JUNGLE CAMPS
2250 RELÉGUÉS

MANA
CONVICT
CAMPS

ALBINA
ST. LOUIS ST. LAURENT

ST. JEAN
RELEGATION

55°   54°   53°

SALVA

Royal Is.

SINNAMARIE

KOUROU

GOLD
MINES

ININI
450 CONVICTS
FROM
INDO-CHINA

Mana R.

GOLD
MINES

GOLD
MINES

GOLD
MINES

DUTCH

GUIANA

Maroni R.

FRENCH
GUIANA

AREA: 60,000 Sq. MI.
POPULATION: 28,000

CONVICTS   3300
LIBÉRÉS   1250
RELÉGUÉS   2250
            6800

BRAZIL   MT. TUMUC HUMAC

55°   54°   53°

DEVIL'S ISLAND: 7 Political Convicts
ROYAL ISLAND: 325 Convicts
ST. JOSEPH ISL.:   375 Solitary Confinement

...TION ISL.

Devil's Isl.

St. Joseph Isl.

CAYENNE

CAYENNE
800 CONVICTS
500 LIBÉRÉS

× ×
× ×
CONVICTS

Kourou R.

Approurgue R.

Oyapoc R.

A T L A N T I C
O C E A N

B R A Z I L

To Amazon River →

0   25   50
Scale in Miles

52°

51°

50°

5°

4°

3°

2°

DRY GUILLOTINE

Fifteen Years among the Living Dead

by René Belbenoit

Prisoner #46635

The text in this volume is based
on the original translation from
the French by Preston Rambo

With an Introduction by William La Varre

BANTAM BOOKS

TORONTO · NEW YORK · LONDON

A NATIONAL GENERAL COMPANY

DRY GUILLOTINE

*A Bantam Book / published by arrangement with
E. P. Dutton & Co., Inc.*

PRINTING HISTORY

E. P. Dutton edition published 1938

Bantam edition published under the title
I Escaped from Devil's Island *July 1949*
2nd printing ...... August 1949
3rd printing ..... October 1949
New Bantam edition published February 1971

Introduction

To THE island of Trinidad, washed up on the tail end of a Caribbean hurricane, had come a slender waterlogged Indian canoe. In it, the *Trinidad Guardian* said, were six starved and almost drowned Frenchmen—fugitives who had, after seventeen days on the tossing sea, successfully escaped from Devil's Island and the penal colony of French Guiana.

Out of curiosity several British colonists and I went down to the military barracks to see the fugitives. They were not under arrest; there is something of the sportsman in every real Englishman no matter how far away he is from home, and the Officer-of-the-Port voiced the thoughts of everyone (but the French Consul) when he said: "I am not going to turn these poor men over to the French Consul. Let him tear his hair all he wants! French Guiana is a plague on the face of civilization. We will feed the fugitives, give them a place to rest, give them a better boat and give them a chance to continue their escape!"

In a large comfortable room six men greeted us with an eagerness to smile that was pathetic. Five of them were big, tremendously powerful men—they might have been prize fighters, Canadian lumberjacks, soldiers of the Foreign Legion. They were men of brute strength, brute living, and brute mentality. The sixth man, in contrast, was astoundingly little, less than five feet, very thin, and weighing under ninety pounds. But he had fire in his eyes, fire fanned, as I was to learn, by fifteen years of living death, by four previous attempts to escape and now by an almost fanatical decision to either make good his fifth attempt or die.

He had with him only one possession, an oil cloth covered package which contained over thirty pounds of closely written manuscript—the detailed record of fifteen years of prison colony life; the most amazing document of biography, of crime and of punishment which I had ever seen.

After I had read many chapters I began talking with him. I wanted to learn something of his earlier history. Born in Paris on April 4, 1899, René Belbenoit was at twenty-one years of age en route to a lifelong exile in the most notorious prison colony the civilized world has ever known. But I was impressed by the fact that he didn't fit any picture I could sum up in my mind of what a criminal, a Devil's Island convict would, or should, be like. Step by step I traced his history, his boyhood, looking for the place where the downward path into his personal hell had begun.

Some children grow up into successful men, some into failures. Why? *Papa* Belbenoit, who married quite late in life, was a good man—a very good man, René Belbenoit told me, who took great pride in his position, won after many years, of Chief Conductor of the Paris-Orleans Express. Three months after baby René was born the young wife deserted husband and child and went to Russia as a tutor to the children of the Czar's family. She thought René's father very unambitious because he refused to accept a promotion which would have taken him from the train which he loved, and the adventure of moving it like clockwork back and forth over the rails. *Papa* Belbenoit did not want any further promotion, did not want to sit in a superintendent's office, and the mother, young, ambitious and dogmatic, left home—for the Russian Court.

Papa Belbenoit was on his train four days each week and young René was entrusted to his grandparents who owned a small restaurant near the railroad station. Until he was twelve years old René was just another good little French boy. He went to school, studied hard and stood at the head of many of his classes. But when he was twelve years old his grandfather and grandmother died. His grandmother died one day, and five days later his grandfather died. Everyone said that the old man loved his wife so much that life oozed quickly out of him as soon as she was not with him any longer.

Four days out of each week the growing boy from then on had no guardian to regiment his life, until an uncle moved to Paris and became manager of a night club, the *Café du Rat Mort* (the Dead Rat) in the Place Pigalle which was to become very famous. The uncle took René to live with him in his apartment over the restaurant. During the late afternoons and evenings, young Belbenoit worked as messenger and errand boy. He was only thirteen years old but he must have been very resourceful. The *Rat Mort* was patronized by women of the theatre and of the *demimonde,* women clad in expensive clothes, and displaying large amounts of jewelry. Montmartre was the great center of Parisian merry-making. The most notorious playboys of Europe were among his uncle's customers as well as the most desired and highly prized women. The beautiful Otero, "Queen of Paris," visited the night club every night. Prince Murat gave Belbenoit a 100 franc note as a tip —merely for delivering a love message to her and getting an answer. Mistinguette, Baron Maurice de Rothschild, the Prince of Wales and many other colorful men and women gathered at the *Rat Mort,* spent money lavishly, and before long René Belbenoit was receiving more money in tips during a week than his father made in salary in three months.

"I had never seen so much money!" Belbenoit told me. "So much careless spending! All the people I had known, all the people my father, grandfather and grandmother had known, worked very hard for money, spent it frugally. Money was something which they struggled to obtain, and went without many nice things in order to save. At thirteen years of age I looked thus into another and different world—an amazing society in which people did no work, had all the money they wanted, denied themselves nothing, spent money furiously, lived in a realm of champagne, silks, perfumes, jewelry and abandon which made me gasp with excitement."

Living at night that sort of life did not make of the youth a good student during the day. He was often sleepy. And when he was not sleepy he was quarrelling with the idea of continuing studies which, at best, would get him only an apprenticeship in the business world that would pay him but a fraction of the money he already was obtaining in the *Rat Mort*. When he was fifteen years old his uncle agreed with him. The successful assignments in which he had been engaged, the delivering of love messages and the arranging of trysting engagements between men and women, had much to do probably with the growing prosperity of the night club. Both playboys and women of the *demimonde* found the boy's services unusually efficient and successful.

But *Papa* Belbenoit was very angry when he found out about it. He wanted his son to get a good academic education and then a technical training; he wanted him, he said, to become a railroad man. Someday when he was too old to work he'd retire and turn the Paris-Orleans Express over to René. *Papa* Belbenoit and *L'Oncle* Belbenoit quarrelled violently and René did not see his father again for a long time.

Some patrons met at the *Rat Mort* during the day. They played games or bet on the races. René carried the money to the bookmakers and his commission when the horses won was considerable. One day a group of patrons announced that because of some secret information they were betting more money than usual on a very long shot—on a horse which would pay twenty to one if it won.

"It's like throwing money away," a friend of René's advised him as the boy was taking the package of money to the race track. "Don't be a fool! Put the money in your own pocket. Don't place it. That horse will surely fall down, or come in last—and the money will be yours instead of the bookmaker's!"

René counted the money. The bets amounted to two thousand, two hundred francs. It would be a shame to give all that money to the already rich betting agents. He pocketed the money and did not go near the race track.

Unfortunately the dark horse won. "I did not return to *Rat Mort* that night," Belbenoit said, "I would not have been able out of my savings to have paid off the bets at twenty to one and I didn't dare face my uncle and admit that I had not placed his patrons' bets but had deliberately kept the money. I walked the streets of Paris all night long trying to think of something I could do. Finally, toward dawn, I worked out a solution. I had failed to place the bets: that was dishonest. But I still had all the money that belonged to the patrons. I had enough savings of my own to pay them double the amounts they had bet. So I crept into the *Rat Mort* through a rear entrance. My uncle glared at me like a tiger when I tried to explain. He grabbed the money from my hand, beat me over the head with his fist. He struck me with a heavy bunch of keys. I ran from the blows, and from his voice calling me a thief, drugged with the disaster which so suddenly had befallen me."

It was a catastrophic day for the rest of the world too. Suddenly the streets of Paris became filled with anxiously reading and talking groups of people. "War!" a former schoolmate cried rushing up to young Belbenoit with a newspaper in his hand. "We're going to fight the Germans. War's been declared! My father has already gone to join the volunteers. Look!" he shouted, pointing down the street, "There's the place where the volunteers register. See how fast the line's growing!"

The schoolmates walked toward the hastily opened enlistment stall. And there, nearly at the head of the line, René saw his own father. He stood out from the other men, for his railroad uniform had been carefully pressed, the buttons, polished. He looked almost like a general. René went up to greet him and ask his forgiveness. He didn't know whether his father had heard about the unplaced bets but he was going to tell him and ask his forgiveness. He would promise to go back to school, study hard, and do as his father wished.

"Stand back from me!" *Papa* Belbenoit said as the boy held out his hand to take the gold-braided coat-sleeve. "Stand back, *thief!*"

"The men in the line all turned to look at me," Belbenoit remembered, "but my father kept his eyes straight ahead, his face frozen with grief and anger. I do not think that any of the volunteers realized that we were father and son. I walked away as fast as I could."

Two days later René Belbenoit stood in the balcony of a small hotel and watched the soldiers march through the street to the place where lorries would transport them up to the front. There at the head of a squad marched *Papa* Belbenoit. He was stiffly erect. His shoulders were back. His eyes were front. He was not the Chief of the Paris-Orleans Express any longer.

"I watched his back," Belbenoit told me softly, "until it was indistinguishable in the river of soldiers and then I was alone. I was very alone. I do not think that in all Paris, where many people were becoming lonely, there was a youth so lonely as I."

In less than a month René Belbenoit was a soldier too. "I was not eighteen years old," he told me, "but I stood up as tall as I could and puffed out my chest. The Sergeant was very eager for recruits and didn't look too deeply into my years. I was still another one who could fire a gun."

The French Army had a gun which was called a *fusil-mitraillieur*. It weighed thirty pounds, fired bullets in rapid succession from twenty circular barrels. In practice Belbenoit became unusually adept at using this weapon and on the replacement train which took new soldiers up to the madly fighting front Belbenoit was in command of a brand new *fusil-mitrailleur* with two assistants. One carried ammunition and half of the gun while the other recruit, a skilled mechanic old enough to be Belbenoit's father, carried the other half and stood by during firing to fix the mechanism whenever the gun jammed.

"The war," he said, "was terrible. But of course it was nothing to what I have since been through. My part in it was that of thousands of unknown soldiers, fighting as directed, charging ahead as commanded, scared to death most of the time of what might come out of the sky ahead of me, wondering when my time was coming. I tried not to look individually at the men I killed. I ran past them with my eyes averted. We went into Belgium and new replacements constantly took the place of those who had fallen. Outside of Roulers, which we were preparing to take from the Germans, I received my promotion. I became a Corporal of the 40th Regiment. Five hours later word reached us that the Armistice had been declared."

While with the Army of Occupation in Germany, Belbenoit saw on the bulletin board of the Cologne encampment a notice asking for volunteers for the Army of the East. He became a Sergeant in the 2nd Regiment of Tirailleurs, the Arab Regiment, and went to Syria. Then at Alexandretta, after the capture of the city of Aleppo, he became Top Sergeant of his company. In the middle of 1920 he became ill with fever and was sent back to France. Of the fourteen soldiers sent on the same ship only five lived to reach Marseilles.

He was sent to Percy hospital at Clamart, and while convalescing he met a young nurse—fell madly, head over heels, in love: Renée and René. They decided that as soon as he was demobilized he would get a job and they would marry. At the end of February, 1921, he was dismissed from the hospital. He went immediately to the demobilization barracks.

"In a military uniform," Belbenoit remembered, "almost any man can look impressive. Rich or poor, we all had the glamour of epaulets, brass buttons, tight fitting tunics. I prided myself on my own fine feathers—the uniform of a Top Sergeant of the African Army. A natty fez was perched on my head, three decorations were on my chest. Renée thought I looked very grand. Jauntily I reported to the authorities for official discharge. I took the three decorations from my uniform, wrapped them in paper and stuck them in the pocket of an ill fitting pair of gray pants which the Supply Sergeant issued to me. It was my *Abrami* suit, a present of the French Government to each soldier who hadn't died. The gray coat fitted me even worse than the pants. Pants and coat, the Sergeant said, cost fifty-two francs. If I didn't want them I could take the money instead. Many wealthy men took the fifty-two francs and used them for a champagne party. Tailors had made them plenty of good clothes. But I had no tailor and no money to spend on clothes. I took the *Abrami* suit."

Thus René Belbenoit, civilian, twenty-one years of age, walked again the streets of Paris. He spent the first night in a cheap hotel. Early the next day he began looking for a job. He signed his name to many application blanks, even though he was told that his would lie at the bottom of earlier stacks. He felt, when the day was over and he went out to the hospital to walk home with Renée, like a ragamuffin.

"I was disgusted at not having quickly found a job, and I was scared that Renée would look at me, in my *Abrami* suit, with different eyes—decide she'd made a bad bargain. But she didn't. She cheered me up. There were many returned soldiers looking for jobs, she said. I should be patient and everything would work out all right."

But ten days went by and there was no job. His money was spent—everything he had saved as a soldier. He hastened to the town of Besançon where he heard that a restaurant keeper needed a dishwasher. Eight francs a day, meals and a room was all the manager would pay. For ten days he worked in the steaming kitchen trying to save every *sou* in order to get capital. On the eleventh evening he discovered that in the locker of the restaurant there was a good deal of money.

"I looked at the few francs I'd been able, by sweating all day, to save," Belbenoit said. "They would not have kept me alive for a week. As soon as the manager was busy elsewhere I reached into the open locker, took the wallet and stuffed it inside my shirt. Outside the door there was a motorcycle. I jumped on it and rode all night over the national highway. In the morning I left the vehicle outside of Paris and with 4,000 francs in my pocket began a shopping tour. I bought two good quality suits and had them altered until they fitted perfectly. I bought shirts, neckties, socks, underwear, shoes and a hat. I bought a suitcase and filled it with the things I couldn't wear.

"I went to see Renée and for a while we laughed together as we had when I had been a sick soldier. She seemed very happy that I had found a job. I was rid of my terrible *Abrami* suit and now looked, as she said, so nice in my new clothes. Tomorrow night, she said, I must come to her home so her mother and father could approve of me. But I was frightened. What I had done lay heavier and heavier on my conscience. I had committed a theft. I was a thief! Already the police would be looking for me. I did not want to have Renée mixed up in such disgrace. I did not want her to know that I was a thief. For two days I did not leave my hotel room. On the third day I wrote her a letter saying I had been sent out of town and went hastily to the railroad station. I boarded the train for Nantes and made myself as small and as unrecognizable as possible in a third class coach."

Nantes at that time of year, he said, was glittering with wealth and fashion. Using his military record book containing many highly favorable credits Belbenoit went to an employment agency which had a fashionable clientèle and within three hours after his arrival at the resort he was being fitted for the garments of valet in the Château Ben Ali owned by the Countess d'Entremeuse.

"Looking backward now," Belbenoit said as we sat in the barracks of Trinidad, "upon that moment of my youth, from across the years of punishment and regeneration through which I have passed, I do not know whether that was the turning point of my fate or not. But I do not think so. I think the turning point began the day my mother deserted my father and went to Russia. At the tasks in the castle I could have found long, comfortable and honorable employment and a good chance of entirely cutting myself off from the theft at Besançon. Yes, I could even have married Renée. The Countess d'Entremeuse was a gracious employer. No one was overworked; there were frequent intervals when we could enjoy ourselves on the beach or in haunts to which other employees of the nobility gathered. But I looked on my days spent as a menial in that fashionable household, and on my livery, as a disagreeable penance and gradually became more and more discontented.

"I had been at the Château only a month when I saw on the Countess' dressing table a red leather case containing her pearls. There was also a package of money, brought to the castle to pay the servants on the following day.

"I took money and pearls, went to the servants' quarters, changed my clothes, and hastily took the train for Paris. The next morning two policemen in plainclothes began walking beside me as I came out of the postoffice where I had mailed Renée a letter asking her to meet me secretly in Paris. I was, they announced, under arrest. . . ."

That, Belbenoit said, wrapping up the bundle of manuscript and documents which he had brought from the penal colony, was the story of his early life. From the Gallery of Thieves he was taken to court—and sentenced to eight years of hard labor in French Guiana. A short time before two other men had stood before the same court for serious crimes. Galmot, the Deputy of French Guiana who had engineered the notorious rum scandal by which he was accused of profiting to the extent of four million francs; and Vilgrain, who was accused of making over six million francs selling the French Army bad supplies. But these two men had many lawyers and influential friends. They were acquitted.

Two big guards took Belbenoit, who began challenging the sentencing judge for such unbalanced justice, by the arms and without allowing his feet to touch the ground walked him quickly to the door of the prisoners' guardroom. There they dumped him on the floor and snapped handcuffs on his wrists. René Belbenoit, not yet twenty-two years old, was on his way to Devil's Island.

"But that manuscript of your life in French Guiana and the documents," I said as he was tightly sealing the oil cloth covering, "why don't you let me send it safely to the United States for you and find a publisher. It's impossible for you actually to gain permanent freedom. You'll be lost at sea or, landing in some unfriendly port, you'll be arrested and sent back to Cayenne."

"I'll make it this time," Belbenoit said. "I am going to reach the United States and I am going to take the manuscript with me."

Twelve months later I was in the jungles of Panama. I saw a little man with a big butterfly net in the forest trail ahead of me. He stood still for a moment and looked at me as though he couldn't make up his mind whether to run or not. I recognized him.

"René Belbenoit!" I said. "Congratulations!"

"Not yet!" he answered. "Panama's only half way to the United States. It's taken me a year to get here!"

"Where are your companions, the others who were with you in Trinidad?" I asked.

"I am the only one who is still free," he said. I could not help but turn over in my mind as I looked at his thin, worn body and face the fact that in the year since I had seen him—the year which for me and most people in the world had been quite routine—his life must have been a continuous nightmare. A whole year it had taken him to get from Trinidad to Panama! We sat in front of his little thatched butterfly hunting shelter, many miles from civilization—ten miles, he said—from the *Chakoi* village in which he lived with primitive Indians. Again I asked him to let me take his manuscript safely to the United States.

"You can't continue lugging thirty pounds of paper through Central America," I said. "You've still to pass through Panama, Costa Rica, Nicaragua, Honduras, Salvador, Guatemala and Mexico, countries that now guard their frontiers with the vigilance of hawks. You've no passports. You're a fugitive. What you are trying to do is impossible. Let me take the manuscript to the United States and get it published. It is an amazing document, and an extraordinary story. The publishers may be able to help you win permanent sanctuary and freedom."

"Thank you, again," he said politely, "but I think I can make it. I want to take it to the United States myself. The United States is the land of the free, isn't it? The Land of Liberty. I have been fifteen years in hell. If I can reach the United States I may be able to put an end to the sufferings not alone of myself but of thousands of other human beings. If I am caught somewhere, if it looks as though I will be sent back to French Guiana, I will send the manuscript to you—before I kill myself!"

I thought I would never see him again, that the story of man's inhumanity to man which he had transcribed painfully during fifteen years of torture would be lost to all other readers, lost in the jungle or in the sea which would be his grave also. But I was mistaken. René Belbenoit, after twenty-two months of superhuman trying and many amazing adventures, finally reached the United States. He crossed the frontiers in rags, but his manuscript was always safely wrapped in oiled paper.

His book, *Dry Guillotine,* begins with his exile from society and civilization. It is the story of Devil's Island, of Iles Royale and Saint Joseph, of Cayenne, the capital of a colony of sin, of *libérés* living like jackals, of men going crazy in solitary dark cells, of life more terrible than death and deaths more gruesome than fiction. At thirty-eight, terribly emaciated, almost blind, toothless, scurvy eaten and fever wrecked, he may not have many more years to live. He says that he hopes the publication of his book will accomplish just one thing. He hopes, with all his heart, it will cause France finally to do away with French Guiana and send no more human beings there to suffer—on the *Dry Guillotine.*

WILLIAM LAVARRE
Fellow, The Royal Geographical Society

The Harvard Club
New York City
Christmas Day 1937

Glossary of French Words

bagne: (the galleys) convict slang for prison or the penal colony.

condamné: a convict.

débrouille: rake off; graft (slang).

déclassé: a convict who has been restored to normal prison life after a term at a punishment camp.

doublage: (doubling) the law by which a convict, after release, has to reside as many years in the penal colony as the length of his prison sentence.

doudou: a temporary mistress; prostitute (slang).

durs (les): the penal colonies (slang).

évadé: a convict who has made an attempt to escape.

évasion: escape; whether successful or not.

forçat: a convict.

fort-à-bras: rough-neck; an old and seasoned convict.

inco: a prisoner classed as "incorrigible" (slang).

libéré: a convict who has served his prison sentence but who is still condemned to reside in the penal colony.

maquillage: (make-up) convict slang for the bringing on of artificial sickness so as to get out of cells into the hospital.

môme: boy-pet; young pervert (slang).

mouchard: spy; stool-pigeon (slang).

mouillage: (wetting) disposing of a convict's corpse by throwing it into the sea to be eaten by the sharks (slang).

plan: a metal or bone suppository used by convicts to hide their money or other small contraband articles (slang).

plan d'évasion: special escape-suppository, furnished with a handcuffs-key and small saw and screwdriver (slang).

prévôt: sergeant-keeper of the jail.

relégué: an exile; a criminal with four convictions against him who has been banished to the penal colony, but without a prison sentence.

stère: a cubic meter of wood—about 35⅓ cubic feet.

tafia: a cheap rum, made for local consumption in Guiana.

vieux (les): old hands; seasoned criminals (slang).

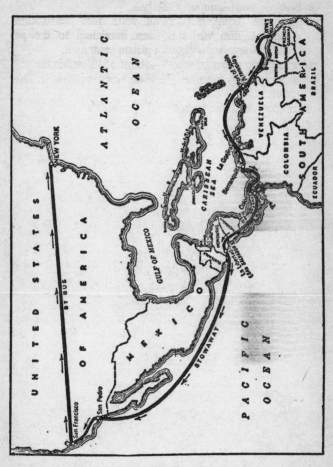

Map showing the route taken by René Belbenoit on his
final escape from the Penal Settlement of French Guiana
(Devil's Island)

Chapter I

THE transfer of convicts who are sentenced to French Guiana to the concentration prison, which lies on an island near La Rochelle, to await the convict ship is effected in the *wagons-cellulaires,* railroad cars which contain nothing but small cells three feet by four. Each cell contains one prisoner whose feet are securely fastened with chains, and a small bench; and it has a sliding panel in the locked door through which food is passed. There are three armed guards in each cell car, and these cars, hitched to passenger and freight trains, come from all points of the nation to the focal point of La Rochelle, stopping by the prisons that lie in their path to pick up all the men condemned to the horror of banishment to the penal colony in South America.

After two days in prison I was taken to Besançon to answer charges for the theft I had perpetrated in the railroad station lunch room—the first step in my fall to crime. There the court gave me a year in prison; my appearance there was merely a technicality and the sentence was incorporated into my eight years' term of hard labor.

When the cell car began its devious journey to La Rochelle I was its sole occupant; ten cells stood ranged at each side of the narrow corridor, and in one of them I sat chained in utter silence. The next stop was Arbois, the town where Pasteur lived. Two of the guards went off to the prison and bright back a convict. They locked him into the cell that faced mine across the corridor.

"Absolute silence! Or I'll slam the panels on your faces and you'll stifle in there," barked one of the guards. Then he walked off to the end of the car where he joined his two companions, who were preparing the meal.

1

I began a whispered conversation with the newcomer. His face, what I could see of it in the panel, was hard and deeply lined; his name was Gury and he had been given five years for stealing. He told me he had served several sentences and that he had been six or seven years in the African penitentiaries as a *condamné militaire*. In the years to come I was to learn the vicious import invariably connected with the African *condamnés militaires*.

The cell car stopped next at Lons le Saulnier; we arrived in the middle of the night, and the guards took us to the prison in the town where we were again locked in cells. When we left the next morning there were two more convicts. One of them was named Joannelly. He was sentenced to ten years' hard labor for sexually violating a woman seventy years old. He said he was innocent of the crime—he worked on a farm and one night when he was drunk he had lurched his way into a house to find a place to go to sleep: the old woman saw him come in and began to scream; he told her not to yell and said he would go away but at that she screamed all the more, so he caught her and stopped her cries by putting his hand over her mouth, and in the struggle they both fell down for he was horribly drunk. After that he fled and left her on the floor; the next morning the police arrested him and he told them just how it had happened. But they didn't take what he said as true because the old woman had many scratches on her thighs. This convict had also been in the military penitentiaries of Africa; and, as was the case with Gury, he had tattooing all over his body—it seemed to me very savage and bizarre. The other convict was named Moyse. He had been given fifteen years at hard labor for repeated theft. He was a war veteran and said he had several decorations and that he held a number of patents for mechanical inventions. It was to finance a new patent, he told us, that he had committed the theft for which he was being sent to Guiana.

At Dijon, our next stop, we took on still another convict, named Richebois: he was fifty-five years old and had been given eight years for seducing and abusing lasciviously his two daughters who were both under seventeen years of age; he was an inveterate degenerate. After this we came to Châlons sur Saône where we were locked into the city prison for two days.

We had each been put into separate cells. I was pacing back and forth restlessly the first day when of a sudden there began a steady rapping of blows over my head. "There's somebody up there telegraphing to me," I said to myself. I picked up the worn broom that stood against the corner of my cell and with its end I began tapping against the roof of the cell by way of answer. Over my head more beats acknowledged my answer. Listening closely I soon discovered that he was using a very simple code—one rap stood for A, two for B, and so on down the alphabet.

"Where're you from?"

"Paris."

"How many years?"

"Eight at hard labor."

"Why?"

"For theft."

"What did you steal? Are you wealthy with loot?"

"No. I stole a necklace, but it was returned."

"Ever been in jail before?"

"No. Who are you?" I rapped.

"I'm in detention. Cocaine traffic. Your name?"

"René Belbenoit. And yours?"

"Georgette."

Georgette! so it was a woman who was in the cell above me?

"How old are you?" I asked. She might perhaps be a dishevelled old hag taken in on a drug clean-up.

"Eighteen. And . . ."

At that moment I heard a key rattle in my door. I barely had time to shove the broom against the side of the cell. The door opened and the guard cried out, "So you're rapping, are you! If you like dry bread there're still plenty of cells that are empty!" I said nothing and he slammed the door shut.

In the afternoon a small pebble fell into my cell. When I picked it up I found a bit of paper wrapped around it, which read:

> *"My dear René—You're going to the 'durs' (the slang name for the penal colony) and it's bad luck, but don't give up. You'll escape! I'm waiting for my court trial and I'll get one or a couple of years in prison. Haven't you got some tobacco and matches? Tie up a little package for me and climb up on your window, and I'll give you a sign when to throw it. Too bad I can't make a hole in the floor of my cell. We might have lots of fun. Georgette."*

I made a little wad of tobacco, paper and matches and tied it to the pebble. Then I pulled myself up on the grill of the window. About fifteen women were circling around in the court below me at a slow walk while a female guard sat at the far end watching them. I had no trouble spotting Georgette, for the girl made signs to me as soon as she saw me appear at my window. She pointed with her hand to the spot where I was to throw the pebble, but made signs for me to wait. I saw her say something to one of the women, who fell out of line and went over to the guard and started talking to her. That was the moment, and I cast the pebble. I saw her snatch it up and hide it in her blouse. The whistle sounded for the end of the walk in the court. She threw a kiss from her finger tips, and then I watched her disappear into a door with the other women.

That night she "talked" to me again: "I'm puffing a cigarette. It's so good. You're a darling. I bet you can love like everything! A thousand kisses. I'll see you again tomorrow in the court." But at daylight next morning my cell opened. The cell car was moving on, and I left without hearing or seeing Georgette again.

There were three new convicts in the car. My first impression on seeing them was that they were being taken to some house of correction, for they were very young; but at the roll call their names and crimes were read out, and I was amazed to learn that all three were

4

going to French Guiana for five years. These three were Julien, Raoul, and Maurice. They had gone off to a near-by village together on a lark and had drunk too much. On the way home they passed a tavern which had closed up for the night; they were feeling hilariously merry and wanted to drink some more, so they banged on the door. There was no response. So they broke the door in and helped themselves to the bottles they found on the shelves! The owner of the establishment heard them and came down in his night shirt to see what was going on. There were words, and in the altercation they struck him. As he fell they saw he had hit his head on something, for he got up bleeding. At this they became afraid and fled, carrying off in their pockets several hundred francs which they had found in the cash register, which they had drunkenly rung up while they had the run of the place. The next morning they were all arrested in their homes. They immediately returned the money and were put in prison. The owner of the place got out of the hospital in two or three days —he was only slightly injured by the fall. The Prosecutor brought them before a provincial Court of Assize, interpreted their somewhat picaresque action as a criminal assault, and pressed the court to brand their young shoulders with a term of five years of penal servitude in French Guiana. Julien was sixteen, Raoul and Maurice seventeen! In Paris they would have been given at the maximum a few months in prison or would probably have been sent back to their families. They were not bad boys. They had never left their village and during the war when their fathers were at the front they had managed the farm. Circumstance had forced them to work and live like men, and they had learned to drink and go to cafés before they developed a sense of responsible conduct. Poor youths, in less than a year the penal colony was to kill all three of them.

Our next stop was Tours where we picked up our ninth cell mate, Maurice Habert. He was a young man, twenty-seven years old, a Parisian like myself, and had been given ten years for theft. Two days later, stopping here and there to take on more convicts, the cell car finally ended its journey at La Rochelle where we were all taken out and locked together into a large cell.

It was good to have space to walk in and, above all, after those interminable days of sleeping upright in the cells in the car, to be able to lie down at full length. I had only a pair of boards to sleep on, but at least I could stretch out!

We nine prisoners for French Guiana were all together now for the first time. Naturally enough, we were interested in each other for we were all destined to be in the same boat, the notorious convict ship. Every man had something to say for himself; often it was in self-defense, and that the court had been too hard with him. In this last respect there was usually some justification, for in those chaotic years in France just after the war the courts were excessively harsh and were quick to send men across the sea when they possibly did not deserve this doom. Among us it was Gury who spoke the most; for he was seasoned to prison existence and was full of talk about the penitentiaries of Africa which, he said, had much in common with the penal colony in Guiana. He dwelt chiefly on the moral customs, the sexual practices, which existed in these penal prisons where he had lived so many years and, as far as I could see, this was something that was deeply ingrained in the life and thoughts of all convicts. His stories and conversation, obviously directed at the three youngsters in the cell, set me thinking. Here I was, now, a convict. What was I going to do about it? Never before had I ever been forced to live alone among men. I was going into an existence where I could not see or have a woman when I needed to. Its full meaning bit deep into my mind. I knew life thoroughly, and all the perversions resorted to and practiced by men and women—but I had always thought of these things as coming from a choice and not as being forced upon the individual by circumstances. In Paris I had known men who were sexual perverts; I had nothing in common with them, but still, the way they lived was the result of

6

their personal preference. The way I had lived, also was according to the preference of my moral choice. But now I was going into a world without women where I would be surrounded by men only for eight long years.

While I listened to Gury's perverted stories and anecdotes, the significance of all this for the first time broke into my reason; and reason, which has grown to be the predominant force in keeping me alive, began its work. In the bleak barrenness of that cell where we all lay together at full length on the boards, my mind began to analyze what lay ahead of me in the future: I loved one girl, and to be with her all my life I had stooped, foolishly and youthfully, to crime. But the thought of her clung in my mind as a living and beautiful image, and to return to her I would escape at the first opportunity; she was all life meant to me, who had been thrown out by my family and had no one else to love. To come back to her and prove to her that I was worthy of her love was the thing that gave me hope and strength.

But this night in that cell gave me a glimmer of the reality ahead of me: I was banished to a life of privation where only men would surround me, men who like myself were forced to lead an unnatural existence protracted through months and years, men who were prodded by sexual desire and had no opportunity to appease it in the normal way, and my mind asked how I would meet the situation. Would the image of the girl I loved so completely sustain me until I came back to her and to the world from which I was being exiled? To the world where man is not forced from the normal by circumstances and is free to live the way he feels! It was a problem which worried me, but I found consolation in the determination to escape from Guiana as quickly as I could.

Julian lay next to me on the boards; he had acquired a certain confidence in me, for I was better dressed than the rest of the lot and was young like himself and didn't look tough. He was loath to believe the erotic stories

7

Gury was telling; he even said so, but old Joannelly confirmed them and vouched for their truth. "I'd rather die than live a life like that," Julien said to me. The stories had put a sort of consciousness of his youth in him. That night he slept between myself and Moyse; Moyse had developed into a friend, because we understood each other and had the same ideas about escaping, which we agreed to attempt together at the first opportunity.

In the morning, chained together and escorted by gendarmes, we were walked through the town of La Rochelle and put on a ferry-boat for Saint Martin de Ré. The passengers surveyed us curiously, and some pointed to Julien and his two companions as they discussed us among themselves, undoubtedly struck by their extreme youth; a few women waved us a *Bonne chance!* or an *Adieu!* with their hand, women whose profession made them feel a sympathy for us. It was an hour's crossing: when the ferry was out in open water the gendarmes took off our handcuffs; a sailor asked if we wanted tobacco, and at this one of the gendarmes told us to smoke as much as we liked because in the prison we would not be allowed to do so. On the advice of Maurice Habert, who said our clothes would be taken from us in the prison, we swapped our overcoats and ties for cigarettes, giving them to the sailor. When we were about to land Joannelly slipped a ball of tobacco in his mouth. "This'll do me three or maybe four days!" he whispered.

The prison of Saint Martin de Ré was, in former days, a grim embattlement from which the musketeers of Louis XIII once repulsed the forces of the Duke of Buckingham. We entered through a great drawbridge into a large court where a detachment of Senegalese riflemen were quartered. At the back of the court stood a high porte-cochère. The gendarme in charge of our escort rang a bell and a head appeared in a sliding panel. The door then opened and we went into the prison. The chief guard took the paper from the gendarme and called our names, and after that he signed the paper. It was our discharge from the gendarmes.

A guard led us to a small court where four other guards stood waiting. These ordered us to undress from head to foot. Then each of them called one of us before him and barked:

"Hold your arms up high!

"Open your mouth!

"Out with your tongue!

"Turn around!

"Spraddle your legs and lean down—down, lean *way down!*

"Cough! Again. Again."

After making each of us bend over and cough, the examiner stuck a rubber-gloved finger into our rectum. Then, on finding nothing, allowed us to pass.

They were looking for our *plans,* or suppositories, Gury whispered to me. A *plan,* as it is known in French criminal jargon, is a hollow cylinder about 8 centimeters (3 inches) long and about 2 centimeters (¾ inch) in diameter, made usually of aluminum but sometimes even of gold or ivory. It is divided in the middle and the two parts are held together by screwing one into the other. In this smooth container which is concealed by inserting it into the anus, convicts carry their money and other articles of small size which are of great value to them. These *plans* cannot be made of any metal which has corrosive qualities, as they would result in physical harm to the individual.

I heard the sound of a vicious smack and turned my eyes that way; old Joannelly held his hand against the side of his face. The guard had discovered the ball of tobacco he had in his mouth!

After this inspection a convict brought us a bundle of prison clothes and clumsy wooden-soled shoes. A guard made an inventory of all we had brought into the prison and said we could send these to our families if we wanted to, otherwise our things would be destroyed. I abandoned all I had in my possession. This made me sad. For I prized the letters and snapshots I had with me—I had thought they would let me keep them—and it hurt me to realize they would be burned. I knew the moment had actually come when I was a convict; and a new life had begun.

The guard who brought us to the compound had been standing aside. He now took us to the prison barber. After we were all clipped and shaved, we were put though the icy showers.

Next we were taken to the *quartier cellulaire,* the part of the prison where the bleak cells are; the guard let us into a large cell and lined us along the edge of the tier of bare boards which served as a bunk. The *prévôt* of the cells soon appeared. He asked us all our names and how many years of sentence we had each; when he came to Julien and had asked him this question he turned to the guard and remarked:

"Young! . . . Pretty skin . . . nice eyes! Ha, some *vieux* will fight over him all right! He'll be snapped up!"

The guard and the *prévôt* broke into peals of rough laughter, and I saw a tear run down the youth's cheek. It must have gone hard with him to see that in Gury's vicious tales there was no bluff.

The *prévôt* put chains on us and the two went out, commanding us to observe a strict silence.

In the morning we were each given a number and sent to workshop Number 3. There were about fifty men there, seated on benches shredding rope; all were dressed in the monotonous, rough prison clothes and they were all closely cropped and shaved. They were being watched by a guard who strolled from one end of the shop to the other, and as we came in he motioned us to a bench, where a convict brought us bunches of rope and showed us how to work. A dead silence reigned, for the discipline was one of iron. For the slightest thing—if a man turned his head, mumbled a word, exchanged a glance with another convict or smiled to him, he was taken to the cells, where the *prévôt* was free to beat him as much as he liked; and this cowardly punishment put fear into everyone, even

10

into men who didn't give a damn about irons or having nothing but dry bread to eat. However, there was a man working on a bench directly in front of us who immediately took an interest in Julien; every day he would roll a little note to him scribbled on a bit of paper. Then one day the guard surprised him in the act and they were both sent to the cells.

Julien was in the cells two days. In the dormitory where we all slept together he was my neighbor, and the night he was brought back from the cells I noticed there were many long, livid stripes on his white back. In the dormitory we could get away with whispering and he told me the *prévôt* had mistreated him brutally but had done nothing to the other convict, who was the cause of his being sent there, because the convict and the *prévôt* were friends.

Julien began receiving scribbled notes from other convicts who proposed their friendship to him. My advice to him was to answer none of them. But a few days after he got out of the cells I caught him reading one of these notes one night; he said nothing to me, and I thought this a bit strange, because he had been consistent in making me his confidant. Then, the next morning I saw him scratch off a reply . . . and I understood. That night he confessed to me that in order to be left alone and have some peace he had given in and accepted: it was the convict whose insistence had sent him to the cells, a hairy middle-aged ruffian called Dédé, and from then on Julien became considered as Dédé's little friend—his *môme,* as the convicts call the passive member of a sexual relationship between two men.

It hurt me to see Julien fall prey to this heinous custom of convict life. However, he told me he had accepted the other's friendship only to escape the constant solicitations of other men; for every few days he received letters from his mother who assured him his sentence would be commuted to a term of prison, as his lawyer had addressed a powerful demand for his pardon to the Ministry of Justice and his commutation would certainly be granted, and Julien felt confident

11

that he would not go to the penal colony. He was sure, therefore, that by favoring Dédé he would be left in peace until he was taken away from Saint Martin de Ré; in the meantime, the stringent discipline of the prison served to enable him to stave off successfully the consummation of the older man's desire. Then, one day, Julien was called from the workshop to the warden's office. "Must be that pardon," I said to him. But when he came back to his place beside me his face was white as a sheet and he looked like a man struck down by terrible news and intense emotion. His pardon had been refused! His doom was sealed. He must have known it too, for I heard his sobs where he lay that night in the darkness a few feet away from me in the dormitory. His two young comrades were in the same difficulty; they were also receiving incessant notes and one after the other they were forced into accepting the favors of some one man in order to have any peace. By the middle of February there was talk of an early departure for French Guiana. Julien's fear now became ungovernable, and he sought to break relations with Dédé; but the other threatened him, even openly at times, and Julien, afraid of the guards and that he would be sent to the fearful beating and kicking dealt out in the cells, fell into submissiveness.

Because I had an attractive penmanship and had some facility of expression, every Sunday convicts approached me to write letters for them; for many of those men in the prison couldn't write at all, or else didn't know how to write a good letter. Most of these letters were addressed to the Ministry of Justice beseeching pardons, others were instructions and details sent to a lawyer in the hope that he could work a miracle at the last moment. I wrote at least forty letters every Sunday, and this gave me an opportunity to learn the histories of a great many of the condemned men.

Early in March the convict ship sailed for French Guiana, but neither I nor any of the others who had been brought to the prison with me were designated to sail on her. When we came the prison was overcrowded,

12

although two months before a cargo had sailed for the penal colony; for in that year of 1923 there were still some two thousand convicts in the various prisons of the nation, although there had been six convoys to French Guiana and more than four thousand convicts had been sent out. During the years of the war the convoys had been suspended, and the total of convicts waiting in the prisons had passed the five thousand mark! There still remained a great many distributed about in various parts of the country. A few days after the departure of this last convoy they began pouring into the prison, and before long the six hundred that had sailed were replaced to the last man—they were to embark with us on the next convoy, which was slated to leave on the 3rd of June.

Four hundred and fifty of us were designated to form the cargo and were separated from the other convicts. We were no longer made to work, and the prison authorities generously gave us an additional quart of wine every day; this was done, I learned, so that we would be in a better condition to stand the trying voyage. A doctor from the Army vaccinated us all for typhoid fever. The guards redoubled their nerve-cracking severity and every day at least thirty men were taken to the cells—the true motive behind this added discipline was that the convicts sent to the cells didn't have a right to their extra quart of wine, and their share thus automatically fell to the guards in charge of them. Four days before we were to embark a medical visit was conducted by two navy doctors; it was a rapid inspection, a very superficial one, for if a man was marked down to go he would be taken on the ship unless he was at the point of death. Out of the total number of men who were to sail only two were classed unfit; one was the son of a millionaire factory owner in Paris and the other, poor fellow, actually died before we other men left the prison!

During the days before departure many of the convicts' relations came to the prison for a last visit with the forlorn who were still so dear to them. The visits were invariably very moving, for almost all the convicts had their eyes red from crying when they came away: it was a wretched time because many were seeing their wives, their children, their mothers and fathers for the last time.

On the eve of departure our canvas sailor sacks, containing two sets of clothing, a pair of wooden-soled shoes and a blanket were distributed to us. The last night had come! Many of us were glad to be off, to flee this prison where the discipline was so awful—most of us felt confident we would escape soon after we reached the penal colony, and this certitude that we would soon manage to be free lifted our spirits a little and made us for a moment happier and more jovial. There were others though, for the most part men who were older and were fathers of families, who were bitterly sad; to them the departure meant goodbye forever—they were too old ever to return.

The morning came for the departure. The convict ship was ready. We were taken out into the court where we were lined into ranks of four. We saw now for the first time the guards from French Guiana. There were sixty of them standing in the court, waiting to take us in charge; most of them were going back to their posts in the penal colony after a leave of absence, but there were some who had just received their rank and were having their first experience with convicts as well as embarking on their first crossing on the convict ship.

Four hundred and fifty of us were listed to go; the ship could not take more because it had to take on convicts at Algiers, where the North African prison was overcrowded. The chief guard from Guiana counted every man; there were some missing in the ranks, but the head guard of the prison showed him a wagon where three men who each lacked a leg and could not walk to the pier were chained, and where another lay, too weak to hold himself up. The count tallied and the consignment of human cargo was signed over. The guards of the prison then withdrew from their posts along our ranks and the ones from Guiana stepped into their places. From this moment on we belonged to the Penal Administration of Guiana. And, as if by a miracle, the discipline changed! We began to talk fearlessly, cigarettes appeared—from nowhere—the new guards even deigned to light them for the condemned. It was a new and totally changed atmosphere.

Guards immediately went out of their way to curry favor with exiled prisoners whom they were commissioned to guard! I was to learn quickly that each guard's mind was intensely active—searching out prisoners who might have obtained, in some manner, money or other valuables, and who were, therefore, likely prospects.

Julien was at my side. His mind seemed remote from the rest of us while he stared vacantly at the back of the man ahead of him. He was going into the unknown, into uncertainty; and Julien was desperately afraid of the man he had thought he would be able to escape.

Chapter II

"SACKS UP!"

Each of us shouldered his sailor bag.

The gate of the old prison opened.

"March!"

Slowly we wretched, sordid-looking men who formed the cargo of the condemned began our last steps on the soil of France. A double line of Senegalese soldiers in field uniform, bayonets fixed to shouldered rifles, kept pace and hemmed us in. We crossed the large, embattled square of the fort and filed over the drawbridge into the town.

Anxious and curious citizens from all points of France were there to watch our departure. Among them were the grief-struck—parents, wives, children and friends—who had come to have a last look at those who were close to their hearts and were leaving for exile. Among them, also, were the accomplices who had come to see their unfortunate comrades go off to Guiana. Newspapermen snapped pictures. Standing precariously on an automobile an individual steadily cranked a motion picture camera.

A wild scream suddenly broke out: "Adieu, Bébert! Good luck, courage!" It was the mistress of a cab driver from Marseilles who had come to see her man depart.

"Oh, my son! Roger!" The crowd was in commotion, for a mother had fainted. The riflemen drew their line closer, and a couple of paces behind me the son of the poor woman growled at a guard who was kicking his mother back to sensibility. "You filthy brute," he said, "I'll kill you for that some day!"

We reached the pier.

Out on the water a heavy cloud of smoke billowed from the *La Martinière*'s stacks. A number of barges waited to take us to her gangplank.

After a long-drawn and nervous delay which made me very nervous the barges pushed off. Julien was at my side. Just then I felt the pressure of a hand on my shoulder, and turned to see Dédé who had worked his way around to where we stood. When Julien looked up and saw him his face became pale. Dédé offered us each a cigarette which in some manner he had managed to secure. Half an hour later we were boarding the convict ship.

As we marched up the gangway we crossed the deck and dropped our numbered sacks into a small hatch where they were stowed away. Then we went down a flight of narrow iron steps. One behind the other we were made to pass into a cage faced with heavy iron bars, through a small opening so low that we had to bend over to go through. Each cage was to hold ninety men. A guard counted us: ". . . 87, 88, 89, 90." I was the ninetieth man. He barred the opening after me, and turned Julien and Dédé into the cage opposite. And that was the seal of Julien's doom. I cursed myself that I had not let him stand ahead of me—and thereby separated him from Dédé.

The portholes were closed and we could not look out at the coast. The line continued to file into the opposite cage, and in the rest of the ship more men were being herded into other cages. In this way, for more than an hour, the human cargo was finally distributed until the caged hold reeked with human sweat and bad breath.

The steamer's whistle roared over us. Some of us were frenzied with despair. We milled in the cage, more possessed by the grief of departure than by the thought of the future. The heavy air, tainted with human smell, was sickening. We were like so many suddenly nervous animals penned behind bars. The ship began to vibrate. We were moving. A hopeless anguish possessed me: Would I ever see France again?

A guard opened the grill and a sailor brought in a pile of hammocks. Each man took one and hung it to the ceiling in the spot which to him seemed the best. Moyse hung his alongside of mine. Then the sailor opened the portholes. And those who had the chance to look through them were able to see, in the distance, the vanishing outline of the country's shore. In a few hours half of the convicts were sick, for many of them were on the sea for the first time in their lives—as well as for the last time.

The *La Martinière* is the old German freighter, *Duala,* which used to make the run between Hamburg and the Cameroon. Since the end of the War it has been used for the transportation of convicts to Guiana. Its predecessor, the *La Loire,* went down in the Adriatic, torpedoed by a German submarine in 1916.

On each trip to Guiana it carries about six hundred and eighty convicts, herded as we were into cages set up in the holds. Each hold contains two cages, one to starboard and the other to port. Between these two cages there is an open space in which, day and night, two armed guards stay constantly. The cages are approximately sixty-six feet long, about twelve feet wide

17

and about twelve feet in height. They contain between eighty and ninety convicts, and there is hardly one square yard for each pair of feet. Their outer walls are the ship's hull, and their sides are the thick sheet-steel partitions which divide the hold of the ship. The inner side of the cages, facing the space where the guards watch, is a frame of heavy iron bars. They are entered through an opening in the center, so narrow that only one man can pass in at a time.

Inside each cage there is a bench which runs the entire length of the frame of bars. This is the "bench of justice." On it unruly convicts are made to sit; it is so high that their feet cannot touch the floor and, with their backs against the bars, their hands are brought around on the outside and handcuffed. The position is unendurable and the toughest ones soon have had enough. For cases of extreme punishment there are the hot cells; these are of sheet-iron and are close to the boilers, and are so small that a man cannot straighten up in them. The heat inside is awful. A man is given only a quart of water a day to drink. The possibility of a mass rebellion has been foreseen: in the ceiling of each cage there are openings through which steam can be ejected; at a word the engineer with a turn of a knob, can send jets of scalding vapor spurting in on the whole convict cargo.

For half an hour every morning the condemned are marched up on deck to breathe fresh air while the sailors slosh the cages with buckets of water. It is a critical moment, the only one when real trouble is possible. Discipline is then strict in the extreme: the convicts are not allowed to talk, move or even turn their heads, and must stand silently facing the sea. They are let out from only two cages at a time and all the guards, with weapons drawn, watch them closely.

The food is extremely bad. For, since the Government allots a sum of only 450 francs per convict for the crossing, the captain very naturally cuts down as much as he can on the quantity of the food he has to serve out. His excuse is that half the men, being ill from seasickness, do not eat. As for the quart of wine each convict is supposed to get on the ship, there are every day whole cages which have to go without it for some reason or another: The guards drink up every man's portion which, by some trumped-up charge, they are free to confiscate.

These guards, I soon saw, were men of a very different type from the ones of the prisons of France. While the latter were individuals who had chosen their calling because it did not demand much of them and were for the most part rough brutes who thought of nothing else but punishing, the guards of Guiana were more approachable and one quickly understood that they had chosen the profession to line their pockets rather than to serve conscientiously in a social enterprise.

Discipline was very lax and we were able to talk, play cards and smoke in the cages. Conversation turned naturally to Guiana and the subject of escapes. There were some in my cage who had small maps of South America torn from atlases and they spent their time studying these minutely, measuring distances and learning names for rivers and towns of the countries which surround Guiana; and the majority of them tried their ability to pronounce words which a few months ago for them did not exist: Paramaribo, Venezuela, Orinoco, Oyapok. . . .

Cliques were formed quickly! Parisians got together, men from Marseilles sided off to themselves, each national gravitated to his kind. There was a distinct group, however, which is composed of men from everywhere. These were the *forts-à-bras:* the heavily tattooed ones, the strong-armed men who had lived many years in the military prisons in Africa and knew all the tricks. They were the ones who, from the very beginning of the voyage had tobacco and other things in the cage. On the second day out they had already organized different types of gambling games which they made ingeniously; playing-cards drawn on bits of paper or cardboard, checkers and dominoes fashioned from

19

kneaded bits of bread or lumps of sugar. They became the leaders and the relentless bullies of the cage; their muscles which bulged on their shoulders like lumps of steel, their scarred foreheads, their thick lips that turned suddenly into snarls, vomiting coarse ejaculations and obscene sentences, were part and parcel with their tattooed obscenities-pictures with the legend "*Ça va! poupée!*" below. The *forts-à-bras!* Their quick eyes had a sinister, sizing-up look and theirs, I realized, was a vicious mentality. Every one of them sought the company of some young convict, and before the third day they all had *môme* companions. They had no scruples and during the night, while the others slept, they stole anything they could. They stole our linen and sold it to the sailors who, for it and other articles, swapped packages of tobacco: from the deck the sailors dropped a weighted line to the porthole of the privy, and each parcel of stolen goods brought five or six packages of tobacco to the waiting tattooed form!

When the time came for food, a few of the convicts in the cage were sent to get it. They would bring it in huge buckets and another would dish it out, invariably favoring his comrades at the expense of the convicts who were weak or old. Moyse and I were sticking together and between us managed to get our share; we had already begun to lay plans to escape through the forest when we got to Guiana, and had no doubts that our decision and courage would get us our freedom easily. On repeated occasions I would look through the heavy bars into the opposite cage, trying to get a glimpse of Julien, but he was always out of sight, buried in that human mass; then, once when I was doing this, a man over in that cage who had seen me several times from where he lay stretched out on his blanket, called across to me: "He's married to Dédé now!"

On the second night after our departure, I was startled out of my sleep by a rough jostling against my hammock which nearly upset me and threw me to the floor. Two men were struggling in the hammock which was strung up next to mine; then the commotion ceased and I overheard their arguing, which was in a low voice. I understood then what had been going on: the rather young fellow in the hammock had innocently swapped notes with the other while we were in the prison, had even accepted presents of food and other extras, believing this was one who liked him and wanted to be his friend—now the other was demanding what he claimed to be his right.

Three days after leaving Saint Martin the ship arrived at Algiers, where it took on two hundred more convicts, for the most part Arabs and natives from the French colonies in Africa. It then headed straight for Guiana. We passed between Gibraltar and Tangiers and went out on the high sea.

One day a quarrel broke out in the cage. Two convicts who had been enemies in the cental prison, wanted to settle matters. Each one had fashioned a knife by sharpening the handle of his spoon on the cement floor. We all lined ourselves against the bars to hide the fight from the eyes of the guards on duty. The *forts-à-bras* began singing a ditty in unison, so that any cries of the struggling men could not be heard outside. The fight lasted about ten minutes and blood ran freely over the struggling bare torsos. Suddenly one of the fighters slipped, and the other was preparing to finish him off when the fallen man's comrades stepped in and held him back. A few of the convicts got some water for him and he washed himself clean of blood. About this time the guards became suspicious that something unusual was going on in the cage and entered, revolvers in hand. Their eyes fell on the blood-soaked loser and they gave the alarm. In a moment a dozen guards were in the cage. They commanded two convicts to carry out the wounded man and demanded that the other man in the fight step forward. The fellow had to denounce himself, for he still bled and knew he would be found out. The wounded convict was taken to the infirmary and, an hour later, he was back again taped up and covered with bandages. As for his adversary,

21

he was placed in a hot cell for the rest of the voyage and there the matter rested, temporarily.

As we reached the tropics the heat and closeness of the air in the cage became terrible. Three-fourths of the men wore nothing but towels about their waists. The water became contaminated and the sailors poured rum into it so it would be drinkable; later when it became worse they had to replace the rum with permanganate. Twice a day we were given a collective shower; the sailors came down into the hold with hoses and, pointing them into the cages soused the steaming men with fresh salt water. It was a delicious relief.

Occasionally the ship cut its engines and slowed down. Then it would regain its speed. The human cargo, we all knew instantly, had been diminished by one. A wretch had died, finishing his term in the cages. One afternoon a convict who had gone to get the soup exclaimed to me, "Do you know who was dropped in the sea this morning?"

"No! Who was he?" I demanded.

"Raoul—little Julien's friend," he replied.

Already one of the nine men who had accompanied me on the prison train had died. Which one of us, I wondered, would be the next to die?

One day, when we had been on the sea about a fortnight, a piercing cry came from the cage opposite mine —then there was a noisy scuffling, accompanied by a series of yells. I was one of the first to the bars to see what was going on. Two Arabs had become engaged in a fierce fight all over the cage; one was chasing the other, who dodged among the men, and every time he caught up with him there would be yells and a furious scuffle while the other convicts tried to get out of the way of the fists and kicking feet. The guards on duty broke into the cage and put an end to the affair—which by this time was being cheered tumultuously by the men. The two Arabs were seized and dragged out into the space between the cages, and an investigation began.

It seemed that one of the Arabs had pounced on the

other while he slept, and bit his ear in two while he held him by the throat with one hand and by the hair with the other. The other Arab had kicked to his feet and, blind with fury, had tried to lay his hands on his assailant who fled from him through the crowded cage. The bite had been brought on by a fit of jealousy over the favors of a young convict. It had all come about in a flash, and the ensuing mad chase, and yells of the enemies every time they closed, had created pandemonium in the hold; for when they yelled in a scuffle the cries and cheers of the other convicts in the cage were taken up by all of us in the other cages and the place sounded as though a cargo of lions had gone amuck! The guards came flocking down the narrow steps, not knowing what was taking place.

The two guards on duty were furious. When they had bellowed, "Silence!" we convicts had only intensified the uproar, and the situation had gotten out of hand. They were mad enough to murder the whole lot of us, and they took it out on the two Arabs, whom they cuffed and handled roughly in the space between the cages. Sarcastic remarks and insults came floating out to them from the herds behind the bars, which only added fire to their anger.

The two Arabs became the butt of their revenge. The guards singled out the one who had done the biting —they went into a conference, and decided to punish him severely, by way of an example to the rest of us. Orders were given that he receive ten strokes with the rope and the punishment was to take place right there between the two cages.

The guards all stood back, so that we could see. The Arab, naked to the waist, was made to kneel while a big sailor wielded the rope. The ship doctor looked on. At the first blow blood flowed, but the Arab did not let out a groan!

Whuahfff! The second fell, raising another long welt across his back.

Whuahfff! whuahfff! The next blows rained down. Blood ran in tricklets down his sides. The man bit his

23

lips, but did not make a sound. He only shut his eyes hard when he heard the rope sing. The *forts-à-bras* were muttering curses at the sailor.

At the eighth blow the doctor stopped the punishment, and the Arab was carried to the infirmary while his enemy was taken to the hot cells.

Over in a corner of our cage two men whose faces were somewhat more intelligent than those of the others talked together hour after hour; they were Sasse and Marquetti, who barely escaped the guillotine for assassinating the Chief of Secret Police of the city of Cette. Alone, and taking no one into their confidence, they were preparing carefully for an attempt to escape as soon as we reached Guiana.

A number of pervert couples had become established, some of whom had had their beginnings in the prison of Saint Martin de Ré and were now effective. The very young convicts, seventeen and eighteen years of age, not having the strength or the will-power to resist, had fallen into the vice because of fear. As the crime cargo approached Guiana, the life which awaited the condemned there became more and more defined, while the guards looked on, and often aided in its development with a smile on their lips.

One morning the shore appeared, and a few hours later the ship came to a stop off the mouth of the Maroni River. It waited for the high tide. Then we entered the river and steamed slowly along the French bank toward Saint Laurent. Twenty-two days had gone by.

We all flocked to the portholes of the cage. All wanted to look. There were exclamations of many kinds.

"Monkeys! Look, over there . . ."

"Look, Toto, a parrot flying!"

"The jungle! Look how big the trees are!"

With so many rude and forceful companions elbowing each other I succeeded in getting to a porthole only for a moment. As I looked out at the high green jungle which slid along the bank, its immensity frightened me, for I knew I had to live surrounded by it, and through it I'd have to take my chance to escape.

The guards ordered some of the convicts out. They were made to go for our sacks, which were distributed to us in the cage.

"Dress for landing," the order came. And every man began to put on clothes, setting his cap on his head as best he could. For we still had a little vanity left.

The whistle blew. Then the ship came to a standstill. I could hear the river water lapping against its side. A little later the guards took their posts and the grills were opened. We began to file out.

Before us Saint Laurent du Maroni, the city of crime, lay still under the morning sun, and its colonial aspect looked pleasant. But many among us turned their heads furtively to look at the other bank, the Dutch shore, and their hearts beat fast for they thought that there, in the Dutch jungles, lay liberty . . . close at hand.

The arrival of a cargo of convicts at Saint Laurent is an event which the entire population comes to see with curiosity. The pier was crowded with officials dressed in white and wearing pith helmets; some were accompanied by their wives.

When the entire cargo had been taken off the ship we were marshalled into a line on the long pier. A group of guards who bore many service stripes on their sleeves counted the convicts, some of whom lay prone on the landing waiting to be carried to the hospital; a short list accounted for those missing from the convoy —those who had been thrown into the sea. A tall Negro, dressed spotlessly in civilian clothes, stood to one side watching the procedure. He was the Director of the Penal Administration.

"Sacks up!" a guard shouted. "Forward march!"

And slowly we marched off the landing. A flock of native men and women who had been kept off the pier stood along the shore and lined our path. The black women laughed freely and gesticulated in our direction. One exclaimed, "Keep your spirits up, you!" Their spontaneity infected us, for it seemed so gay after the long trial of the crossing. There were also many white men, but they presented a miserable front. We could see they were little excited by our arrival. Most of them were barefoot; they were all shabbily dressed, and some were bare-armed and had on torn undershirts. A few wore dirty, frayed hats. Then we saw the convicts in red and white stripes and wide straw hats. One of them drew near and asked, "Any from Marseilles in your cage?" Two others came up and walked along with us. One of them had recognized in my neighbor a boyhood friend, and I overheard him say: "I'm the Director's cook—I'll send you a note tomorrow. If they ask your profession, say you're a painter!" And I saw him hand his newly arrived friend a pack of cigarettes and some money. One of my companions, who had also overheard the conversation, whispered to me: *"Eh bien,* I'm going to say I paint, too!"

After we had filed along the bank of the Maroni for a distance of several hundred yards we were turned to the left.

In a high wall, there was a huge gate before which were a number of guards. Over the opening gate I read in large letters:

CAMP DE LA TRANSPORTATION

"C'est le bagne!" the man behind me murmured, in a voice that was already weary and, seemingly, robbed of all hope, "So this is where I'll live—*until I die!"*

Chapter III

A SECTION of the Saint Laurent camp was ready to receive us and, as soon as we arrived, we were locked into barracks in groups of sixty men. Under no pretext whatever were the old convicts in Guiana to communicate with the newly arrived men. This order was official. But there was no official order which has to be strictly observed in the French penal colony. That was one of the first things I found out.

A few hours after our distribution in the barracks and when the doors had been locked, five men came up to the barred windows.

"Tobacco?" they whispered. "Coffee! Bananas!"

We were tempted. "But how are we to pay?" I asked. "I have no money!"

"With your clothes," they answered and then quoted their prices. A pair of pants was worth 40 sous; a blouse, 30 sous; a blanket, 5 francs.

Many of us hesitated. We were afraid of the punishment that would follow if we were found without our complete outfit of clothes. But the convicts outside assured us through the bars saying: "Here things are different; the guards pay little attention to whether you have clothes or not! And then," they insinuated, "you can always say the stuff was stolen from you on the ship!"

This, unfortunately, had been true enough for many of us. The deal began. One new arrival sold a pair of trousers, another a blouse . . . And that night everybody had his pack of cigarettes—and a few bananas to eat!

The next morning at reveille several men discovered that even the clothes they had retained in their possession had disappeared. The thieves did not have to be looked for: they were the same ones who had done the stealing at night on the ship. As for the buyers, they had been the turnkeys* on night duty around the

---

*NOTE: These turnkeys are convicts, for the most part Arab, who are detailed to help the guards. They open and lock the doors of the barracks and cells; they search the men at the command of the guards; and when there is not a guard available to accompany a small gang of convicts to work they take his place. They are often useful to the convicts for they get many things to them which they are forbidden to have and cannot obtain, this depending on a financial remuneration, of course. They will also close their eyes when they search a convict, if he makes it worth their while. A Governor has said of them: "A turnkey is a functionary, and his position is not a sign of good conduct."

barracks who had bargained for the stolen effects and obtained them for a small price. Seeing this, the men hesitated no longer. Rather than be despoiled of what remained of their clothes they preferred to sell them, and the trading continued.

On the second morning after our arrival, the Commandant of the penitentiary at Saint Laurent assembled everybody in the compound and made the following speech: "You have here two paths to follow, the good one and the bad one. Those of you who content yourselves with quiet behavior may hope to be pardoned: at least it will be possible for you to serve your term without suffering unduly, and to better your condition every day. Now, there is the other path; the alternative the majority of you, I know, are firmly decided to take —escape. Here in Guiana you enjoy a great amount of liberty, and you can try to escape whenever you like. But we have two constantly watching guardians who are always at their post; the jungle and the sea. In the jungle it will be death for you from hunger or under the knives of your own comrades: at sea the sharks will get you. I know what you are thinking about; I've been here sixteen years and I know your minds even better than you do! I know that in less than fifteen days many of you will be off into the jungle; I know also that these will return soon and I'll see them in the cells or in the hospital, except for those who are lying as skeletons picked clean by ants at the foot of some tree.

"To those of you who are men with good intentions, I wish luck." He finished, but then he added as he turned away: "Just to show you how impossible escape really is, I will not punish the first attempt!"

A few days later our names were entered on the penal roll. "Belbenoit, René: 46635"—the figures burned like a brand into my mind. I was the forty-six thousandth, six hundred and thirty-fifth condemned man who had arrived in Guiana since 1852!

Julien was given the number right after mine on the penal roll, and we were now put into the same barrack. I was able to talk to him again. He had learned about the miserable death of Raoul at sea. It had been a painful shock to him. I refrained from asking him any questions about how he fared on the crossing for there were no doubts in my mind as to what the poor youth had been forced to put up with. That same night when we were together again in this barrack, he got a note from Dédé telling him he was going to be changed to another barrack next day; and on that very next morning Julien was changed over to Dédé's barrack. The latter had given the convict who was the bookkeeper at the camp a few francs as a bribe to transfer Julien! The youth made no effort to fight back, and went off quietly to the sexual brute whose victim he had become. He'd once said to me, "I'd rather die than live a life like that." I was never to see him again. In five days he became sick and died in the hospital shortly afterward. I learned later that Dédé, vulture and corrupt brute that he was, had sent Julien's few personal effects to his forlorn mother, begging her to please send him some money to have a slab put on the tomb of her son; she sent him several hundred francs, never suspecting that they were for the pockets of the beast who had killed her boy.

Then came the medical inspection. It lasted hardly two hours. Nine tenths of the convoy was classed in good physical condition, capable of any work. Those who were very weak were classed for light work and a few (those who lacked a limb or were crippled) were classed as incapable. As I presented myself before the doctor I showed him my title to a war pension and he classed me for light work: this saved me later from many a misery.

At the end of a week we were distributed among the labor camps in the jungle. I now had to part with Moyse, with whom I'd made my plans to get away from the penal colony at the first possible moment. He was sent with a group of other convicts to install a radio station in the village of Saint Georges in the region of Oyapok on the frontier of Brazil. All our hopes and plans had been of no avail! He wished me good luck before he went. I was never to see him again: news reached me later that he was drowned attempting to escape in a dugout with six others soon after he got to Saint Georges.

Only a few of the men of my cargo remained in Saint Laurent. The others were all sent into the jungle to labor. The Administration makes no distinction whatever: whether a convict is young or old, is sentenced for life or for five years, is condemned for murder or for desertion from the Foreign Legion; whether in civil life he was office clerk, laborer, artist or business man: all are set to the same tasks. Since we had just arrived and were stronger, supposedly, than the anemic convicts already there, we were set immediately at the worst and hardest tasks.

Most of the men of my cargo were put to work in the jungle. Most of them were men accustomed to city life in the temperate zone. Men who had never had an axe in their hands were put to work chopping down huge trees in the heart of the tropics. For them a miserable existence now began, a frightful life under which more than half of them would quickly break and die. Of the round seven hundred that arrive each year in Guiana, four hundred, the records show, die in the first year.

In the timber camps, at five-thirty in the morning while it is still dark, the guards awake the prisoners. Tools are distributed, convicts go off in gangs into the jungle. The task imposed by the Administration is one *stère,* one cubic meter, of lumber per man for each day. The convict has to chop down the tree, cut it up into pieces and pile his *stère* in a designated spot —which is often hundreds of yards away from any place where there is standing timber. He has four days in which to learn how to do the work; if, on the fifth day, he has not completed his task he is given only dry bread when he comes from the forest.

The convicts at work are not accompanied by a guard. Each is free to chop trees wherever he likes.

For, when you think of it, where could he go—with only an axe? The guards, at three in the afternoon, visit the place where the *stères* are to be stacked to see if every man has done his job, and the ones who have not finished by that time will go hungry.

One has to see these ragged creatures trooping off into the jungle, their feet bare, carrying their axes awkwardly on their shoulders with just half a pint of black coffee in their stomachs, to realize the depth of despair to which they have sunk. Drenched in perspiration, striking with all their might at trees which often are so hard they turn the edge of the axe, they sob and swear; they know nothing of jungle timber, and will sometimes try valiantly to cut down a tree which steel will barely bite into. One should see them at noon, working continuously in the hot sun or in the close, mushy dampness under the shadows of the great trees, with sweat streaming at every pore, and mosquitoes biting every inch of exposed flesh; working frantically to have their task finished on time so as to get something to eat. And when they return to camp all wet there are no clothes to change into, for they have none; they have either bartered them away for necessities, or someone has stolen them before they came to the camp.

For food, this is what the Administration issued to us: In the morning, at five-thirty, half a pint of black coffee. At noon, 750 grams (26 ounces) of bread, a pint of broth which contained no vegetables and was little more than hot water, and 90 grams (over three ounces) of boiled beef, at least part of which we had to throw away. At night, we received five times a week 60 grams (over two ounces) of rice, which is the bare equivalent of six or seven spoonfuls. That is all. If there were no rice, we received 100 grams (three and a half ounces) of vegetables—either dry beans or dried peas. Every Frenchman, proverbially, must have bread in the morning to eat with his coffee, but there was not a convict in ten who could manage to save a little piece for his breakfast next day! The bread was given out in loaves to be divided between two men, and the practice was to take turns each day with the other man at cutting one's loaf in two. The man who wasn't doing the cutting would take his pick of the two halves. Yet the men were so pressed by hunger that bitter disputes and knife blows would arise over a mere crust of bread. Albert Londres, a French newspaper man who visited the prison colony, has said, and very rightly: *"Le forçat vit sur sa faim."*—"The convict lives on his hunger."

For the men of my cargo a miserable life now began. They had no money to buy even a little tobacco, and were obliged to barter away the stick of soap the Administration issued them every month.

There were also the diseases prevalent in this climate to which they were not accustomed. These unfortunates who came from a cold climate and were made to work in a humid jungle, who had to endure the burning sun, who were bitten incessantly by mosquitoes and other pests, who were drenched from head to foot by the daily rains, found themselves undernourished, badly housed and indifferently treated; all down through the years, since 1852 it has been the same.

They see their companions falling sick and perishing all around them. Often, in the morning when they wake up, they find their feet soaked in blood: they were victims in the night of the silent-winged vampire bats which infest the jungle barracks, and it is only a matter of weeks before they are so anemic they can hardly stand up. Also after they have been in a camp a few days they are full of *chiques,* tiny insects like fleas which dig their way into the human flesh under the nails of fingers and toes, and deposit egg sacks; when the sacks swell up and burst, or are punctured, infection and blood poisoning set in. One month after the arrival of each human cargo the hospital is filled, and every night five or six bodies leave for the "Bamboos," the cemetery of unmarked graves at Saint Laurent.

To the physical exertion in the heat and dampness of a hostile climate, is to be added the mental suffering of which they are quick victims, in the monotony of their life. The psychology of the place at first frightens them: for the axiom of life in French Guiana is every man for himself; self-interest reigns supreme and is at the bottom of every action. Each man revolts inwardly against everything. Reduced to a struggle for bare existence, they shut themselves up within themselves for refuge. They are miserably lonely—but, to each man, each other convict appears incapable of sympathetic understanding or appears to be an evil character: for they all, with a warped perspective, see each other at their worst, when they are looking with their hearts for someone unattainable to talk with, to confide in, to lift them out of that Hell. They hunger for someone "all right" to talk with. But they withdraw within themselves and encase themselves in a world of their own. Many acquire the habit of talking to themselves; it is a sort of a safe communion which, to some extent, brings relief. There is no helping of one another, no coöperation; for there is lack of good faith, lack of trust, among men of this type, particularly in this environment where life is stripped of all civilized sentiment. Individualism, egotism, take the leading role in guiding their actions, and every prisoner suffers in this exile from the devouring restlessness which is one of the factors in his obsession to escape.

The convicts in Guiana say that one cargo of convicts replaces another. This is true. For every year seven hundred new men arrive—and the total number of prisoners does not permanently increase. When a convoy comes the total rises to 3,500; the hospital overflows, some disappear in the jungle, and in the twelve months before the next ship load arrives the count has dropped again to 2,800. The policy of the Administration is to kill, not to better or reclaim. To the Administration the men who arrive on the convict ship are things to be disposed of.

Many of us newly-arrived convicts remembered this remark which the Commandant had intentionally saved for the end of his speech to us, and of course

most of us thought to ourselves: "The silly old fool—
I'll be gone in a week!" And almost every man, when
he thought he saw an opportunity, made a break for
freedom. They left their camps, taking along a few
lumps of bread and whatever food they could manage
to lay their hands on, certain that with courage and
will-power they, although others had failed, would
succeed in getting out to freedom. Some tried to swim
across the Maroni River into the jungles of Dutch
Guiana, others started off through the French jungle in
an attempt to reach Brazil. The first were quickly arrested: if they succeeded in getting beyond Albina, the
Dutch outpost, they were caught further on; at all
events, only a few got beyond Paramaribo. The others
wandered about in the jungle days and days, often
weeks. Many became lost and perished. Most of them
came back of their own accord, hungry and shaking
with fever, to the camp from which they departed.
Others got caught when they sneaked into a prison
camp at night, looking for food. Some were captured
by the relentless *chasseurs d'hommes* who hunt convicts in Dutch Guiana for the reward they get per head.
And all who came back had to be taken to the hospital,
gravely ill: for they were bitten and cut, were suffering
from dysentery and fever and other diseases, and many
of them died in the hospital. The Administration had,
indirectly, struck another group off the list of men.

This procedure is not followed every year, but every
Director of the Administration has his own way of getting rid of a certain proportion of the unadapted new
men who do not know how the game is played and
are ignorant of the dangers of the environment—it
never fails. Within six months after they arrive in
Guiana most of the convicts are reduced from a civilized state and live a daily life little—if at all—better
than that of primitive beasts.

They become accustomed to going barefoot, for the
wooden shoes given out by the Administration are un-
suitable for the environment and for the work which
has to be done, and there is hardly one convict who

will continue to wear them. Governors, many times, have protested and insisted that this type of shoe be changed, but no other type has ever been sent out from France. In addition to having nothing on their feet, underclothes and socks are now a thing of the past and, with handkerchiefs and towels, cease to exist for them. They do not even wash themselves in the morning, for this is often impossible—the water in the barracks is never plentiful. What little there is must be kept for drinking. As for a tooth brush, this is a luxury which is never seen. A rapid stripping of customary habits crushes self-respect in many men, and is the beginning of their degeneration.

They write home less and less frequently. For one thing they must buy paper, envelopes and stamps when they are miserably destitute and are pressed to use what money they get their hands on for the relief of smoking, a distraction which becomes a vice in Guiana. Yet that is not the fundamental reason; the real factor is the environment and the distance between them and their former life. It takes four to five months for as answer to reach them, and they are further cut off from interchange with their former connections by being forbidden to receive packages or money. Some are lucky enough to get mail and money sent to them in care of a guard—who takes half for the service, but in time the convicts become estranged from those who were close to them, and the gulf grows wider between the present and the past they used to know back home, for they are ashamed to continue to write about their existence and find nothing else to say. Relentlessly, the environment absorbs them and they soon fall into a mental attitude which makes it impossible to share their thoughts with those outside; it is too much for their pride, it is hard for them to tell of their existence and they shrink from writing. Little by little the urge to communicate with the outside is supplanted by the actuality of the insufferable conditions they are subjected to, and they cease writing altogether.

There is no religious provision or observance for the

convicts; no church, no priest. There are no books for these thousands of condemned men who are banished from civilization for the better part of their lives, or forever.

The prisoner must be equipped with a strong constitution and temperament to resist and override these physical and moral exactions which most of them can not endure—and from which many perish. Those who are not dead at the end of the first six months are the ones who have adapted themselves to a bestial existence. For them life will be a little easier; but, even so, many of them are destined to die before their first year is up, or in the next . . . or in the next. Three out of the eight men with whom I had walked into the prison at Saint Martin de Ré were already dead—and the other five were to die in less than two years. I was one man in a cargo of seven hundred, little, physically weak, unused to hardship—how long would it be possible, I wondered, for me to last?

Chapter IV

EIGHT days after my arrival at Saint Laurent I was told that I would be sent with a dozen other new convicts to Nouveau, a camp in the jungle.

When he had handed each one of us our food rations for the day, the chief guard of Saint Laurent called over an Arab turnkey and told him to show us the way.

We crossed the town and were soon trooping down a shoddy street leading to its outskirts.

The turnkey halted us as we passed a small store, where a Chinese leaned in the doorway watching us, and remarked: "If any of you want to buy tobacco or food before you leave the town you can go into this store." And he added, "He's got a good rum!"

Two of us had a few sous resulting from the sale of our shirts but the rest were penniless. Nevertheless, we felt strongly tempted to go in the store. Such a thing had not been allowed us for so long! It was the enjoyment of a little liberty.

The turnkey, realizing we had no money, proposed to buy our clothes. I sold a pair of trousers to him and the others sold various other odds and ends of clothing. Then we went into the store. A package of tobacco, a loaf of bread, a glass of rum . . . and my trousers were liquidated.

When we came out of the shop the Arab led us to a place where a narrow path disappeared into the trees. There, at the edge of the jungle, he said to us: "You have to follow that path. This afternoon you'll be in Camp Nouveau—it's only fourteen miles from here." And he went off and left us.

We stood there amazed. We could not believe we would be left alone that way to proceed unescorted into the jungle! We looked around furtively, and gazed over at Dutch Guiana across the river. Surely there was a guard hidden somewhere, watching us, we thought. This must be a sly way of checking up on our intentions!

We started off on the trail. As we walked along we expected to find a guard beyond the next bend waiting to pick us up and follow us to the camp. But there was not a soul in sight. We seemed to be alone in the jungle.

When we had been on the way an hour or so, we passed by the first camp. It was Camp des Malgaches. Fifteen convicts were stooped over in the dirt road digging weeds, while a few yards away a guard stood chatting with a turnkey. They all looked at us when we came up, and one of the convicts asked us where we were going. The guard pointed to a new trail and told us to keep moving.

Later we encountered a group of half naked men coming toward us carrying axes, who jog-trotted along and seemed in a hurry. But they stopped a moment to talk with us, for they saw by our light, untanned faces that we were from the new cargo. They had finished their *stère* of lumber and told us they were going back to camp for their nets. Then they would go into the forest again and catch Morphos and other butterflies, which, they said, brought a little money when sold to the prison officials. It struck me as bizarre that those tanned axe wielders in order to smoke and buy food had to chase the delicate, beautiful winged creatures which flitted so ethereally across my path. Little did I realize then that I was to make many a franc, in the long years to come, at the same strange occupation!

Around noon we came to Camp Godebert, which was about ten miles distant from Saint Laurent. A few convicts stood near the path as we were passing, and one of them called out my name. I looked at him in great surprise but failed to recognize him. He noticed this, and spoke his name as he came up to me. "I've gotten thin, no?" he remarked.

He was an old acquaintance of the prison, at Saint Martin de Ré; he had been brought out in the cargo just before mine. He was hardly the same man—his face was haggard, and he could not have weighed more than one hundred pounds. "I think I'm going to leave my bones here. It's the fever!" he said in a hollow voice. "At Nouveau, where you're going for light work, it's a little better. You won't be chopping trees out in the jungle. That's what kills a man, that and the fever. Look at me—back home where I was a lawyer's clerk I'd never even seen an axe: now they make me chop eight hours a day, here on the equator!" A guard came up and told us to get moving, and that was the last time I was to see him.

The early afternoon was stuffy. We were now in no hurry, as we realized that, between the camps, we were not being watched, so we loitered on the trail. The day had been oppressive to us who had just come from France, and we were tired after the morning's walk. We would often sit at the foot of the big trees or whenever we came to a clear spot on the trail. We saw a number of snakes with their heads mashed in. We would pick these up and examine them with interest, for they were new to us. There were monkeys jumping about in the high trees and we would stop and gather together to watch them. We saw several beautiful birds and strange-looking parasitic plants dangling from the trees. All these things captivated our attention, and life did not seem so bitter to us then.

As the afternoon progressed the going became cool. Around four o'clock we reached the Nouveau camp. In the jungle sea fifty acres of trees had been cut and burned—and many years of toiling men had trampled the mud into a sunbaked plaza. Thatch and tin-covered barracks—in which thousands of men had existed like animals, and other thousands had died—stood in the clearing.

We went directly to the bookkeeper, as we had been instructed to do, and he, after registering our names and numbers, indicated to each of us the barrack in which we were to live. There were five barracks and I went into one that looked as though it had once been a pig pen.

Darkness fell.

It was my first night in a convict camp out in that equatorial wilderness. I was anxious to find out what sort of an existence I had been condemned to serve.

Stretched at full length on my back on a hard, bare board bunk, I watched what went on in the barrack. An oil lamp burned in the center, over the passage between the two tiers of boards on which the men slept; its pale light shed a glow over a radius of several yards. A number of the men had little lamps of their own which they had made from empty tins, and they were working by the light of these at something or other; one mended a butterfly net, another was sewing his trousers, another took bugs out of his feet. Some played cards. Outside, I could hear a group talking in front of one of the openings which serve for doors at each end.

The bell clanged for turning in. The men outside entered and a few moments later a guard appeared, followed by a turnkey.

"No one missing, Chief—thirty-one present," announced the convict who was keeper of the barrack. In every barrack, I learned, there is a convict who is officially termed "the keeper," and his duties are to watch the things in it and keep it clean. Every morning he goes to the kitchen, and brings the coffee and distributes it to the men; while they are at labor he sweeps, goes to the river for water and fills the water barrel, and stays in the barrack to see that nobody steals anything from it. The keeper of the barrack is in a position to carry on a profitable trade with the other convicts who sleep there. He sells them tobacco, matches, oil which he saves from the regulation lamp, vinegar, onions and anything else they need. Most of these things he has the turnkeys bring to him from Saint Laurent when they go to the town to take reports or to bring food supplies for the camp; he buys wholesale and makes his money selling piecemeal to the convicts at night. The keeper is not chosen for his good conduct or for any other such reason: it is work like any other, although it is one much sought after by the convicts. "All present!" the keeper of my barrack said.

The guard went on to take the count of another barrack.

Little by little the individual lamps winked out, and after a while the only light in the place came from the dim regulation center lamp.

I was unable to sleep. The hours dragged, for I wanted dawn to come so I could see what the routine would be. I stared vacantly at the gloomy outline of the men humped on the boards, lying in the sweaty clothes they had worked in all day; they were all asleep, worn out with fatigue—worn out from the work imposed by the Administration and by their efforts to catch butterflies. For in those days a blue Morpho was worth 2 francs.

I had been lying there, musing and staring into the half-gloom many hours, when I saw a man rise and go over to the lamp where he made believe he was lighting a cigarette. Mechanically, I followed his movements and then suddenly I saw him blow purposely on the flame. The light went out.

Fear gripped me. I knew what such convicts were capable of doing; I was young and I was afraid I might be attacked. So I drew my feet up, ready to kick out with them at the first sound close to me in the darkness, and held a knife, which I had acquired in Saint Laurent, lifted to strike.

For minutes I held that position, prepared for defense. My muscles tightened at every sound while I tried to pierce the darkness with my eyes. I could distinguish shadows moving and heard whisperings. There was something going on in there, there was no doubt of that. And I prepared myself for anything.

An hour went by.

Then a voice began muttering. I recognized it; it was the voice of the keeper of the barrack.

In the darkness I saw his dim form rise from where he had been lying on the boards and go over to the lamp, then it loomed in the glow of a match while he lit the lamp. "The damn wind," he mumbled, "it always puts this damn thing out."

And the night passed, a long and nervous one for me.

At *réveillé* I discovered what had happened. Five men were missing at the roll call, and there were four more gone from other barracks in the camp. There had been an *évasion*—an escape!

That filled my heart with hope. I wouldn't be in Camp Nouveau long, I promised myself. I, too, would escape!

Chapter V

I WAS assigned to the workshop where wide straw hats for the convicts are made. With a pile of *awara* palm fiber in front of me I had to sit and plat a braid

41

twenty yards long which would later be fashioned by another convict into a hat.

I started work before dawn and usually had my task finished every morning by ten o'clock. Then I went into the jungle. I was attracted there mainly by the new things which I never failed to see in the rank vegetation of the great rain-forest which submerged the trails that led out of the camp; but at such times I was all alone and walked in the forest, where I could think things out with myself.

I had begun to realize it would be impossible for me to escape—it was a thing which turned in my mind constantly—with the other convicts there in the camp, for, in the first place, I had no money to put up for my part in a planned *évasion* and, lastly, I did not know how to get any. So I made up my mind to escape alone into Dutch Guiana.

At the Nouveau camp there were many convicts who had been in that neighboring Dutch colony across the river and had been brought back. Every night I chatted with them, and I learned from them all the details of the route I was to take. Yet all of them, without exception, tried to convince me it was a folly I was bent on doing; they explained to me that I had no chance of getting through the Dutch jungle and they assured me that, in all events, I would get myself arrested at Paramaribo, the capital, if I was lucky enough to get that far. But I would not listen to them. Dutch Guiana seemed, from all I could find out, to be full of trails and native jungle villages—just because they had run afoul of the authorities was no reason why I should also.

In the first days of August I struck up an acquaintance with a young convict, Leonce, who was also prompted by a strong desire to escape. He was the object of incessant homosexual proposals from the older more vicious convicts in the camp, for he was good-looking and under twenty, and from this came his urge to get away from the place. He had a little money and I had secured useful information, so we agreed to pool the two and try together.

We decided on the 14th of August as the day we would set for our dash for freedom; for I had been told that the day after would be the birthday of the Queen of Holland and that on this date a holiday was declared and on such an occasion no one would bother to trouble us in Dutch Guiana colony. Each afternoon Leonce and I would leave camp separately and go down to the edge of a creek a few miles away, where we secretly made a raft with bamboo trunks and tree vines.

On the 14th we quietly left Nouveau camp after the noonday meal. Down by the creek we uncovered our raft, and pushed it out into the water and let it drift down on the current. We had with us for provisions, half a dozen lumps of hard bread, some tins of sardines and condensed milk, salt, tobacco and a bottle filled with matches; these we had collected in the camp, one thing at a time.

We both felt extremely happy, for, in our youth and inexperience, we were certain we were going to liberty.

Night came. A pitch-black night, which did not even give us time to build a shelter, it came so quickly. We could not see to navigate the raft through the creek and we had to make a halt.

It was our first night out in the jungle alone. We were afraid to make a fire for there might be someone already pursuing us down the creek. We drew the raft up against the bank and hid under a tree.

Mosquitoes buzzed about us by the thousands. We slapped and slapped, and it was not long before our hands were smeared and sticky with blood. Our faces itched and became swollen with knots from the maddening bites. Repeatedly fruit would fall from the high trees or a branch would crack near us and we would be startled, for we thought some animal was walking about our hiding place. Buried in between the huge, flaring roots of the tree, pressed against each other in the cold damp night, we dared not talk. The immensity

43

of the jungle, the deep solitude, our uneasiness because we were running away, all these things melted together into one long nightmare and filled us with dread.

Suddenly my companion caught me by the arm in a vise-like grip.

"Look there!" he whispered, "a tiger!"

Two glowing eyes watched us. They were hypnotic. My tongue stuck to the roof of my mouth, and Leonce was shaking violently against me. The two eyes seemed to fasten on us, moved slightly. Then, suddenly the eyes separated, one going one way the other another! Two fireflies had been courting together on some leaf —and that, in the silence and loneliness of the strange forest, had scared us until we were alternately too cold and hot in our spine to relax into laughter.

But the worst fear came a short while before dawn. Needless to say we had slept not at all during the night, for there was always something to fire our inexperienced imaginations. We were both humped together between the roots in a dulled stupor of cat-napping when a pandemonium—a veritable hell—of noise broke loose all around us, plunging us into stark terror.

We jumped up and started to run. Then I saw scores of shadowy forms moving in the trees. They were giant-sized red-monkeys—the kind we were to become used to hearing close at hand, and know as "Howling Baboons."

At last dawn began filtering more and more through the foliage and the jungle came to life. Birds began chirping and butterflies came out and flickered along the creek. Our fear of the night was dissipated like magic—as day came we seemed in another world.

After eating some food we pushed out the raft again and continued toward the Maroni River.

When we came to the river we drifted down the current for a while, and then decided to wait until darkness set in before attempting to cross it. There would be less danger then of being seen.

When the tide started running up river we decided it was time to try to get to the other bank, as there was less current to buck. It was almost dark, so we made up our minds to take the chance.

I had made a small paddle with a forked stick over which I had slipped the end of my sleeve and, steering carefully, we ventured out into the current. We now got into real trouble. Neither one of us knew anything about rivers. The Maroni, at the point where we were attempting to cross, was almost a mile wide. First one current dragged us toward the Dutch bank, then another would take us over in the direction of Saint Laurent. In spite of all our efforts, we could do nothing to steer the raft, and it looked as though we were going finally to drift into the river's eastern bank at Saint Laurent! Leonce, who could not swim, hung on to a short branch of a tree we had stuck up in the center of the raft, so as to have something to tie our bundles of clothes and food to, and with his free hand he tried to paddle in the swirling water which splashed continually over the sides of the raft.

When, after many hours of struggle in the dark night, we were beginning to lose hope entirely, another current caught us again and carried us obliquely toward the Dutch shore. After two more hours of hard work we finally reached the Dutch bank, a few hundred yards below Albina. We jumped on land with our bundles and let the raft go. We hid ourselves and waited for light to come. Clouds of mosquitoes piled on us until we could hardly breathe.

The convicts in Nouveau camp had told us that there was a path which led from Albina to a tribe of "Bush Negroes" who lived on the edge of the Cottica Creek some twenty-five miles west of the Maroni River. Fumbling around in the jungle we searched for the trail; and we foolishly came out into the clearing where a group of Carib Indians were at work. They saw us immediately and started toward us. We could see they had shotguns and machetes. But we realized it would be useless to flee, for they would surely overtake us.

So we waited where we stood and, when they came up, we tried to induce them to leave us alone. We gave

45

them the little money we had, hoping to buy them off. But they held their guns on us, stuck the points of matchetes in our ribs and motioned for us to march ahead of them. They took us to Albina, where we were put in prison. The next day a launch carried us over to the French side of the river and dumped us at Saint Laurent!

The Commandant had us locked in the blockhouse, on the charge of arrest for *évasion*. The Director's final remark in his nice speech—about not punishing us for our first attempt to escape—seemed to have been forgotten.

Our escape, a childish thing, as I realized later, had lasted only thirty-nine hours!

Chapter VI

THE penitentiary, or prison unit, at Saint Laurent is divided into two parts. One is the camp itself and the other is the disciplinary section, called the blockhouses. This disciplinary section is as large as the camp. It consists of four blockhouses each large enough to hold fifty convicts, and ninety individual cells.

There are usually about two hundred and fifty convicts in the disciplinary section. Some fifty of these are undergoing punishment in the cells. The others are locked up in the four blockhouses, waiting to be tried for their crimes by the *Tribunal Maritime Spécial,* which sits three times a year. Three fourths of these men are in detention for attempting to escape, guilty of *évasion;* the others are guilty of theft, murder, refusal to work, insulting a guard.

When we came to the blockhouse a turnkey searched us carefully, and then took our clothes and all we had in our possession away from us and gave us each a pair of trousers and a jumper made from flour sacks, on

which were painted, in red, "L.D." *(Locaux Discipli-*
naires).

We were then locked in. Convicts, in the blockhouse,
most of them completely naked, got up as soon as he
closed the door on us and came around with questions:

"Where were you arrested?"

"What camp did you escape from?"

"And so and so, is he still in the Nouveau camp?"

After a few moments, realizing our escape held no
interesting or unusual information or anecdotes, most
of them went back to their places.

Of the forty men in my blockhouse the majority
were in confinement for *évasion* and had been brought
back from British or Dutch Guiana. One had been
extradited from Cuba. They had sold all they possessed
for tobacco and not one of them had clothes. A few
had a piece of rag wrapped around their loins. Some of
them continued talking to us and I quickly understood
from their manner what was holding their interest—the
youthfulness of my companion, Leonce.

We were given no blankets, so we stretched ourselves
on the bare boards just as we were. In these blockhouses there were two long tiers of boards raised two
feet above the ground on either side of a center walk;
the men slept on these in rows with their heads to the
wall and one ankle in an iron lock. The heat was
stifling in the blockhouse, for it was but fifty feet long
by sixteen feet wide, and had a height of only twenty
feet; the only air entered through six heavily barred
small openings in the walls about twelve feet above the
floor. A nauseating odor permeated the place. It came
I saw from a bucket for human excrement over in a
corner—a bucket that was emptied only once every
twenty-four hours!

It happened to be dry-bread day, so Leonce and I
who had saved no food and had no money, had nothing to eat. At five o'clock in the afternoon about a
dozen of the men massed around the heavy door of the
blockhouse, which was being unlocked, and waited.

An order broke the silence: "Push!"

And the men dashed into the court to grab the best of the small buckets for the night, to use as latrines when they were in irons. There were not enough for all, only one for every three men. A convict warned me to get mine right away, but the best ones had been seized already and I had to content myself with one which was battered and leaky.

A turnkey called Leonce and myself over and handed us each an ankle lock for the nightly placing in irons of every man in the blockhouse. Then the chief guard commanded the men to go back inside and drew the heavy door shut.

Then followed the procedure of being put in irons. We got up on the boards facing each other in two rows, and fitted the locks over one ankle. As the long *barre de justice* was pushed into the blockhouse from the outside, each man caught the end of it as it came to him and shoved it through the rings in his lock and, when the bar came out through a hole at the other side of the blockhouse, it was secured with a padlock. The guard made the roll call, inspected the irons, and the door was then bolted until the following morning.

The irons clicked and rattled with incessant monotony.

The temper, and attitude as well, of these men in isolation is terrible. It is caused primarily by the abject misery they have to live in while they are locked up in a blockhouse, where they have no distractions, nothing to do, and no money for tobacco or with which to better their ration of food. When a newcomer comes in and they discover he has money, if he is weak, he is soon plundered if he refuses to divide what he has with the others. Then there is the fact that they usually come back in a group from an unsuccessful attempt to escape and blame each other for the failure of their dash for liberty, and quarrels break out which usually end with knives. Murders in the blockhouses are a common thing; often enough the stretcher is brought in to fetch a convict who is cut open or stabbed beyond hope of recovery.

The men slapped mosquitoes. A small oil lamp cast its feeble light after dark, and we all sweated in the heat. There was the smell of decomposing offal in the tepid closeness.

The men knew there were only two guards on night duty and that these were under official orders not to enter any blockhouses at night. So a few of them slipped off their irons: they had exchanged their own for a larger one of someone who died or went to the hospital, or else they had a precious bit of soap with which they lathered their ankle and painfully squeezed their foot free.

One or two had tobacco and they smoked a cigarette which they passed around for a puff to five or six comrades. The conversations turned around the coming session of the *Tribunal Maritime Spécial,* even though it would not sit for another three months.

Life in the blockhouses, I was to discover, never changes from year to year. Many of the prisoners will be dead when the day of trial arrives—after weeks of waiting and suffering, of longing to get out. In detention for months, they show the wear of the close confinement. There were some who were veritable walking skeletons. Continued existence in a place where there is so little light, and where they have to lie around breathing a tainted air which is hot and saturated with humidity, soon makes them anemic. Their digestive systems do not function properly, they lose all desire to eat. They suffer from dysentery, from hookworm, from malaria—they need medical attention and exercise. By day they pace up and down and fret: for these are the men who have rebelled at conditions, who had the courage and will-power to face the dangers of *évasion* rather than see themselves exterminated and degenerated in the cesspool which is the prison colony: any other civilized nation would have given them a chance to remake their lives, instead of sending them to death. Some of them committed a first felony in an excess of folly, caught in a cycle of circumstances, as so often happens in life, and are in no sense criminals; they are men who have energy, moral fiber and self-respect, who lost in the gamble for liberty with the odds all against them, and are now locked up like animals in close quarters with assassins, thieves and perverts. They are all men of action, and the confinement goes hard with their temperament.

Those who have made a try for freedom pay dearly when they are put there. Hardly one of them gets a chance to go to the hospital; for the men in the block-houses are considered the troublesome ones, they are the damnable and rebellious, and are given last call for medicine or doctors. And so, week by week, those who were once strong become weak. The ones guilty of *évasion* who survive for the trial will be sentenced to solitary confinement on the dread Saint Joseph Island off the coast, for periods ranging from six months to five years, and will then be classed incorrigible. The Administration, frowning at the fact that they came back alive from their attempted escape, weakens them in the long months of confinement in the blockhouses and then sends them to Saint Joseph to die.

"Sing something, Lulu!" called out one of the men.

Lulu sat up. He was a former cabaret singer from Paris, condemned to seven years for killing a man with a bottle in the course of a night of revelry. He was tubercular and his days were numbered, but, nevertheless, either because the memory of his profession lingered on in him, or because he was not aware of his condition, he was frequently gay and ready to sing.

"Keep quiet, and don't move, anybody," said a convict, for the noise of the irons was distracting.

Lulu hummed for a while, then broke into some old French songs. He knew hundreds of them, many of which brought memories to the men listening to him, and his voice was good.

"Bayard! Sing L'Oraput!" somebody demanded.

"Yes, L'Oraput!" half the blockhouse chimed in.

Bayard was now in his twenty-fifth year in the prison colony. He had been in the terrible Oraput timber camp, the former camp of the incorrigibles about which the great song of the prison colony was written, composed by the poet who died there. Bayard drew himself up on the boards and hung his free leg over the bar, and in a voice which was rough but full of feeling he sang this song which, set to the tune of the Eucharist, tells of the life and the miseries of the convicts who worked and died like flies in the death camp of the jungle:

ORAPUT*

There goes the bell! Up, all of you! Five o'clock, fellows!
The night mists are still hanging low over Oraput,
And the foulbats, drunk and heavy with our blood,
Are flapping slowly towards their hiding places for the day.
A fearful awakening for most of us: our spirits
For a little while have been drifting under kindlier skies,
But the infernal bell has called us pitilessly back
To another day's suffering in this Hell.

Out we go, our tools over our shoulders,
Stumbling in and out among the gloomy trees
Like a row of drunken devils
—For *this* is the real Hell, not Satan's—
On past the rollers we go, falling and getting up again,
Down among the stumps and the mud which there's no escape from,
And all the encouragement we ever get is: "Keep going or rot,
The next ship will bring us plenty more of you."

In vain the sun tries to struggle through the sagging clouds
That press darkly down on us and stifle us.
It rains—God, how it rains! It is always raining in this filthy hole.
O France—for just one glimpse of your blue skies!
Hurry up! Get to the *biseau* and fix the ropes,
Then start a chorus, you miserable dogs, to get the thing going.
Hooray, hooray, fellows! the damn log is moving!
It begins to travel, while the guards look on and sneer at our efforts.

At last we have got it up to the timber chute:
Then, without even a pause for breath, back again to haul up the next one.

---

*NOTE: *The French original of this chant will be found on pages 291–92.*

And on top of the strain and the pain, comes the worst, the
   ultimate insult:
The Arab guard barks at us, "Get moving, white men!"
Day after day, day after day, we suffer this!
O sons of proud Gaul, is *this* what you have fallen to!
When even the strongest of you must hang down your heads for
   sheer shame.
Weep—weep for yourselves, you cowardly convicts: you're not
   men any more!

This sad song, which I heard there in the blockhouse
for the first time, moved me to the verge of tears. Then
strong blows on the bolted door brought me back to
reality with a jump.

"You'll be on dry bread tomorrow!" a guard's voice
said harshly through the door. "Shut up!"

"Owooooh!" The men sang back at him. They were
not afraid; for we were already on dry bread that day
and they knew we could not be put on it the next, as
the regulations prohibit two consecutive days of dry
bread.

After a while, quietness fell over the blockhouse.
Occasionally one of the men, out of his ankle lock,
would bring water from the big barrel to a comrade or
for a sick man. One after another the men fell asleep
or sank into a drowsy stupor. Only snores broke the
stillness, the groans of the sick, and the incessant sound
of irons clicking on the steel bars when a man changed
his position.

At six in the morning the turnkey drew out the bars
and each man freed himself from his iron. After this
came the exercise in queues around and around the
courtyard for half an hour. Then we were locked up
again until late afternoon, when we were let out for
another short period.

The days were long for me, they dragged intermin-
ably in the stench and heat, in the monotony of the
noise of irons and the same dying faces week after
week. The only distraction was when the French mail
boat arrived in the river, which was usually once a
month, as more often than not it brought *évadés* back

from the neighboring countries, and these were interesting for a few days because of what they had to tell.

Since it was the first time I had attempted to escape, word came from the *Tribune Maritime Spécial* that I was to be punished with only sixty days of cell, and when these came to an end I was sent back to the Nouveau camp—from which I made up my mind that I would try to escape again, this time by sea. For during my stay in the blockhouse I had talked with escaped men brought back from Surinam, Guadeloupe and other places, and I had absorbed many facts from their unsuccessful experiences. I had decided that there was only one way to escape which offered a chance to reach liberty, an escape by way of the sea, and not by way of the jungle!

Chapter VII

I WAS sent back to the Nouveau camp, under guard. For a week I worked in the hat shop, then I had to go to the infirmary because my feet were full of *chiques* and had become so badly infected that I could no longer stand up.

During this period I was more unhappy than I had ever been at any other time in my life. I had absolutely no clothes to put on, for the Administration had none to issue to convicts. The storehouse, I learned, had been emptied as the result of the operations of an unscrupulous official who had sold the government blankets and clothes, which had been sent from France for the convicts, to men who were working in the Soom gold mines up the Maroni River and to Indians. A scandal had broken loose also in Cayenne, the capital of the colony. A Commandant there had been arrested for selling a thousand of the commissary blankets to Brazilian contrabandists. He was condemned to five years in prison; and a high official who was his accomplice hanged himself in his cell while under arrest to escape dishonor. The Governor of the colony, M. Chanel, as a temporary measure in the crisis, authorized us convicts to clothe ourselves as best we could out of our own pockets and to wear whatever kind of clothes we wanted, until a new shipment could be sent out from France. This order solved the situation for the convicts at Cayenne, who, since they usually have some money, were able to go into stores and buy trousers and shirts; but as for the unfortunates who, like myself, were buried in the camps or were in the blockhouses at Saint Laurent, we had to wear our old clothes until they fell apart. We went half naked for months until the matter was finally attended to in France.

Albert Londres has nicknamed the Nouveau camp, *"La Cour des Miracles"*! There were about four hundred men there, of whom at least a hundred were cripples, lacked an arm, had elephantiasis, were blind, or were hunchbacks—in a word, all the human deformities imaginable walked about in rags and none of them were excused from work of some kind or another.

When I was well again and out of the infirmary I returned to my barrack, and the chief guard decided he would send me to work in the jungle clearings where they were trying to grow vegetables. The first day of my labor there I was literally devoured by huge black ants, and the next morning I was so swollen and feverish that I reported sick and asked to be again given a cot in the infirmary.

But the doctor rejected my petition. So I then reported myself sick every morning; but this only after I had drunk my coffee, for the sick who are not going out to work do not have any coffee. So I would wait until after the coffee had been distributed, and when the moment came to start I would fall out of line and say I was not well enough to go! I thought I had found a good system. That went on for a fortnight, then the disciplinary commission arrived on its rounds.

Every fifteen days the Commandant of the prison

unit at Saint Laurent visits all the camps under his jurisdiction to preside over the disciplinary commission. He sits with a civil employee of the Administration and is aided by the chief guard of the camp. Every time a convict commits an infringement of the rules a guard writes a report against him, noting his name, number and what he is guilty of. The Commandant reads the reports to the convicts as they appear individually before him, and lets them speak to defend their action before he decides on the punishment to be inflicted. Unusually he is rather generous and will give only 15 or 30 days in the cell.

It was now my turn to stand before him. "Belbenoit, 46635, has reported himself sick after drinking his coffee—" read the Commandant from the reports that the guard had written against my name. I had twelve of these reports, and they were all alike. So the Commandant, looking at me sternly while I made an attempt to account for them, gave me six punishments of 4 days in cell for the first six reports, three of days for the next three, two of 15 days, and one of 30 days for the last one; a total of one hundred and eight days in the cells.

And that same night I lay in irons alone in a small cell.

I was most certainly better off there than going to work in the clearings under a parching sun and subject to the painful bites of those ants. In the mornings I had only a glass of water, instead of my coffee, but after a while I became accustomed to this. I did not mind being on dry bread for two days out of three; not being a heavy eater, it did not affect me much. As for the irons, I found that one could become habituated to them after a time.

The 14th of July arrived: I had then completed sixty-five days. The chief guard came and announced that the Commandant had pardoned all those who had been sent to the cells, and told me to pick up my things and go back into camp.

My things! They consisted of a bent mess-tin, a

spoon and a dented aluminum quart cup; I had absolutely nothing else, no clothes except those which were on me and which were in tatters—no blanket even.

I refused to get out of my cell. "Tomorrow I wouldn't go to work anyway," I told him, "and you would have to bring me back here. So leave me alone."

"You may come back tomorrow," he answered, "but you are to come out today."

I had to obey. I returned to my barrack where I had been absent more than two months, during which period I had seen none of the convicts I knew; not one of them had even sent me a package of tobacco or anything to eat during my time alone on dry bread. I stretched out on the boards, waiting for the next morning to come to go back to my cell where I decided I would be far happier.

In the afternoon the chief guard sent for me.

"Belbenoit," he said, "are you ready to go to work?"

"No," I replied.

"And why not?" he demanded.

"Because I make nothing while I am working out there and I have no love for going into that sun and having myself eaten up by the ants. In the cell I am in the shade and, furthermore, I am not exposed to the mosquitoes and malaria."

"You are frank," he said. Then he added, "And if you had some interest in what you were doing would you prefer that to the cell?"

"Yes, if it permitted me a means of getting my tobacco and to better my food."

"That is good," he said. "Tomorrow the infirmary attendant returns to Saint Laurent and you will replace him. I hope you will conduct yourself well!"

"Thank you, sir," I said. "That's better than working in the sun!"

My work consisted of sweeping out the infirmary, keeping fresh water always by the side of the sick, and bringing them their medicines.

One day, as I was going for water in the garden of the chief guard, I noticed a large orange tree full of fruit. And the next day, instead of going after the water in the morning I went for it at the time when he was making the roll call in the camp, and filled my buckets with oranges which I sold later in camp for 2 sous apiece. I made 5 francs, and right away bought myself a shirt. The next day I did the same thing again, and was able to buy a new pair of trousers. Some of the convicts at the Nouveau camp had spare clothes, for they were men who had become sick at Cayenne and had bribed the bookkeeper to have them sent there so they would have three months rest from hard work.

On the third day my luck failed me, for the chief guard surprised me in his orange tree.

"Is this your idea of behaving yourself?" he exclaimed. He looked annoyed.

"I'm destitute of clothes," I said, "and I have need of some. When the doctor comes, do you want him to find a half naked attendant in the infirmary?" I asked earnestly.

"So! Well, tonight you return to your barrack," he said tersely.

In the afternoon he appeared in the infirmary. "The oranges belong to me, understand?" he told me. "When you need any to sell to the sick you will come tell me. But you can gather all the chestnuts. I give them to you."

So I began a trade in chestnuts, which I roasted on a piece of tin and sold at 2 sous for twenty. From that I earned 20 sous a day. Then I dealt in tobacco, bread and even in rum; for the convicts who earned money hunting butterflies spent many sous for a glass of *tafia*, as the cheap rum made in Guiana was called. They would sell these butterflies very cheaply to the chief guard, who made a big profit sending them to buyers abroad.

This chief guard was in some ways a splendid individual, and he had a deep knowledge of the psychology of convicts. But, poor fellow, he was unlucky; accused of receiving a sum of money for a spy who had planned to escape, he was put in prison, and hanged himself in his cell at Saint Laurent. His tragic end impressed me very much, for toward me he had conducted himself with unusual humanity.

Little by little my capital increased.

Three months later, by the middle of October, I had got together the sum of 500 francs, and also had a sufficiency of clothes, and I began to talk of escape with some acquaintances who also had saved up some money earned from the sale of butterflies. We started with the greatest secrecy possible to prepare for my second attempt to escape. I now had more knowledge, more experience—and having been in French Guiana for over a year I was hardened to both the climate and the primitive conditions of existence; this time, I told myself, I would not fail! Yet, even with knowledge and the resources which I now had this second undertaking was to have far more serious consequences for me than my first one.

Chapter VIII

IT WAS the night before Christmas, and we who were about to attempt an escape numbered nine, sworn to the last man to gain liberty or die. As the eight o'clock summons bell tolled we slunk out of the Nouveau camp. Through the blackness in the silent jungle we hurried until we arrived at a creek where a long canoe had been hidden. Quickly we jumped in and pushed off into the dark stream. We were certain that this night our chances would be excellent, for the guards had a big supply of bottles and were already beginning to celebrate Christmas noisily.

The preparations for our get-away had not cost us much. One of us had stolen the dugout, an Indian pirogue thirty feet long, in the Chinese quarter down by the river in Saint Laurent; it was a well selected one, made from the trunk of a huge rubber tree, and we had fixed it up well for the voyage. The sail had been fashioned from old trousers and some cloth hammocks which a *libéré* from the village had sold us. Our water tank was a privy barrel of the camp which we had submerged in the creek for several days to remove its bad odor—after we had burned it out well with fire and tar. As for food—coffee, rice, tapioca, tins of condensed milk, some dried beef and a bunch of bananas —that had cost us in all about 100 francs.

We reached the Maroni. But this time I was in a canoe, manned by eight eager paddlers and not dependent upon a current and a raft. Three hours later we had traveled the thirteen miles down the river and were at the mouth, with the open Atlantic in front of us.

Marseillais, who had been steering, spoke to the convict who lay in the bottom of the dugout: "Basque!" he whispered, "We are at the end of the river. Take the paddle and steer!"

"I feel sick," Basque answered. "The sea here is all right. You go on steering a while, I'll take it later."

This answer did not surprise any of us, for we all knew that Basque had just come out of the hospital and was still suffering badly from malaria.

The water was calm and Marseillais kept the canoe heading into the swells without trouble. He knew nothing at all about handling a boat at sea even though he had been the leading man in helping me organize the escape. But it was not necessary to be a sailor, a navigator as Basque had claimed to be, to keep a dugout pushing onward in that almost still sea.

It was a still night and we drifted slowly out to sea. The tide was going out and there had been no high wind to stop us at the mouth of the river. We were soon out upon the open sea.

We set the sail. The light on Point Galibi fell off behind us as we slipped gently forward.

"Sing something, Robert!" said Big Marcel. And Robert sang the Angelus of the sea while we listened to him with swelling hearts. And when he had finished that he had to sing another song, and another. We were all happy—we were going toward liberty!—and were full of hope.

"In eight days we'll see the light of the Barima beacon at the mouth of the Orinoco!" exclaimed Big Marcel enthusiastically.

Old Poletti, who was making his ninth try, sang out; "This time . . . yes! This, *mes enfants,* will be the lucky one!"

"Damn right," rejoined Marseillais in the stern, "in eight days we'll all be free men!"

The sail began to fill. We went faster and faster over the growing waves. I was drowsing where I sat, for the excitement and preparation of the night had worn me out. Then suddenly I heard Big Marcel's voice. He cried out, "Listen! It sounds like thunder!"

We all listened closely. There seemed to be a hollow rumbling in the distance.

"Can't be thunder . . . it's too steady," remarked Marseillais. "Besides," he said lightly, "there are stars up there!"

But Big Marcel was in no mood for such things. "That shows how much you know of the sea," he answered. "A storm could rush up and drown you while you were looking at stars! You've been too long in dungeons!"

The sound gained slowly in intensity. After a while it lost its far-away tone . . . it rumbled nearer—nearer, louder and louder.

Then it was that old Poletti suddenly stood up in the canoe and exclaimed, "We're in the rollers!"

We began listening anxiously now. Marseillais, especially, was deeply concerned. And so was I, for that matter, for there was no doubt in my mind that the heavy sounds were coming closer.

Marseillais shook Basque roughly, for the latter still lay at full length in the bottom of the canoe. He yelled at him: "Here, take the paddle! We're getting into rough water!"

Basque groaned that he was too sick. Marseillais

then shoved him with his foot. He shouted excitedly: "We're in danger, Basque! I don't know a thing about a boat, and you—you were brought along as navigator! Take the steersman's paddle. Take it, I tell you!"

Basque sat up. He began moaning and begged me to forgive him. He knew nothing about sailing, he said. He confessed that he'd posed as a navigator just to get us to take him with us. He had no money to chip in his share of the expedition. "I've never sailed a boat!" he cried. "I lied!"

The terrible truth of our predicament stared us in the face.

He had hardly ended his excuses. A good breeze was up and we were skimming along rapidly, when a huge roller heaved ahead of us without warning and crashed in from both sides. Marseillais yelled from the stern. The dugout slit it like a knife, and the forward length spanked down on the water with a vicious slap which nearly snapped our heads off. It was the saving of Basque who had betrayed us—there was now no time for us to pounce on him. The dugout was full of water. Big Marcel's wrist had become dislocated with the first impact. We had to grab everything in reach and bail rapidly.

"We're in them now!" old Poletti screamed. "They're driving us in behind the rocks . . . they come ripping in with the tide through these shallows . . . we didn't go out far enough!"

Just then a second roller, higher than the first, drowned us again. The canoe floated almost level with the water. It was a wonder the thing did not split when the great mass of water, hissing viciously at us out of the night, struck it with a solid crash! Fortunately, the rollers were coming in far apart, with tranquil periods between them. This gave us time to bail some of the water out of the wallowing dugout. We bailed silently and furiously while Marseillais, clutching the paddle, drove us straight ahead.

Soon a third surge of water descended over us, showering down on our backs. The dugout sliced through and leaped out into empty air. I thought we were done for. The mast snapped in the jolt and the sail fell down on us as we bailed for our lives.

"We're going under!" cried Big Marcel.

In our desperation we shouted and tore at the sail, almost knocking some of our number overboard in our efforts to get it out of the way before the next roller bore down.

Marseillais shouted things from the stern, and all was hectic confusion.

Just at this point, when I was steeled for the next oncoming surge, I heard Marseillais: "We've passed the last line of them, I think," he shouted, "Keep bailing! Get all the water out!"

Moments passed—they seemed an eternity. But no more rollers loomed out of the night. The dugout was lapping quietly in still water.

"We just made it by a miracle," said Big Marcel. "And he's to blame, that fool!" he said, as with a curse he kicked at Basque's prostrate form.

We discovered that the rudder had been torn away. Now we had neither rudder, sail nor mast! Our water supply was ruined, for salt water was mixed up with it. We had lost practically all our food!

There was a slight breeze, so we took off our shirts and rigged them on two paddles, into a makeshift sail. The dugout slipped forward in silence. Hardly nine hours had gone by since we had left the camp.

Dawn broke slowly for us, and then the sun appeared golden over the horizon.

We saw the low jungle shoreline a few miles away. The wind was with us, so we made straight for it. There were no rollers now in sight. This was due, I imagine, to a happily different condition of tide and wind.

The canoe was leaking badly, and we shoved it on a muddy beach in sullen silence. But no sooner had he set foot on the sand than Marseillais said to Basque: "I don't want to kill you now, but somebody ought to." He looked at him coldly a few moments and then pointed to the trees. "Get going before it's too late," he said, and he took his long knife out of his waistband.

I think the rest of us would have pardoned Basque and allowed him to stay with us, but we hung dejectedly in a circle and said nothing. Basque looked at the threatening knife and then without a word walked slowly away with hanging head and disappeared in the coastal jungle. Without comment, we turned our thoughts to our own problems.

We took stock of our situation. With the exception of a heavy sack of condensed milk tins, practically everything had been washed out of the canoe. There was some tapioca, but this was all sodden; we spread it out to dry, however, for even though salty it could still be eaten.

We decided that we could not now continue our escape by the sea. None of us knew how to sail a boat, and the dugout looked too battered. Its bow was split, and we had no means of repairing it or of making it seaworthy.

We agreed to rest on the beach until the next day and then set out for Paramaribo overland through the jungle. There we would try to get a boat and enough provisions to go on to Venezuela. We divided what food remained.

Then we stretched out on the sand and slept.

Next morning, just as we were gathering ourselves together for the start, greatly to our surprise we saw Basque come out of the trees and walk toward us. When he was about fifty steps away he stopped and called out: "Everywhere there's flooded savannah land, I can't get through!"

Marseillais looked at Big Marcel, and in that look I recognized Basque's death sentence. Marseillais got up and walked toward him.

Basque stood motionless. He knew probably that it was death, but he was too weak from fever and fear to run.

Two yards in front of Basque, Marseillais stood still facing the man who, by claiming to be an experienced navigator when he was not, had upset all our own hopes and plans. There was a moment of motionlessness while the two looked at each other.

Then, with a curse, Marseillais leaped and struck.

There was a piercing scream and Basque sank to the ground. Then Marseillais, as if nothing had happened, took his body by the heels and dragged it to the edge of the water, where the tide would claim it and take it out to the shark scavengers in the sea.

It was the first crime of our escape and we hadn't even been gone as much as two days from the penal colony! However, to men of my companions' type that was in essence not murder but execution. Basque had not hesitated to risk the lives of eight men in order to gain an opportunity to save his own. Yes, I think he deserved his fate.

That day we set off on foot, keeping as close to the shore line as we could. But here and there we had to go several hundred yards into the muddy forest for it was impossible to follow along the edge of the water because of mangrove marshes.

Just as Basque had reported, there were flooded savannahs everywhere. We had to plod along in water and mud and when we got into heavy growths of mangrove roots our faces became covered with blood from the constant biting of swarms of sand flies. We tramped all day. At night we built a lean-to on a little hummock of soft ground. It began to rain and we were unable to make a fire. Without a smudge the mosquitoes became a torment to us. We took big handfuls of black mud and smeared our faces, necks, arms, hands, legs and feet—but it did little good, and the mud smelled so foul I couldn't sleep.

As soon as dawn broke we resumed our march. We were in an exhausted state, but we were glad to get away from such a pest-filled place. Toward noon we saw the sea ahead of us; so we swung sharply to the left—inland, as we thought.

An hour or so later, we saw the sea again directly ahead of us! Robert and I, who were small and light, climbed to the top of mangrove trees to have a look round. We discovered that we were wandering along one side of a wide, flat peninsula which spread seaward from the land. To cross it we realized we would have to fight our way through miles of mud and tangles of mangrove roots before we could reach the coast and continue on firm ground!

So we now began retracing our steps. All our plodding had been for nothing! The way back was just as wearying as the struggle forward had been, and the following night, in a miserable condition, we arrived at the place where we had spent our first night on the strip of beach beside our useless canoe. We chopped it up, and out of its remnants built a fire to keep the insects away. I looked out over the sea but Basque's body was nowhere in sight.

Next morning after a long talk we decided to get back to French Guiana as quickly as possible!

This might seem to have been a foolish resolution, but it was really the safest thing to do. Our food was almost exhausted, and we had no means of securing more. If we struck out for any other destination we would have to plod across great mud flats and afterward cut our way through wide expanses of jungle; and the jungle, contrary to general belief, is not a place where edible things are found at every turn. Without a gun we would either starve or poison ourselves trying to eat the things we might find. On the other hand, the Maroni River was not more than thirty miles away, and we knew our food and strength would last until we got to its banks. Once at the river, we planned to spend several months catching butterflies and, from the sale of their wings, we would get together the money necessary to organize another escape. We had friends we were sure of in the various camps, on whom we thought we might depend to help us hide out.

So we set out toward the east, hoping to reach the Maroni by the following night.

Progress became easier now, for, after wading a short strip of swamp, we emerged from the mud and mangrove into higher ground and started cutting through the jungle. Big Marcel and Marseillais were in the lead, slashing out a trail with machetes. I followed in their rear with three others, and a short distance behind us were Gypsy and Robert. The going was rough, as the region was very broken and uneven. We had to scramble over stretches of rock covered with slippery moss and we encountered many large clumps of bamboo which we either had to circle or painstakingly dodge and bend our way through.

Gypsy had a wooden leg—he was a War veteran—and this slowed him down considerably; he fell often on the rocks and had difficulty bending low to avoid the vines. Robert, a man even smaller than I, and Gypsy had long been companions in the camp, and now, drawn closer by their physical handicaps, they walked in the rear and helped each other when the need arose.

All that day we pushed forward through the snarled jungle taking turns at the machetes when Big Marcel and Marseillais got tired. Gypsy and his little companion were exempt from this work for they were too slow with the blades and made us impatient.

At nightfall we came to a stream and there we spent the night. By the fire we ate a few handsful of tapioca and sipped some condensed milk. Marseillais had caught a small turtle. Our meal was less than a taste of food. For men who had struggled all day it was nothing, and we slept that night hungry and exhausted. Big Marcel and Marseillais, who was also a big fellow, suffered most: they were ravenous. We had not had a square meal since the day we left the Nouveau camp—and we had started off with 100 francs worth of food!

Early next morning we started again into the jungle. We were on higher ground now, and sometimes we found the going easier. In many places there was little undergrowth. The towering old trees soared to a tremendous height, and their foliage met high above to cut off the sun from us below. Mosses and long-leafed parasitic plants hung over our heads. In these places we walked with comparative ease and had little need for the machetes, but there were quantities of low plants whose broad, thorn-bordered leaves constantly drew blood from our legs and ankles as we attempted to step among them. We endeavoured frequently to creep up on a bird or throw sticks at iguana lizards, but had no luck.

At noon there was nothing to eat. We drank some more condensed milk.

In the late afternoon we reached a good-sized stream and decided to spend the night there where the ground was less damp than under the trees.

Gypsy and Robert were still behind us on the trail. The six of us stood around and tried to figure out just where we were. We agreed we had hardly covered half the distance to the Maroni River; and this was a discouraging admission, in the tired and famished condition we were in. We made up our minds to start at sunrise and push eastward as fast as we could, for the sooner we reached the Maroni the better it would be for us. We stood a good chance here of finding an Indian village, where we could secure food and dugouts; for we all had money, and we knew money would get us anything we wanted from the Maroni Indians.

Soon Gypsy came out of the trail and joined us. He was alone.

"Where's Robert?" Marseillais asked him a few minutes after he had stumped up to where we stood.

Gypsy said that Robert had lagged behind because he was feeling sick. He'd be along presently.

An hour went by.

Robert still did not come. We called after him in the jungle but there was no answer.

So Marseillais decided to go and look for him. He disappeared in the trail, calling, "Robert! Robert! . . ." at the top of his lungs.

He traced back almost a mile. And he was about to give up and turn back to camp when a number of cut branches piled on the edge of the trail caught his eye. He had a sudden suspicion and stepped closer.

There was Robert's body under the branches—it was still warm! His face was all bloody, and when he turned him over he saw where the back of his skull had been split by a terrific blow; and Marseillais remembered the heavy stick Gypsy always carried to steady his wooden leg. Close at hand lay Robert's food bag. It was empty. Gypsy had murdered his little friend and companion for a few mouthsful of tapioca and milk!

Marseillais was a hardened individual. He returned to camp and told us he had found no trace of Robert. But, unnoticed at the time by the rest of us, he got Big Marcel off to one side and, as I learned later, revealed his discovery to him. The two men, Marseillais and Big Marcel, because of their size were close companions.

The rest of us talked about Robert's disappearance, advancing various opinions as to what might have happened to him. There were some who thought he might have become turned around—and gone in the opposite direction; they said he would surely discover his mistake and catch up with us sometime in the night. Others feared a jaguar had killed him and carried him off. Gypsy, all this while, stood leaning against a tree, resting on his good leg. He did not have much to say, but we all attributed this to his sorrow over the loss of his friend. I, for one, tried to console him. I caught his eye roving after Marseillais constantly and, every time Marseillais came near, Gypsy would ask innocently what Marseillais thought could have happened to Robert. "He was my friend!" Gypsy almost cried. "He was my *good* friend!" But Marseillais wouldn't answer him. He was very taciturn, and busied himself getting the camp in shape before dark.

Marseillais was busy cutting palm leaves to protect us from the rain. He was hacking around with his machete, approaching nearer and nearer the spot where Gypsy was standing.

Suddenly he passed behind Gypsy's tree and the latter, still suspicious, for he must have been wondering if Marseillais might not have seen Robert's mutilated body—it had not been well concealed, for he had not expected any of us to go back to look for Robert!—turned his head to keep an eye on him. At that instant Big Marcel leaped on him—and planted a long knife squarely in his heart!

Gypsy crumbled to the ground. "You got me, Marcel!" he wheezed—"Take my food . . . " His last thought was that he had been murdered for the same reason he had killed his best friend—for food!

The others and I had witnessed this sudden scene in complete bewilderment. As Big Marcel wiped the blood from his knife Marseillais told us of his discovery on the trail.

We looked in Gypsy's bag: It contained the can of milk little Robert had hoarded so preciously against the last day.

I remember even now, many years later, every detail of the horrible scene which followed.

My companions were all large, husky brutes, demoralized by the life they had had to live so long in this Hell and by the primitive necessity of the moment. They were utterly famished. They did not know exactly where they were nor when they would be able to eat. Alone, among us, I will say frankly that I was the only one who was not suffering greatly from the need for food—possibly because of my slight physique.

It was Dédé, the brother of Big Marcel, who proposed it. "We ought to roast his foot," he said.

Marseillas agreed. "He was but a beast—and beasts can be eaten!" The others approved. I did not join them in cutting Gypsy's body open. I had no heart, or stomach, for such work. Half an hour later Gypsy's liver, skewered on a stick, was grilling over the fire—which, ironically enough, had been kindled with Gypsy's wooden leg.

"One might think it was wild pig," declared Big Marcel, who was the first to taste the meat.

And then they ate. . . .

In such a situation as this, with men of this type, one's life is in danger if one refuses to be one of the crowd. Although I was not tormented as much as they by hunger, I was unwilling to expose myself to their dislike and hatred. So—and prompted, even by a slight curiosity—I tasted a small piece of the human flesh. I still had a handful of tapioca and one tin of milk, but I had to be as one of them, or else I might jeopardize my life by incurring their dislike. None of us knew what lay ahead, and I could not afford to take a chance of making myself an outsider, an outcast of the group, for, if necessity came, I would then be the next in line to fall.

Marseillais chopped off Gypsy's good leg and placed it on the coals to broil.

They had left Gypsy's body lying a few yards away from the fire. But Dédé, who was a degenerated and coarse fellow, went over to it, saying he was going to quarter it.

Soon he came back into the circle of firelight. He squatted by the edge of the coals and set two of the emptied milk cans down on the hot ashes.

"What're you doing there?" asked Big Marcel.

"It's his blood—I thought we might dry it and take it along," Dédé answered. "We'll be hungry again tomorrow!"

Later that night we stretched out, exhausted by the day's struggle, to try to get some sleep. That night there was no talk—not even the most cynical, I believe, could get away from the horrible events of the day. Three bodies lay now in the trail of our escape.

Two days passed. It was morning, and we were still marching through the jungle, keeping the sun on our right shoulder. Rain had fallen all the previous afternoon, and we had again, somehow, turned off our course.

We were cut, bleeding, and our wounds were festering. Marseillais limped badly. We had cut up Gypsy's thigh and each of us carried a piece of human meat in his own shoulder bag. The flesh was beginning to decompose in the hot dampness of the jungle, and occasionally a revolting whiff came to my nostrils from the ones ahead. But no one dared suggest we throw

away what we had with us, as we had been made desperate and grim by the stark fear of hunger.

Suddenly, we saw prints of human feet in the mud!

We followed the trail, and soon arrived at an Indian
village—we had reached the bank of the Maroni!

The men of the village happened to be away. There
were only women and children in the thatched houses
and they ran off when we approached.

We walked up to a hut. A thin old woman sat in it.
She must have had some knowledge of convicts and of
the white people of Saint Laurent, for she seemed unafraid. It is possible that she just took pity at our sight.

Marseillais pointed to a string of dry fish hanging
from a pole, and she gave them to us. For a few pieces
of money she gave us a large bunch of ripe bananas.
We gulped food as fast as we could. Unnoticed I went
down to the river and threw the lump of smelly human
meat, which I had been carrying, into the water. We
visited other huts and any food we ran across we immediately ate. In half an hour we had gorged ourselves
to capacity, and we sat down in one of the empty huts
and drowsed in its shade.

Some of us had fallen asleep when the men of the
village came back. They had fish with them, and must
have been off fishing along the river. The women most
probably had gone to warn them of our arrival. They
showed no pleasure over our presence. Marseillais held
out a quantity of coins, hoping to gain their friendship.
They took them, but our gesture did not help to change
their attitude.

We lay around in the same hut all that day, stupefied
from the food we had gulped down. We had no plans.
The Indians left us alone. We felt safe and were all
imbued with a feeling of immense relief.

But while we dozed the Indians were not idle.

Several of the village men made a fast run by canoe
down to the police post on the Wana creek and brought
four Dutch soldiers back with them.

Those Indians must have set out soon after they
came into the village and saw us, for the soldiers were

there soon after nightfall. They took us by surprise, pistol in hand. We made no resistance for we realized it would be of no use.

That very night they packed us, tied together into a large pirogue, and took us down to the post on the Wana where we were locked up. And the next morning they took us to Albina.

After we had confessed who we were, we were taken in the police launch across the Maroni River to Saint Laurent, where we were hustled at bayonet point to the blockhouse.

Chapter IX

BACK again in the blockhouses at Saint Laurent—my second escape a failure—we were in a miserable condition. Marseillais' foot, torn by razor-edged vegetation, and on which he had been limping when we were captured, rapidly became worse from infection, until he could only just hobble around. He was suffering badly from the pain. But it happened that he found himself assigned now to a blockhouse in which an old accomplice in the crime for which both had been condemned was a prisoner. There was bad blood between them for some reason, and Marseillais' former accomplice, seeing that he was in a bad way, now started bullying him behind the closed iron doors. One night Marseillais squeezed out of his leg iron and drove his knife into his new adversary. Then gangrene developed in his infected foot and he had to be taken to the hospital. Six days later he died of blood poisoning.

The rest of us were locked up in a weakened condition, also, and the smell and lack of air in the house were again unendurable to me, after the days I had spent out at sea and in the deep jungle. It was a fearful contrast, and there were moments when I wished I had died on the escape rather than have to pace the floor in that stifling close stench of human sweat and excrement.

Our well-planned effort to reach freedom and life had failed completely. But in the blockhouse we stuck together, for we attributed the disaster to Basque, our "sailor," who in the mind of every one of us, had wrecked our chances so we were still friends, and agreed we would try again at the next opportunity.

It was lucky for us we were in harmony, for there happened to be numbers of *forts-à-bras* and other dangerous and vicious types of convicts in the house; we all had our money, of which fact some of them were certain after they had talked with us and decided we had not touched at any civilized point. Big Marcel knew most of these bad characters by sight, and warned us all, immediately, to be on constant guard, but when they saw we were hanging together, they left us alone.

There were men in there whose bare bodies were baked a red-brown by the sun. There were some old convicts among them who were burnt almost black, and others, the *forts-à-bras,* had blue and red and green tattooing on their bodies and faces. Mixed in with these were the white bodies of newly arrived men. To some, whom we had known before trying to escape, we parted with a little money to get them tobacco: we had to, for in there, where tempers are tightened by so much waiting and misery, friendships hang on a thread. In the blockhouse one has to sleep with one eye open in order not to be robbed or killed, even though all are supposed to be ironed. And even in the daytime, the *forts-à-bras,* if a man is weak and has no comrades, will take what he has by force—and then kill him the next day if he complains. Men in the blockhouse become beasts even though when they are outside they may conduct themselves with their fellow-convicts in an ordinary half-friendly fashion.

The weeks passed. In time, the filthy stench and heat in the blockhouse grew more endurable by dint of living in it so long.

A month and a half passed . . . uneventfully. Then,

rumors began to circulate among us that some men were going to be executed in the court yard of the blockhouse; this was a momentous piece of news to us, for the court was along one side of our house, and could be seen from the barred windows. Someone said that Hespel, the executioner, was going himself to be one of the guillotined! This piece of information created high excitement in the blockhouse, for the beheading of an executioner is always an event in the prison colony.

News ran from word to mouth, there in Guiana; it reached even the solitary cells. Before long the current rumor was confirmed: the guillotine was to be set up on a certain morning, and two men were to lose their heads. Yes, one of these two men was to be Hespel, "the Jackal," as we called the cruelest executioner the prison colony had ever known!

Hespel's story was discussed and repeated in the blockhouse. I heard it time and again before the day arrived on which he was scheduled to die. He had been the executioner at Saint Laurent for several years. In 1923 he, a *libéré,* had escaped into the bush with the intention of making good his escape and it was then he had gained for himself a dreaded nickname: the "Vampire of the Maroni"! For, at this time he owned a dugout, and he made a business of taking escaping convicts over to the Dutch side of the river for 25 francs. But many of these *évadés* had been found dead by the edge of the river: they had been murdered and, in every case, their abdomens had been cut open. These crimes had all been pinned on Hespel, who was suspected of having killed them, and then cut them open to grope in their bowels for their suppositories which, without doubt, contained money! For they were in the act of escaping, and no convict will try to escape unless he has money on him. Hespel was caught, and put in detention on the charge of—not murder, but *évasion.* He tried then to escape out of the blockhouses, but a turnkey stopped him. Hespel told the turnkey: "Before long, I'll have your hide!" And the next day when he

74

was let out with the others for exercise in the court yard he attacked the turnkey with his knife and killed him. This was his third witnessed murder in the Saint Laurent penitentiary and this time he was given the death sentence.

The eve of the execution finally arrived. Rain fell heavily on top of the blockhouse all night, and the dank air was close with humid, lush heat. Mosquitoes entered in quantities through the high, barred windows above our heads, as was usual when there was a storm outside. Those of us who had tobacco smoked continuously, in a futile effort to keep them away.

A group of us talked in a low murmur, hunched on the boards. In other parts of the house the men had slid their ankle locks along the bars, and whispered in groups. There was a monotone of murmurings, an atmosphere of tenseness, and the irons clicked more restlessly than usual. Throughout the house conversations centered about the subject of executions.

Rivet—we called him The Claw because of his long, hard nails—had slipped his leg iron and sat near me among a group of whispering men. He had a powerful but emaciated body; with vivid gestures, which made him grotesque against the dim light of the lamp, he told us how one of his best friends had lost his head.

"Deleuze . . . Hah!" he exclaimed. "He and I, we were *good* friends. He came out with me in the same ship. We liked each other from the first day. He was a quiet fellow—they sent him for ten years because he killed a neighbor in some sort of property quarrel.

"Well, when he got here he had a big surprise. He found one of his old regimental buddies here in Saint Laurent—but his duddy was a guard! In spite of their difference of position, they became fast friends again, just as they had always been. And his friend kept cautioning him to watch his conduct so he could be promoted to a second-class convict. He could then take him out of the cells and make him a servant in his house, where he would have things much easier. Deleuze was having an awful time but he watched his step and led a

75

quiet life, just waiting for his chance. He avoided getting punishments, and he put up with everything, with just one thought in his head—to get to be a convict of the second class!

"After a while he got to where he had twenty-three months already done, without one punishment! That had been hard for him, for he'd had to take a lot from the Corsican guards. He needed only thirty more days with good conduct to get the higher rating. Then one day he was reported by the captain-at-arms because he sneaked some bananas into the barracks. He would get several days in the cells for that infraction of the rules, and that meant he'd lose the promotion—after all of those twenty-three months when he'd fought off his temper!

"Deleuze got depressed. It just about drove him mad, the thought of going all through it again. Poor fellow! He was frantic. He went after his friend, and told him all about it. And his friend went to the captain-at-arms and asked him if he wouldn't tear up the report. But the captain had something or other against Deleuze, and he wouldn't listen. So Deleuze then, himself, went to the chief guard at the camp and asked him to fix it so he wouldn't have to come before the Commission. But the chief said: 'You're guilty, and you're going to get punished.' They all knew what Deleuze wanted by then, and they were mainly intent on keeping him from his goal.

"And so that night Deleuze was sulking when he went to his barrack. He was pacing up and down, in a bad temper—he was a quiet fellow, but he had a foully hot temper when he got mad!

"There were two young convicts in the barrack and they were making fun of him. He told them: 'You'll see tomorrow how a *man* acts!' He'd made up his mind what he was going to do. He was out for revenge!

"As soon as the turnkeys opened the barrack door at five the next morning, he went out. In the crowd of exercising men nobody noticed him especially.

"It was still dark, and he went straight to the house

76

of the captain. The captain was sitting at his desk writing reports. Deleuze came up behind him quietly and drove his knife into his back twice! He left the captain as soon as he was sure he was dead, and making his way behind the barracks went to the other side of the penitentiary, where he knew the chief guard always stood when sending the men out to work every morning. Sure enough, the chief guard was there, watching the men as usual; and Deleuze sneaked quickly up behind him and brought him down with his knife, and raced for his barrack before anybody, he thought, saw what had happened. But one man did see him, though! It wasn't the chief guard, for he was badly wounded and had been taken completely by surprise. It was a turnkey, Labib: he saw Deleuze jump on the guard, and he denounced him. Everything was against Deleuze, and he was brought to the blockhouse. In a couple of months they had sentenced him to the guillotine.

"All the time he was in detention, his friend the guard sent him tobacco and did everything he could to help him out. Some of the men, for we had all found out about it, sent him things to cheer him up.

"And then the day arrived. His friend the guard didn't go out in the morning to count his men, he was so dejected he stayed at his house. The chief guard, whom Deleuze had tried to kill, asked permission to see Deleuze's head fall off, but the Commandant wouldn't let him leave the hospital.

"Deleuze was led to the scaffold. I was one of the convicts who had to witness it on bent knees. Hell, it was hard to see him there—by this time, poor devil, after the weeks in the blockhouse, he was a mass of scurvy. He had asked twice to be sent to the hospital, but they knew he was going to die anyway, so it was refused. He hadn't eaten a thing for five days. The executioner had to help him up to the knife, he was so weak. He was just weak, it wasn't that he was scared. Humm, not Deleuze—he was iron right down to bottom! He might have been all right, if he hadn't become obsessed with the idea he had no chance in this damn hell.

"All he said when he put his head in the loop, was: 'Don't hurt me any more,' because he was already in such pain because of the scurvy!

"The official executioner (it was Carpentier then) happened to be in detention at the time, too. He was also cook for the blockhouses. He went back to the kitchen after the job was done, and got the rations ready. Hah! when the soup came at ten, nobody touched it! 'We aren't going to eat the soaked food!' the men said. 'It was made with hands still wet with the blood of a comrade!'

"The chief guard then went to the Commandant about it. And he said if the men didn't want the food, that was their hard luck! And it was; but I was glad, for that day nobody in the blockhouse ate a thing because Deleuze was dead.

"And another thing," Rivet continued "—and this shows how much his friend the guard liked him. In less than ten days he handed in his resignation! Yes! And somebody told me when he got back to France he wrote a lot of true things against the Administration. But one voice crying against the wolves didn't accomplish anything at all!"

We had listened to The Claw's vivid account in utter silence. Some of the convicts now started making comments, and discussions sprang up.

It's a strange thing, but always on the eve of an execution, these convicts, most of them men capable of committing great crimes, become seized with a vague nervousness—I have never known it to fail. It is a type of uneasiness; explainable, in a sense, by the fact that there is not one of them but feels that he himself may go up to face the polished knife some day. I have felt that way myself, many a time, for, in the nip and tuck struggle between the corrupt Penal Authority and the condemned man, a convict can never know when he suddenly may find himself facing capital punishment. The convicts waiting during the night know that a man, like themselves, is going to have his head sliced off at dawn; and they also know that they too are helpless beings, subject to an authority which would be unquestioned if it chose for any reason to cut one hundred heads off instead of one! A man who has seen the knife flash and the spurt of red blood when the guillotine falls is struck with a terror that never really leaves him. He hates bitterly—all the convicts do, and no one can blame them for it—the man who as official executioner lets the knife fall.

Out of the dim night Georges, a tattoed *fort-à-bras*, asked The Claw: "Do you remember the execution of Gautier on the Islands?"

"I wasn't there," answered The Claw, "but I heard the story."

"Well, I was," said Georges. "And I was one of the men they brought out and made stand around the instrument to watch it happen!"

"Go on!" several of the men in our group said, "What happened?"

"Gautier killed a guard when he was in solitary," Georges said. "Any of you remember him?"

"Yes," said The Claw and several others.

"One afternoon, the captain-at-arms on the Saint Joseph Island came to the cells to pick out thirty men who were to go to witness the knife fall. I was one of the ones chosen. It was going to be done in the morning.

"About five next morning we were let out of the cells, and six guards took us into the court. The guillotine had been set up there. The Jackal (Hah, he'll die tomorrow) was putting the last touch to the frame.

"After a while day broke. The guards had us all get down on our knees around the instrument, and we had to cross our arms over our chests. It was the first execution I had ever witnessed and I began to feel sick all over.

" 'At the moment of the execution,' the captain-at-arms said, 'all of you bend your heads.'

"The Commandant of the Islands—he was Garagnon—now appeared. A big turnkey and two guards went with him to Gautier's cell.

"Then it was it happened! The Commandant announced to Gautier that his plea for a pardon had not been granted by the President, and that the hour was now at hand for him to die under the knife. While he was speaking this formality, the turnkey took the irons off Gautier. Gautier had listened respectfully to the Commandant's words. But when the irons were off, he drew his feet up slowly as though he was going to get to his feet. Then he did it! With one bound he was on the Commandant! He struck him with something: The Commandant brought his hand to his throat, where a stream of blood spurted, and cried, 'He's killed me!' The guards rushed on Gautier, while the prosecutor and the chief guard carried the Commandant off to the infirmary. Ha! it was a tense moment; for we could hear the commotion, even though we couldn't see actually what was taking place. The guards who were watching over us, on our knees there in the courtyard, drew their pistols and menaced us, crying: 'Any man who moves will be shot where he is!"

"We stayed that way all around the guillotine, on our knees in the court, with our heads bent as though in prayer. It must have been for about half an hour: my knees were paining me terribly but the guards were so nervous I didn't dare move an inch. Then the prosecutor showed up. He went in to see Gautier in his cell—he was in there all ironed up again, poor devil. The Prosecutor questioned him on his motives for attacking the Commandant.

"I learned later what Gautier said. 'For more than a month I've been on dry bread only—yes, only dry bread! They never gave me water to drink. I've been in a stupor from thirst. It was the Commandant's orders.'

"He would answer none of the questions about where he had obtained the knife.

"When he got up on the platform, he cried out to us:

80

'There'll be one less of the sons-of-bitches to bother you fellows! Ha-Ha-Ha, he died before me, the cur!'

"A few minutes later his head rolled from the instrument.

"They found some bits of wax in his cell, which led them to believe he'd had the knife a long time. He'd pushed it up inside of him like a suppository, sheathed in a coating of wax! Some trick, I say! It was a small knife, but a good one, made with an old razor.

"But the Commandant, however, didn't die!" Georges added. "He lost his voice, though—could never say a word after the knife cut his throat. So Gautier got even with him—I guess!"

When Georges finished telling about Gautier, other stories followed, and there was talk on and on into the night; for nobody in the blockhouse wanted to sleep. There was too much restlessness, too much heat, and the mosquitoes were terrible.

The rain, with occasional lulls, kept pounding down until that expected hour before dawn when we began to hear noises in the court—that hour of half gloom for which we had all been waiting and listening.

I had slipped my iron, and as I was the smallest and lightest of the men loose from leg irons in the blockhouse, I was lifted up to one of the windows on the shoulders of taller men to watch what went on and pass the word down to everybody. Another convict was hoisted up to the other window. When the men underneath us got tired, others took their places, so we could rest our feet on them while we clung to the grills.

Absolute silence reigned in the blockhouse, for all of the men inside were straining their ears to listen to what I and the other observer would report.

The executioner, aided by two turnkeys, was putting the finishing touches to the guillotine. There was enough light now for me to see them plainly in the courtyard.

Bang! . . . He dropped the knife to see if it was working well.

"Dieu!" murmured someone below me in the house.

81

Soon some guards appeared. Then the Commandant.

The Jackal's cell was in the row across the court. The door was unlocked, and they brought him out.

There were convicts in a circle around the instrument. They had been brought out in a lump from the blockhouse on the other side. "Kneel down!" The order barked and every convict witness knelt hastily.

When he found himself before the instrument, the Jackal stopped and addressed the executioner—the man now at the knife had been his former assistant.

He said to his former aide. "You see," and his remark was so distinct the men in my blockhouse overheard his words, "now the executioner becomes the executed! My predecessor also at last gave his head to The Widow! Be careful, some day will come *your* turn!" And after a slight pause, he saluted his executioner and added: "Do it neatly, *mon enfant,* just like I showed you how the job should be done!"

In a few seconds the Jackal's head lay in the bloody basket.

"Ca y est!" (That's it!) cried the men in the house when they heard the knife clatter. There were whistles and cat-calls; they hated him, every one of them, for he had cut off thirty heads.

As soon as Hespel's head had rolled into the basket, a cell near the one he had occupied was opened and the other man who was to die that morning was brought to the guillotine. This fellow was a *libéré,* a free convict in exile for life, named de Delorme. He had assassinated the agent for the Cie. Générale Transatlantique at Saint Laurent, who had surprised him stealing a box of cargo on the pier.

I had noticed that quite a number of civilians came into the courtyard to witness this execution, and I recognized the son of the murdered agent among them. Delorme, when he saw the young man, fell at his feet and exclaimed *"Pardon, M. Ouradou! Pardon!"*

Then Delorme turned suddenly to the executioner: "Well, do it quickly!" he shouted, "Hurry up—I'm not here for fun."

The executioner nodded, the knife dropped. Another head was in the basket.

Three days later they executed a Chinese, but this time the guillotine was set up at Saint Jean on the Maroni. The Chinese made the trip from Saint Laurent on the same wagon with the death instrument; and they say he rode the distance leaning his back against the crate in which the knife was encased.

The weeks rolled on. My detention of many weeks in the blockhouse had rendered me excessively anemic. I could not eat, and would sell my ration of bread and meat for drinks of coffee. Day by day I rapidly became thinner.

Every time I presented myself at medical inspection, the doctor would hurriedly prescribe for me some general medicine which could not possibly cure my condition. I realized this, and reached such a state of desperation that I was sure I was going to die in that stench and damp heat. There came a time when I could not even drink coffee; and I calculated then that a man could live twelve days without eating, and that if I went beyond that time it would mean certain death for me.

One morning, after six days had gone by that time I had eaten nothing at all, I again presented myself before the doctor. He gave me, as he had done before, a quantity of quinine. I knew that quinine could in no way help my condition, so in the afternoon I wrote a note to the chief doctor, begging a special visit or some attention to my case. He took the trouble to answer my note formally: "The doctor who makes the visits at the blockhouses," he wrote, "is qualified to know whether a man is sick or not. Request refused."

I was frantic. I saw myself dead in another week, for I saw no hope of getting to the hospital or of receiving any treatment. Three days later I reported at medical inspection again. I could hardly walk, so two of my companions supported me between them. And that day, barely glancing at me, the doctor wrote in his booklet: "Hospital." Then, realizing I was the fellow who had dared to ask for a special visit, he crossed out "Hospital" and wrote: "To be given milk."

Seeing this, I found strength to cry in his face, "You are a devil!"

The guard standing by his side immediately called the turnkeys and had me put in a cell.

A few minutes later the guard appeared outside the cell and told me he had made out a report against me, for outrage and insult against a doctor who was exercising his duties.

But, on the following morning, by a personal order of this same doctor (I hated him so by this time that the thought of him was harder on me than the disease from which I suffered), I was taken to the hospital. My condition was such that I had to remain six months. The doctor realized his mistake—he took personal care of me, and he also put in a request that the punishment given me for the recorded insult be reduced to the minimum: six months in prison.

Chapter X

UNCLEAN and fetid, the hospitals for the condemned in Guiana are dilapidated and inadequate structures. Except for the handful of doctors in charge of them, the personnel is untrained; and a few doctors who do the best they can in trying to relieve pain and disease are the only thing about them which deserves a favorable mention.

Each prison unit has its hospital: there is one for the convicts in and around Saint Laurent Penitentiary; there is another on the Islands, and another at Cayenne where the convicts are cared for in a special building of the colonial hospital. The total hospital enrollment varies between four hundred and five hundred men, and to this is still to be added another hundred and more who are in the various infirmaries—a figure which represents one-fifth of the total number of convicts in the prison colony. Constantly one-fifth of the convicts are incapacitated and seriously ill! Of these sick men, most of them suffer from fever, dysentery, or anky-lostomiasis and, above all, they are victims of growing anemia.

The doctors are French army doctors detailed for a period of two years of colonial duty in Guiana. Usually, they are humane and treat the convicts as sick men and not as animals—it is fortunate when a convict, sent into a hospital at last, finds that he can obtain, for the first time, some degree of human sympathy.

Every two days in the penitentiaries, and once a week in the remote convict camps, a doctor makes the rounds. The sick man comes before him completely stripped; this is not to facilitate the medical inspector, but because once a convict killed a doctor with a knife concealed in his clothes when he refused to send him to the hospital. The convict is allowed to tell the doctor what he thinks he is suffering from. The doctor ex-amines the convict and writes in his booklet, by the side of the convict's name, what he thinks is the necessary prescription; the medicine the man is to have, the num-ber of days of rest he should be given, or the official order for him to go to the infirmary or to the hospital.

The hospital wards contain some twenty beds each; no springs, merely three boards and a mattress. There is only one sheet on each bed and when a convict leaves the hospital, dead or alive, the mattress is aired in the sun a few hours, and is then ready for the next man. By each bed there is a small table and at the foot is placed a container for bodily needs. This is usually an old tinned-beef can and, since most of the sick suffer from diarrhea and dysentery, one can well imagine for himself the smell which prevails in the ward in the mornings. The ward is swept every day by the atten-dant, who sometimes runs a mop over the floor. Once a week he sprinkles it with creosote.

The sick eat on their beds, for although there is a table, they have nothing to sit on. The diets, such as they are, are divided into two types. That given to the men who are in a better condition consists of a half-pint of coffee in the morning, and 400 grams (about 12 ounces) of bread for the day; at noon, half a pint of bouillon, another of vegetables and 60 grams (about 2 ounces) of meat; at night, the same as at noon. The diet for the men who are in a worse condition consists of 250 grams (nearly 9 ounces) of bread, coffee in the morning, and porridge, meat and vegetables at noon and night. Then there is the milk diet for the men who are about to die; three and half pints of condensed milk and water; the attendant is supposed to make this quantity with one tin of condensed milk—but he makes five pints with it, and sells the surplus in the ward. For he must smoke, also! It is his graft, or as the convicts call it, his *débrouille*.

The doctors have each from one hundred to a hundred and fifty patients to attend to. They have visits to make, operations to perform, and they do not have time to attend closely to the condition of the men. Added to this, is the fact that very often they do not have the medicines they require. Quinine often runs short, due to the theft on the part of the guards, and often the bandages give out and it is necessary to wash the old ones and use these again. On the Islands, in 1926, there was no more iodine or permanganate, and the attendant could not make any injections. Often, on the Islands, there is no milk for the sick for one and two months at a time, and it is necessary for patients, bleeding internally from the ravages of dysentery, to eat solid food or starve! Very often the prescriptions filled out in the pharmacy by a convict working there are diluted or else they are simply lacking the necessary ingredients which should go into their composition.

If a sick man does not die it is not the fault of the care he receives. As soon as a fever stays down three or four days, the patient is put out of the hospital and returns to his camp—where his fever will not be long in starting up again. I have known convicts who had ten hospital periods in less than a year, and at the eleventh one they left feet foremost. In fifty per cent of the death reports of these hospitals at the prison colony the death entry reads: "Death from physiological weakness." At the age of twenty-five, could a man die of physiological weakness? At the Ministry this did not seem probable, and so now in the reports this citation is replaced with "Died of pernicious anemia." It looks better!

The attendants are all convicts. Although most of them have no notion whatever of the qualifications which their jobs demand, there are a few who seem to have the proper inclination and acquire a capacity for it. There were, for instance, Mandat, the leader of the band of Parisian *apaches,* Marcheras his accomplice, and Pelissier, who were all three attendants capable of cutting a leg or an arm just as well as any surgeon, and they learned how to cure ulcers and attacks of pernicious fever properly, saving, in many instances, patients whom the doctor in the hospital had given up.

Death comes often in the wards.

I remember one case vividly. The man lay at length, unclothed, under a single sheet in which the holes showed his bony body. At the foot of his bed, his sweat-soaked nightshirt lay drying from his last fit of fever.

"He will catch the tide!" commented the attendant that morning.

The dying man looked at the attendant for a long time and then dropped his head toward his neighbor on the other side of his bed from me, and said feebly: "Roll me up a cigarette, please."

The other sick man hastened to his neighbor's aid for this meant he could roll one for himself also. He got up and felt under the dying man's mattress and drew out a package of tobacco and a box of matches. He rolled a cigarette, lit it and stuck it between the lips of the near-corpse. Then, after rolling another for himself, he put the tobacco back in its place.

The sick man sucked on the cigarette and his throat

rattled at every draw. He was too weak to lift his hand to it.

"Look!" a convict who was watching him exclaimed, "I think it is come . . ."

The dying man had let the cigarette fall on his sheet, still burning, and his head fell backward with the mouth gaping open. From my bed, next to his, I could see his eyes fixed on the roof above his head.

One of the convicts in the ward approached his still form and shook him. Then he lifted one of his arms, and it fell heavily.

"Dead!" and he shook him again. He picked up the cigarette, puffed on it a few moments, then leaned down and picked up the dead man's shoes; then he turned to his own bed and hid the shoes under his mattress.

Another convict got up and snatched the small sack the dead man kept his possessions in . . . an Arab took the eggs which lay on his table . . . his neighbor, across on the other side from me, found the tobacco again and kept it for himself.

Then the attendant came along. With one glance he understood, and he turned pale! For in that one glance he had seen that the man was dead, and, what was worse, that everything he had possessed had disappeared. It was that that affected him most, for the looting of the dead was his due, it was part of his graft, his *débrouille*. Nevertheless he did not dare say anything, for he was not a strong individual and in the ward were two or three giant *forts-à-bras*. He approached the bed of the dead man and stuck a piece of glass before his mouth. That formality over, he searched under the mattress, hoping to find something the others had missed. Nothing! Furious, he went away. Ten minutes later he was back again with another attendant carrying a stretcher. He picked up the body and placed it on the stretcher without troubling to close the man's eyes, which were still staring wide open, and covered the body over with a sheet. Again, the attendant felt all over the mattress and raised it up—but there was nothing. So he picked up his end of the stretcher and, with his colleague, they took the body out to the amphitheatre.

"What's happened?" demanded a sick man at the end of the ward.

"Just another!" somebody told him. "That makes two this morning."

"He was a pretty good fellow," someone said.

"A rat—a piece of foul rubbish," another man insisted.

"He was soon to be freed," a third voice suggested.

"*Oui*," a harsh voice laughed, "Well, he is free now."

The next day nobody thought about him any more.

In the amphitheatre, the attendants put the bodies on a mortuary stone, one beside the other. The convict who is working on duty there watches the attendants go away; when he knows he is alone he picks up the feet of the dead man and moves the legs rhythmically —he is not trying to bring them to life—not by any means! He is hoping the corpse may still be carrying a suppository filled with money. This is his *débrouille*.

Then will come the hand-drawn wagon, pulled by two grumbling attendants (at Cayenne it is the same wagon which is used for gathering garbage in the streets), the two or three rough coffins will be piled one on the other and will go to the burial ground with no mourners. And it will be dropped into the "Bamboos," a pit in the mud with a cross without a name! They have finished suffering; from now on they will be happier and better off. They are dead men!

On the Islands it is even simpler. The bodies are taken out on the sea at sunset, where they are thrown to the waiting sharks that flash their broad fins around the death boat.

I had for a neighbor in the next bed a rather old convict whose name was Sigaut.

Sigaut had come to the *bagne* with a sentence of eight years in 1912, but now he still had twelve years to do before he would be a *libéré*, for he had tried to escape five or six times without attaining his cherished freedom. He had gotten to the point where he cursed eternally at the guards, at the Administration, and even at other convicts. He was in the hospital under treatment for hemorrhoids, and he was to be operated on one particular morning at nine o'clock, immediately after the medical visit.

To be brief, Sigaut was very much perturbed. Where was he going to hide his plan until the operation was over? The suppository contained 800 francs—a fortune —and for him it was more than a fortune; it was liberty, for he had made arrangements to embark on another escape the following week, hoping that this time luck would be with him. Therefore, Sigaut was deeply perplexed; it was a serious problem. Should he risk trusting it to the attendant, or, perhaps, to another convict? This seemed a dubious matter to him, for in the thirteen years he had been in the prison colony he had never come to have any friends and he did not trust a soul. In that environment where one is assassinated for 25 francs, why should he confide 800 francs to another man?

Should he hide it in his mattress? But, what if they changed it? It was a deep problem, and the clock had come around to eight and he still found no solution.

He got out of bed and went to the privy.

While he was there, his eye fell on the water tank up on the wall over his head. An idea came to him then. Up there, he thought, nobody would think of looking for it! He raised himself up and put his precious container on top of the tank, where it could not be seen from below. Then he vacillated. But what if some other fellow tried to hide something there!

While he stood in perplexity, the attendant called out from the ward: "Everybody in bed for the medical visit!"

Sigaut had no time to think, and he did not hesitate —hastily he placed his suppository in its usual hiding place, and hobbled back to bed.

He was taken to the operating room and stretched on the table. The attendant dropped the ether mask over

his face. Sigaut said later he saw thousands of suppositories spiralling all around him as he became unconscious.

"Pass me the knife," said the doctor to the attendant.
Then he proceeded to operate. All of a sudden he
breathed an exclamation of surprise: "Ah, par example . . . !" He had encountered his patient's suppository. He held up the object between pieces of
cotton, opened the tube and examined its contents.
There were the 800 francs. So he put them in his pocket
and continued with the operation.

Half an hour later Sigaut came to in his bed.

"Don't say a word about the suppository," the doctor
had cautioned the attendant. "I'll have you sent to the
cells if you do!"

Sigaut was on a diet for two days. He wanted very
much to eat, not because he was hungry, but because
he wanted to have to go to the privy so he could verify
the safety of his fortune. On the third day, the doctor
allowed him a light diet—and before long he was on
his way.

When he came back from the lavatory his face was
pale. His suppository had disappeared!

So Sigaut then started reconstructing everything minutely. "I had that suppository when I went to be operated on," he said to me. "When I came back I was
bandaged, and I didn't remove the bandages until the
third day. It disappeared when I was in that operating
room, and it's the doctor or that attendant who stole
it!" And he went to interview the attendant.

"You know very well I am above stealing 800
francs," said the attendant, "particularly when it comes
to you, who have been my friend for ten years!"

Sigaut remembered then that, true enough, he had
known Pelissier to have had often 12,000 francs in his
own suppository—undoubtedly, he was above such a
robbery. Furthermore, he enjoyed a good reputation
with the other convicts, and he would not be stupid
enough to turn thief and earn their hate and mistrust
for 800 francs.

"And as for the doctor, now, he is certainly above it," Pelissier told him with a tone of finality. Then he observed: "It seems to me your suppository is stuck. With a good purge you'll probably find it!"

Sigaut followed the attendant's suggestion. He took castor oil. He had to visit the privy four times. But there was still no suppository. The old convict was almost beside himself with worry and anger. The next morning, during the medical visit, he asked the doctor for permission to speak with him privately. The doctor motioned away the guard.

Sigaut proceeded to tell him about his troubles. The doctor listened and finally he told him to lie flat on his back.

Sigaut stretched himself out, and Pelissier, who stood near, put his sleeve over his mouth so the poor convict would not notice how he was about to burst with laughter.

The doctor then proceeded to press and tap Sigaut and then declared: "Your suppository is right there—I can feel it. A good purge, and it will certainly come out!"

Sigaut followed what, this time, were the doctor's instructions. Hopefully he made the necessary frequent visits. Still nothing! So he asked to speak to the doctor again. This time the doctor said to him gravely: "Your suppository must be lodged. It will necessitate an operation, otherwise there may be complications—fatal complications! What do you say?"

Sigaut remained pensive for a while, and then he declared: "Well, if that's the *only* way I will see my 800 francs again, then, sir, go ahead and operate!"

"Very well," said the doctor. "You will come into my office after the visit to sign the authorization."

That morning, when Sigaut walked out of the doctor's office, there was a smile all over his face; and in his funny provincial dialect he said to me, while he sat on the edge of his bed: 'What do you think of that! He made me clean myself, like a gun barrel, from end to end—and then he told me I had to let him slice me in half! Some joke! But he's not a bad fellow: He gave me back my suppository. He prescribed me a whole quart of rum. I'm getting quite fond of him!"

I was well treated in the hospital, because of the doctor's special attention, and when he announced that he was leaving for France I asked permission to speak with him. I asked him now to excuse my attitude, a thing I had not done before—for when a man has nearly lost his life through that sort of thing, he is not inclined to forget about it quickly. He was very decent about it all; he even thanked me warmly for forgetting how he had treated me at first. He was at heart a conscientious person.

"It would be necessary to send everybody to the hospital!" he exclaimed to me. "For all of you are sick! If sometimes I do not do my duty, it is because it's impossible for me to do so; you men confined in the blockhouses come last, for I am ordered to give hospital space to the other convicts who are more obedient. I suffer morally in the face of my helplessness as much as you convicts suffer physically from your miseries. I'm resigning and going back to civilization!"

I understood how he felt; but hard as he thought his lot had been, he had never been a convict and could not realize how terrible our end of the penal situation was.

When I had been in the hospital several weeks, the time came to appear before the *Tribunal Maritime Spécial*. I was to stand trial, with those who had been sent back from Dutch Guiana with me, for a second attempt at escape.

"This time things will not go so lightly with you, Belbenoit," a guard said. "Two attempts to escape are one too many!"

Chapter XI

CONVICTS who commit a crime or any other offense are tried by the *Tribunal Maritime Spécial,* the T. M. S. as it is called. This criminal court is composed of a President who is an officer of the army, usually a captain on duty at Cayenne, and two counselors, of whom one is an official of the Administration and the other a judge of the colonial civil court.

At every sitting of the T. M. S. about a hundred men, on an average, are tried. They are put through at the rate of twenty a day. The procedure is very rapid. The President questions the convict. Then the prosecutor has his turn, always demanding the maximum punishment. The defense for the convict is conducted by a guard who has no facility for speaking in public, and so he usually contents himself with saying merely: "I ask the court's indulgence for my client." That is all there is to the trial. The twenty men pass in four hours: after they have all come before the court and it has tried them, their punishments are read to them in a group.

The punishments dealt out are as follows: for offenses such as stealing, fighting and wounding, verbal outrage, insults, and refusal to work—from one month to five years in prison. For crimes such as assassination, murder, and striking a civilian or a guard—from six months to five years in solitary confinement, or capital punishment. There is no intermediary punishment between five years in solitary confinement and the death penalty! In fact, the bridge is even greater, for a man given five years in solitary confinement can obtain a conditional liberation from it when he has done a quarter of the punishment, or fifteen months, with a record of good conduct; so the court really has to decide between fifteen months or death for him. It is a vexatious dilemma for the court and an uncomfortable predicament for the prisoner. He usually goes to the guillotine, particularly if he is guilty of assaulting a guard or a civilian.

The crime of attempting to escape, *évasion,* is punished with one to five years in solitary confinement for convicts who have a life sentence, and, for all the others, it is from six months to three years in solitary confinement. When an *évadé* is brought back and placed in a blockhouse, a guard enters a report of *évasion* against him: "When did you escape? From where did you escape? Why did you try to escape? Did you have money? Did you have supplies? Have you any statement to add?" This report is then sent to the Governor, who decides if the man is to be brought before the T. M. S. or not. The *évadés* always have an excuse: They say that they had some sort of quarrel, and attempted to escape so as not to be killed by the other convict; if they are young men, they say they were prompted by the solicitations from older convicts; others say that they got lost in the jungle and wandered out of French Guiana; others that they wanted to get home to see their mother before she died; and some say that they were so miserable they took the chance, hoping the genuine excuse will move the authorities. There was a time when these reasons and excuses held, and the men were punished lightly, for the Administration hoped they would try again and not come back—that they would die in the attempt. In the past few years, however, since the newspapers and other agencies, by publishing the first-hand story of those who escaped and lived to tell about the horrors of Guiana, have drawn attention to conditions in French Guiana, the prison authorities have found, in this desire to escape and live, an excuse to kill off all such men by punishing them unreasonably. So the criminal court now punishes *évasion* with the maximum penalty, and, after the first attempt, this means from three to five years of internment on the Islands.

When we had been brought to the blockhouses after

our disastrous attempt to escape, I had told the chief guard that I had been prompted by desperation: for, I said, I had learned I was about to be sent to Camp Kourou and I felt that would be certain death for me because of my weak health, so I had preferred the other alternative. My army disability pension backed my claims, and, because of it, the court acquitted me for this *évasion*. But I was classed as incorrigible, and was given six months of prison because of my episode with the doctor. Big Marcel was acquitted also; for he invented some story to tell the court and, whether they did or did not believe it, they let him by, for it was his first time. He and I are the only two of the group alive today. The rest were all given the customary penalty: two years in solitary confinement for those with a life sentence, and six months of the same solitary confinement for the others. I was to learn, however, that the penalty of being classed as an "incorrigible" was a very severe punishment.

Chapter XII

THE "incorrigibles" of the prison colony—the rebellious, the ungovernable—are all men with unbroken wills, men whose thirst for liberty is supreme; some who are deeply cynical and have no care for what happens to them, others who are out-and-out villains and criminals: all of them individuals who are desperate and unafraid. For the classification "incorrigible" means that they will not bend weakly before the terrible authority of the prison guards.

The *incos* as they are called are, for the most part, convicts who have tried repeatedly to escape. The regulations state that automatically at the third attempt to escape a man is to be classed as incorrigible, after he has finished the punishment given him for his *évasion*. Other *incos* may be men who are headstrong, unruly

workers and bad characters who, along with the confirmed *évadés*, are lumped together under conditions
where the chances are very good that death will overtake them quickly. Any convict who, in less than three
months' time, has been given cell punishments of 108
days, is also classed as incorrigible and is sent to the
dread camp—if he survives the 108 days in semi-darkness on a ration of dry bread two days out of three.

Until 1926, the *incos* were banished to the terrible
Camp Charvein, which was known, along with Camp
Kourou, as the "Camp of Death!" Then, when this
camp was suppressed, the *incos* were put on Royale
Island until 1935. But today they are again on the
mainland, segregated in another camp which is just as
deadly as Charvein, but has another name: Camp
Godebert.

I was sent, at the direction of the *Tribunal Maritime
Spécial*, to Camp Charvein. It was then the most terrible camp in Guiana. Situated in the heart of the jungle
and about fifteen miles from Saint Laurent, it was in a
region where malaria and dysentery raged. The guards
were protected by nets and screens from the mosquitoes
and they were also protected from the menace of bad
water, but not so the convicts. It was a low swamp
region, and the men had to work with their feet wet
all day; and many of them had large ulcers on their
legs and feet.

When I arrived at Camp Charvein, there was an
inco crazed by the existence there, who was determined
to get out of the camp at any cost. One afternoon after
we had been locked up in the barrack he approached
me and held out a piece of needle in his hand:

"Here," he said, "make a hole in my eye!"

"Why, you're stupid, man!" I said in amazement.
"What good would that do!"

He said lowering his face and holding open his red
eyelid with one hand. "No, I mean it. Do it for me—
just a punch."

I simply could not do it. Finally, under the insistence
of the man an old convict took the blunt needle and

stabbed gingerly at the other's eye. We were all grouped around. The eyeball pushed back into the socket for the needle was not pointed enough to pierce it. After a few moments of looking on I had had enough of the gruesome sight. Some of the men told the old convict either to punch it in, or use a pointed knife. The old man was afraid that with a knife he would punch a hole in the other's brain, and he gave it up, but there was blood streaming down the other's cheek.

The next day the convict did the thing himself so he would be sent to Saint Laurent to the hospital.

There was another fellow there who, anxious to get out of the camp also and knowing the hospital was the only way, spread sperm on his eyes to get an infection; but he so overdid it in his desperation, that he became totally blind.

The *incos* were driven in a manner that was not human. The way we had to work was unmerciful. We had to cut down and chop up trees from morning until night. We were given no rest. For one in good physical shape this would have been hard enough, but we were all suffering from diseases, against the ravages of which we were given no medical treatment.

We had to work entirely naked, with only straw hats on our heads. This practice was instituted so as to reduce our opportunities of escape. Yet it did not prevent a good number of the *incos* from fleeing into the jungle completely naked. Their desperation was often so intense that, like naked animals, without even food, they ran into the jungle seeking escape or death. I have known several who escaped naked without a thing, and miraculous as it seems, one of them eventually reached Europe! The guards at Charvein, because of the nakedness of all *incos,* had to be single men or, if they were married, they were required to leave their wives in Saint Laurent.

My life at Charvein? A day among the Incorrigibles went on somewhat like this:

Five-thirty in the morning, *réveillé.*

We had been in irons all night. The turnkeys drew

98

out the *barres de justice*, each *inco* disengaged his ankle lock and slipped it back on the bar—this last was a necessary precaution, otherwise the *incos* would see to it that the ankle locks disappeared in the camp. All the men would then take off the clothes they had slept in, for, contrary to the normal custom in life, the men at Charvein would dress when they went to sleep and undress when they went outside to work. Then an *inco,* the keeper of the barrack, would go to the kitchen and get the coffee.

A few minutes after this, the gang was off to labor. The work might be in the forest or in a clearing. We proceeded in single file, carrying picks, shovels and axes on our bare shoulders. Guards, armed with rifles and girded with revolvers, escort us. These guards on duty over the *incos* are the meanest of the lot at Guiana, and most of them are hard-boiled Corsicans.

In every group there would also be a number of Arab turnkeys; these, chosen for their speed, were called by the *incos* "the running camels," for, in case any of the convicts fled into the jungle, the Arabs would chase after them with machetes and guns.

"Point of direction, clearings!" one of the guards commanded this morning, motioning which way our gang was to start.

Once at the clearing, the guards placed us in a line, five yards apart from each other. Our task was the making of ninety mounds of earth, each three feet high: they were to be used for potatoes, which later would be planted in them.

At each end of the line of toiling men, two turnkeys took up their stand, and in front and behind a guard held himself in readiness with his rifle under his arm, prepared to shoot in case of trouble, for the instructions were to fire on any *inco* who made a break to escape.

It was still early—around six in the morning. It was cool, and everybody worked easily. But, little by little, the sun came up over the clearing, and perspiration was soon flowing freely over bare insect-bitten bodies. The men after a while were blotched and streaked with earth, in a few hours they looked like animals which had been rooting in the ground. The line, which was straight when we started working on the furrows, became broken for some were stronger than the others and worked faster.

The guards look on.

"You, there! Lascret, I'll send you before the commission!"

One of the guards had noticed that the *inco,* who was in advance of the line, was working over on his neighbor's row, intending to help the slower man.

"What do I care!" answered Lascret. "The hell with you and your reports!"

"You'll get another report, for impudence," barked the guard, taking his notebook from his pocket.

"Make it three, if you want to!" snapped the *inco.* Then, after a while, he let his tool fall to the ground. "I'm sick," he said.

"Turnkeys!" cried the guard, in anger.

The Arabs came around Lascret and put handcuffs on him. He was made to sit on a stump, out in the center of the clearing under the burning sun, until it was time for the gang to start back to camp.

"You'll go to the commission, also, for another!"

An *inco* has picked up the stub of a cigarette which the guard has flipped near his feet on purpose, so as to catch him in the act.

"Can't you get it into your head," the *inco* replies, "that I don't give a damn what you tell the commission!"

So the second man is handcuffed to a stump in the burning sun.

Noon! Of the twenty-five *incos,* fifteen have finished their set task.

"In line, assemble!" barks the chief guard, while the other guards jot down in their books the names of the men who have not finished.

"Direction, the creek!" the guard commands.

When we reached the stream the men went into the tepid water to wash themselves. No diving was allowed;

100

for there have been some who have continued to swim off under water and escaped into the jungle on the opposite bank!

We returned to camp. The two who had talked back to the guard and those who did not finish their task have to go hungry, and are locked up in a special barrack.

Food at noon, and again at five o'clock; the ration was always reasonably sufficient, for the cooks in the camp never pilfered the food allowance of the incorrigibles.

At six o'clock the irons went on. Each man put on clothes as soon as darkness fell. Talking was prohibited, but we did talk in low voices; we talked of *escape,* naturally, for that was all we thought about. For freedom all of us had already staked our lives at least once—and we were ready to do so again at the next opportunity. Perhaps there is a little tobacco in the barrack bought at a high price from one of the turnkeys, and the carefully rolled cigarette was passed from mouth to mouth, the butt stuck finally on a pin until there was nothing left of it; for among the *incos* there is a certain amount of mutual misery and comradeship. After a while we fell asleep and the only sound that remained was that of irons clicking on the bars. This is the only moment in the 24 hours that these miserable beings find any relief from their sufferings. Some dream they are free: others lie awake and plan their next attempt at escape.

The regulations state that for an *inco* to be restored to the normal life of the prison he must have served six months, and in the last three of these he must not have any punishments marked against him. The guards in the camp, either because they take a dislike to a man or because they are simply bullies, do their best to catch one tripping, especially when a man has only a few days more of good conduct before losing his grade of Incorrigible. At night, after the men are put in irons, a guard will roam stealthily around or simply stand outside the barrack so as to surprise a man in the act of speaking, solely to make a report against him! If an *inco* is caught committing an offense he must start the three months all over again; another eternity, during which he is prodded and goaded and kicked, to endure without a single error before he can be *déclassé* or restored to normal prison life. Many of the prisoners get so desperate they make themselves targets for the guards' bullets, others eventually fall victims to disease, some manage to live whole years there before they escape from the "Incorrigible" class. There was one of them, Meurs, who stayed eleven consecutive years at Charvein, with a total of 2,300 days in cell on dry bread two days out of three!

There was one *inco*, Peploch, who was what one might call the king of the confirmed *évadés*. Peploch, condemned to five years at hard labor in 1902, was still there when I arrived. He had brought upon himself a grand total of thirty-six years of supplementary punishments for *évasion*. As an *inco* he escaped six times into the jungle, and this he did completely naked! The guards fired fusillades at him, and never succeeded in wounding him; but, poor fellow, he would be brought back every time, sometimes from Venezuela, other times from Dutch Guiana or somewhere else. And each time he came back they would give him two or three more years, and back he would be in the hell at Charvein. He was hated by every guard, for, each time he escaped, the ones that were on duty with the gang would get suspended for thirty days without pay!

A Corsican guard whom the convicts called "The Assassin," because he had five killings to his credit, would often ask Peploch, "Is it today you're going to escape?" He hated Peploch.

"No," Peploch would reply, "But the day soon comes —I'll warn you!"

One morning Peploch went off to labor with shoes on; this was unusual, for the *incos* almost never wear shoes when they go to work, although it is the only piece of garment they are permitted to wear.

The guard asked him, "Well, Peploch, I guess it's today you're going to escape, eh?"

"Yes!" answered Peploch. "Today's the day!"

The guard took up his post behind the working gang, with his rifle under his arm ready for trouble. He unbuckled the strap over his pistol so he could draw it quickly. An hour went by. Two hours went by. All of a sudden two *incos* started a violent quarrel. The other guard cried out, "Turnkeys!" At that same instant Peploch, hurling a shovel of dirt into the face of the guard as he stood behind him, yelled to him, "Goodbye, son-of-a-bitch!" and raced off at top speed toward the jungle.

It happened in a split moment. The guard was so blinded by the dirt in his eyes that he lost his head and did not fire until Peploch had already reached the trees. It was then too late! Peploch was not seen again in the penal colony until, eight months later, he was sent back from some point far along the coast to the west. But he got his laugh at the cocky guard, who had again been suspended for thirty days without pay.

In 1925 while I was at Charvein the dean of the *incos* was old Laporte, whom they called D'Artagnan. He was sixty-two years old. Laporte had been condemned for five years in 1887. Shipped to New Caledonia, he had escaped several times and was arrested in France, and was sent out next to Guiana when the former penal colony was suppressed because it was too far away and less convenient for convict transportation. From Guiana he escaped six times and lived in Colombia and Venezuela, but had the hard luck to be arrested and sent back from both those countries. He finally died in prison, being mowed down by a guard's bullet. The youngest prisoner at Charvein then was Roger Pecquet, who was less than seventeen; you will read about him further on.

Classed as "incorrigible" in June of 1925, I had the good fortune to be *déclassé* in August by favor of a new Director of the Administration to whom I sent a petition. I was thus spared, after eighty tormented days, from certain death. In the rundown and anemic state I was in, I should certainly have died there before the expiration of my full sentence. I had addressed a petition to the new Director stating the condition of my health and asking that I be released from the incorrigible class. I had been so classified unfairly, I said—according to the regulations three *évasions* were necessary, and I had only two against me! However, though freed from the Camp of Death, I still had my sentence of imprisonment for insulting the doctor to serve, and I had to go to Saint Joseph for a term of six months. And so, I was embarked for the Islands . . . for the Islands of Hell.

Chapter XIII

IN THE courtyard of the blockhouses at Saint Laurent, some sixty men, chained two and two, were waiting on that August afternoon to be embarked for the Islands. They had received punishment for *évasion* or for murder at the hands of the T.M.S.—banishment to the feared solitary confinement cells on Saint Joseph. There were three who were sick and were not in irons; of these three two of us were being sent by the doctor to convalesce for a few months in the hospital on the Royale. The other was on a stretcher and was going to solitary confinement, in spite of his condition: he had on only a pair of trousers, which were soiled by his dysentery. He was groaning, but no one except myself and one or two of his friends paid any attention to him.

We moved out of the penitentiary and proceeded to the landing, where the night steamer, the *Mana* smoked, ready to push off. The small coastal boat connects Saint Laurent with Cayenne, the capital of the colony, on the northeast coast. The passengers went aboard first. These were all natives, who did not even look at the gang of chained convicts, for they were thoroughly accustomed to such sights. The native women had on bright-colored dresses and checkered handkerchiefs wrapped around their heads. They talked and laughed gayly. There was a clutter of baggage on deck: reed baskets, pans and other cooking utensils, *vases de nuit* in all colors, dogs, pigs and babies some of whom were a bit too white. We chained men were then shoved below deck into the hold. In a few minutes the boat was out in the Maroni River, and had begun to nose downstream in the thick muddy current.

When we reached the mouth of the river, the turnkeys came down and removed our handcuffs. This was done, however, only after we were well out at sea, for it has frequently happened that condemned men, going to the Islands, have leaped out of the hold and into the river and escaped under the bullets of the guards. When night came, a dim lamp was lit in the hold. Some of the men got seasick and stretched out where they could; they vomited everywhere, and the hot stench was foul. Someone sang in a minor key; he had a good voice, and knew some new songs, for he had come to the prison colony in the last cargo from France.

Most of these men with me, thrown into the hold with bags of cement and other freight, were going to the Islands—Royale, Saint Joseph's, or Devil's Island to stay for many long unendurable years in solitary confinement, or to the prison on Saint Joseph, then to be transferred to Royale and interned there until their crimes were forgotten or their conduct showed they had mended their ways; or, more probably, until there got to be too many men on the Islands, and the Administration would find itself forced to clear some of them out. When this situation arises, the Administration selects those convicts who have been on the Islands longest— whom the Islands can't destroy—for it knows that these restless men will have but one objective when they get back to the mainland, that which they have been thinking of and planning to execute so long— *escape*. Then the Administration can punish them again, and *this* time they will probably die!

After eighteen hours of shaking and chugging the boat came to a stop. We could see the group of three islands outside our barred portholes in the morning light. It seemed a lovely picture. Green and studded with palms, they looked like a miniature paradise. A large rowboat, manned by brawny, tanned convicts, with a guard standing at the helm, came alongside. It began going back and forth, taking twenty convicts at a time, and in a short while we were all landed on Royale. We looked pensively at the *Mana* chugging off in the distance; and in every man's mind was the thought: When will it take me back again?

Ten miles from the mainland and thirty miles west of Cayenne the three islands rise from the blue sea. *"Iles du Salut!"* . . . a name ironical to the condemned. They were named thus three centuries ago by the first colonists sent by Louis XV to Guiana. Having founded a colony at Kourou on the mainland, they were rapidly decimated there by a devastating epidemic of yellow fever, and so they took refuge on the small islands they saw out at sea. The pure air on the islands brought health back to many of them, and from this comes the name, "Islands of Salvation." But to the condemned they are now "The Islands of Hell!"

The largest one was named Royale to please the French King; the island neighboring it was named Saint Joseph, for the saint under whose protection the original expedition had set out; the smallest one, on which the early colonists never went, because the current made it unapproachable, was called Devil's Island because they attributed the fury of the sea in the narrow channel between it and Royale to the devil himself. It is very difficult even today to get to Devil's Island; the Administration has connected it with Royale by a cable which serves to take the provisions across to the political prisoners.

The first prisoner on this island, which is a large rock covered profusely with coconut trees, was Captain Dreyfus who lived on it alone in a hut for five years. His famous case attracted the attention of the entire world, and it was through it that the existence of the most terrible prison on earth was made known to the general public, which still confuses the penal colony with the tiny island on which Dreyfus was confined and which has given it its name. When he was proved to be innocent and taken back to France, Devil's Island remained uninhabited for about twelve years, until 1910. In that year Ullmo, an officer in the navy, was brought there and lived in Dreyfus' cabin for fifteen years. After the Armistice, some twenty political prisoners were brought to the island. Today there are only six. Each one lives alone in a small cabin. They have better food than the other convicts. But theirs is a lonely, barren life on the sea-surrounded rock, and is a sadder life than that of the other condemned men in the colony.

Only some fifty men have been put on the island since 1852. Every night each prisoner is locked into his cabin from dark to dawn; they are not made to work, and spend their time doing what they want to do: most of them sit and fish all day long. They must cook their own food. Their only duty is to gather the coconuts on the island for the Administration; this they must do if they wish to get their ration of wine.

Royale and Saint Joseph are about the same in area, having a respective shore line of one mile and a quarter in circumference. Devil's Island is only about twelve hundred yards in circumference, and one can almost circle it while smoking a cigarette. Seen from a distance they have all a pleasant aspect, covered with palms and whitewashed buildings which have red tiles on their roofs. From the sea they look like a paradise, but in reality they are an island hell, where 850 damned souls suffer eternally in torment.

In the first years of the penal colony the Administration was established on the Islands. It was there that the first convoy of convicts was landed in 1852; then, a few years later, when the prisons were built on the mainland at Cayenne and at Saint Laurent, the Administration made the Islands a unit for repression and punishment.

The normal number of convicts on the three can be divided up as follows: On Devil's Island: political prisoners—11. On Saint Joseph: convicts in solitary confinement—300; turnkeys—30, convicts sent for disciplinary measures to prison there—70. On Royale: convicts freed from solitary confinement and held for a period of time on the Islands as punishment for *évasion* —350; turnkeys and convicts sent there for other crimes—100.

Life on the Islands, I was to discover, was entirely different from the routine of the mainland prisons and camps. On the Islands, there is no work: On them, there is only punishment and waiting . . . great suffering and great restlessness. While a convict is on them he must put off all his projects connected with *escape,* and he resorts to making his idle time pass as best he can. Two vices flourish there with greater ease than they do on the mainland; gambling and immorality.

Two convicts carried me on a stretcher from the landing to the hospital of Royale. I wonder, even today, how I ever endured that trip from the mainland in the stifling hold of the *Mana,* for during the entire crossing my jaws clacked with fever and I vomited incessantly.

The doctor of Royale ordered me to be put in a partitioned-off room reserved for the very ill.

My temperature went up and up. I could not even swallow bread, and everything else I tried to eat would not stay down. What was wrong with me? The doctor diagnosed my sickness as "some sort of stomach trouble," and prescribed milk and eggs with laxatives as medicine.

Even this nourishment I could not eat. Only chocolate, and now and then an egg, would stay with me. I could not touch bread, an indispensable food to me. The doctor tried to get me to eat it dipped in coffee, with butter on it, with chocolate, in chicken broth; but I couldn't keep it down, and day by day I grew alarmingly thinner. Then I developed diarrhoea. I weighed around eighty pounds—was really nothing more than a listless bundle of bones. More than once the attendant, I knew, thought I would die in the night. But my will to live stuck by me, and that is probably what pulled me through.

I experienced at this time a state of deep depression. Four years had passed since my arrival in Guiana. Long years of physical privations and mental torture—dragging years of pain, hunger and illness. My former life had faded slowly in my memory: France, my family, Paris and Renée herself . . . all had lost their vividness in my thoughts, which had become absorbed with the obsession to escape and to live. And here I was now, dying! There were moments, rare ones, when the past would surge up in me and my mind would turn to all which I had lost—which seemed hopelessly lost. Then I would be steeped in melancholy. But those vivid retrospections, fortunately, were not frequent, I thought of the men who had come with me to Guiana, and there was a long list—a very long one—of dead men. I, too, like the few others who had survived, had now become regimented among the uncivilized. I was now an established convict, familiar with the ways of the prison colony. Little by little I had grown to know and understand the attitude and mentality of the condemned, terrible because of the utter lack of anything remotely resembling frankness or friendship, and the ever-present sexual corruption which brooded like a black miasma over it all.

Only those individuals continually bent on *évasion*, on escaping, seemed worthy of respect, for they did not abandon themselves to vice and had only one thing in mind—to get out of that Hell at any cost.

In my mind, I had divided the convicts amongst whom I had to live, into three classes: those who thought only of escaping, and were prepared to gamble their lives to regain their liberty; those who did not think about *évasion*, because they were too old or were resigned to their fate, and the ones who were apparently content, because they were like animals. These last

were, for the most part the *forts-à-bras,* who were the
curse of the prison colony for any self-respecting man,
prisoner or officer. They were vile, steeped in moral,
physical, and sexual degradation.

I had also come to understand the underhand work-
ings of the Administration; I realized that good conduct
meant nothing; I knew that only if I had money in my
possession would I have a chance and, if I had it, I
could get everything I pleased. I had seen for myself
how, frequently, convicts sent 25 francs to the wife of
the Director of the Administration so as to obtain a
favored position, and had obtained it. I had learned
about the incredible rackets practised by the guards—
incredible, but, nevertheless, true. Lying there in the
hospital, I was utterly disgusted and shocked. I found
nothing, absolutely nothing to cling to, and I knew I
had to get away, if I hoped to remain a man, a self-
respecting individual, before it was too late. The abuses
of the Administration revolted me as much as did the
vileness of the convicts. It revolted me even more, for
there was no excuse for it, and it was a hideous advantage taken by a crooked governmental system over poor
men who had no powerful friends, no redress.

One day I happened to notice on my temperature
chart the letters "T.B." Tubercular! I, tubercular? For a
few moments I was surprised. Then I became frantic.
The attendant was passing by and I gave him 20 sous
to go get the convict who was the bacteriologist, to
come and talk with me.

After a while he appeared, and I asked him if it was
true I was tubercular.

"Oh, pay no attention to that chart!" he said. "The
doctor has been doing the analysis himself, and you
know how he sees everything around here as a tragedy
—I'll make the analysis for you myself—for ten
francs!"

A few days later he came back and assured me there
was nothing wrong with my lungs, and he prompted
me to ask the doctor to analyze my sputum again,

which I did. The "T.B." disappeared from my chart, much to my relief!

The doctor was very good to the convicts; he was really too good, for our suffering so upset him that he put everybody he could in the hospital and gave all the sick copious quantities of medicines as well as monumental diets. He was going a little crazy himself, I often suspected. Within a few short months he emptied the pharmacy and the food magazine as well, and the Administration lost no time in seeing to it that he was replaced.

As a contrast to him in technique, there came Doctor Rousseau. The fact that the hospital for the Islands has no running water, that all its windows are broken out and the floors about to fall in, and that he had to leave to the next day the patients he could not get around to who were in agony from dysentery, typhoid, malaria and tuberculosis, only brought out his spirit instead of causing him to adopt a philosophical and resigned attitude. When there was no chicken and no broth for the men in the hospital, he would calmly take his rifle and go into the chicken yards of the guards, and *ping! ping! ping!*—he would have twenty chickens for the men. And he would tell the furious guards they had no right to more than a few chickens when there were dying men in need of food. He would have the men in solitary confinement brought to the hospital for a month's respite, at the end of every three months in the awful cells. He never hesitated to tell the guards, and the Commandant also, when, how and where to go to the devil—and when he said anything he meant it and insisted on it, and it was done!

He began his duties on the Islands by emptying the hospital. He found one hundred and twenty men in it, and he arbitrarily decided that in the future there would not be more than fifty! When he got to my case and investigated my diet, he was openly astounded by the quantity of food his predecessor h d prescribed for me, and he suppressed almost the whole diet. It was that which saved my life. The miracle happened! I was soon

111

able to eat a little bread, and before long I gained weight. Every week I gained six or seven pounds, and, when I stood on the scales, I was happy; for I felt again that I was not destined to leave my bones in Guiana.

In the middle of March the doctor talked of putting me on the outgoing list but I asked him to let me stay until the first of the month, which was the date when I would have been six months on Royale and when, in consequence, my punishment of six months would be ended. This would save me going to solitary confinement for even a few days! He understood and was kind enough to keep me in the hospital until the first of April.

When I was sent out, I went to the office of the chief guard of the Islands, to sign my release on the jailbook, and he put me in the Second Platoon of prisoners and sent me to the Royale barracks . . . the Crimson Barrack, where many famous prisoners have died.

Doctor Rousseau is probably the only man (with the exception of Governor Siadous) whom the condemned still talk of and know by name: But he was recalled to France. The day he left the Islands, the convicts made and gave him a huge bouquet of flowers as he got into the rowboat. He has never been forgotten by the condemned.

Chapter XIV

LA CASE ROUGE—the Crimson, the Bloodstained Barrack: it is the most colorful barrack of the entire penal colony of French Guiana, the prison quarters of the Second Platoon. For the men assigned to them are usually the most dangerous and vicious convicts in the prison colony.

When a man has finished his prison term for a crime committed in the prison colony he is sent there. When he is freed from the dark cells of solitary confinement on Saint Joseph, where he has been imprisoned for many months—or many years—for a knife thrust or an attempt to escape, he is brought over to Royale and locked up in this barrack of the Second Platoon. The incorrigibles, also, if they live to be *déclassés,* are brought there. It is here, that, likewise, the criminals whose crimes caused sensations in France are confined by the Administration, which is ever fearful that these particular individuals will get away and cause another stir in the press against the unspeakable conditions in Guiana; they, the notorious criminals, are brought to the Crimson Barrack straight from the cargo when the convict ship arrives.

It is here, in this barrack of evil reputation, that the celebrities and heroes of the colony have spent much of their time. Dreyfus was kept there before he was taken to Devil's Island. Dieudonné was imprisoned there for many years, together with his friend Jacob, who was the leader of the Amiens gang which used a Browning gun in France for the first time. The famous Mandat, France's first *apache,* lived there and he performed the duties of attendant in the hospital, and Paul Roussenq, the "king of the black cells," stayed there most of the time he was not in a cell. In recent years, new names have been added to the roll of the *case rouge!* Baratand, the millionaire murderer against whom the town of Limoges made a mass demonstration because he was not given the death sentence; Peter Klems, who became a Moslem and, as lieutenant for Abd El Krimm, commanded the Moroccans against French troops and was finally captured by the Foreign Legion from which he had deserted; Pierre de Reyssac, the count who feared scandal and drowned the child he had had by one of his servants, who later revealed his crime; Boppé, brother-in-law of Maurice Barrès the famous writer and member of the Académie Française, who created a major scandal among the wealthy aristocracy of France when his criminal attempt against his beautiful wife was openly denounced by his family; the three Oustachis, who took part in the attack which caused the death of King Alexander and the French Minister, Barthou; and others, many others. Composed of famous criminals, *évadés* and men who have committed the worst crimes in the prison colony, this Second Platoon has a special flavor of its own and is set apart from all the other island convict groups.

The barrack of the Second Platoon is about forty yards long by six wide, and the number of men in it varies between sixty and eighty. The convicts are admitted into it through a grilled door made with enormous iron bars. To look at it casually one would think it might be some kind of crude zoo—that there were gorillas inside. At six in the evening, when the roll is called, the guards fasten the door, bolting it heavily. They will not open it again until next morning at *réveillé,* unless during the night a man has been seriously wounded and has to be taken to the hospital, a thing which happens with consistent frequency, much to the pleasure of the Administration; for every convict who dies in this barrack is a man of whom the Administration is more than glad to be rid.

As soon as the great door is closed, things take on their personal aspect within, such as even the guards do not know. Little lamps, lighted in the darkness, flare up and fling a little light over each convict as he devotes himself to his personal occupation. Two rows of hammocks are strung up, and in the narrow passage between them men pace back and forth. The little lamps are all of a standard model, a condensed milk can in the opening of which the owner has inserted a small socket made from a piece of tin: they give a light necessary to see and work by, which the regulation oil lamp in the center of the barrack does not provide. The men buy the oil from the keeper of the barrack, who is the lamplighter, who always has some to sell, because of his economical use of the oil for the regulation lamp. This is a part of his *débrouille,* his kerosene graft!

Look over my shoulders, while I show you around.

Over there, a man naked to his waist and his skin

blue from tattooing, is weaving a rug out of a pile of aloes. It is *Le Masque,* The Mask, an old *fort-à-bras*— he has been given this name because of the tattooing with which he is covered from head to foot: his face is all blue, he has a red mustache on his upper lip, and his skull which is cropped like mine, is blue.—He says that this tattooing is his hair! On each cheek he has an ace of spades and on his forehead an ace of clubs is tattooed. Beyond him, another prisoner is carving a design on a coconut. Near him four or five men play cards on the floor. Under another lamp a shoemaker squats at the foot of his hammock, mending a shoe which a guard has given him to patch. Another convict sews on a pair of pants for which he will get a few sous, while his neighbor plucks a tango tune on a mandolin made from a bit of wood which he has found on the island. One man is writing, with frequent curses, to his lawyer in France. There is another convict sitting in the light of his lamp, reading an old newspaper which he has found in the garbage can when he swept the Commandant's yard. In the passage between the hammocks, a few naked men talk about their last *évasion,* and plan their next one. Others discuss a bit of *débrouille,* some graft combination through which, tomorrow, they will get some sous to add to their funds, for they are all whiling away their time and thinking of something which will get them money—escape from there and acquisition of money are their predominant preoccupations. From time to time, above the sounds made by these seventy-odd men while they talk, comes the cry, "Ho, Carpette . . . two coffees!" "Carpette, three coffees!"

Carpette is the keeper of the barrack. For 4 sous, he sells coffee made from the leftovers from the kitchen; he mixes it with beans, and it is sweet and hot, and it is good although it has a taste which is only slightly reminiscent of coffee. When an order is called out, he sends his protégé around with the coffee. Carpette is a man of business, and this is part of his accepted *débrouille.* He also sells tobacco, cigarette paper, matches, salt, pepper, oil, vinegar and onions; in short, all that a convict may need to improve his ration, he sells for a few sous. He has stolen these things from the Island supplies. In addition he is the owner of the only "library" on the Islands, comprising twelve hundred volumes which he has persistently collected in the course of many long years: gifts from *libérés* who are at Cayenne and at Saint Laurent, discarded novels handed him by the doctors, volumes which the Commandant has read and does not wish to keep any longer, magazines and books which the guards have turned over to him: a library where the novels of Nick Carter and Buffalo Bill rub elbows with the *Odyssey* and the *Iliad!* There are books for all tastes; Nietzsche is a good neighbor of Victor Hugo, and Jack London of Tolstoi. And Carpette, the scoundrel, rents his books at the price of 2 sous for three days, payment in advance! He was sent to Royale for eight years in 1912. He has four or five more years to do before he will become a *libéré*—eight attempts to escape have cost him sixteen additional years as a convict.

The rattling of a tin box filled with sous is heard. It is the signal for the *la marseillaise,* the favorite gambling game of the convicts. The men start gathering toward the persistent sound.

A strumming of instruments has started up. It is "Sasse's Orchestra," getting ready to practise for the dance that will be held on Sunday by the guards. Sasse! Because he was accused, but without proof, of attempting to murder Gomez, the President of Venezuela, that country closed its doors to all other French *évadés*. He had come back here, at the end of three years in the most dreaded and notorious Venezuelan prison, "La Rotonda," with twelve other escaped convicts who had been rounded up in Venezuela, and the scars of the irons they had put on him were still visible on his legs. Mandolin, banjo, violin, and guitar strike up the latest songs, with a fine touch of originality; for, after all, the musicians have been there so long they do not know how a modern piece should sound! The music lasts until the nine o'clock bell, and then because silence is ordered by the guards, the musicians put away their homemade instruments and join the gambling game which will last until dawn.

Everywhere in the prison colony there is gambling. It is one of the only distractions at night—the convict is tempted to try his luck constantly to gain a few francs. The most popular of all the games is the *la marseillaise*, a form of baccarat. The man who holds the game as the banker has to be a strong character, an individual who is not afraid to receive knife blows or to give them; he is usually a *fort-à-bras* or a Corsican, or a man from Marseilles. He deals the cards and supervises the course of the game; and, when disputes and quarrels arise, he has to exercise his authority by taking it upon himself to settle the differences and bring order back to the game. The money bank is his and into it goes at every play, as his gain, one tenth of the winnings; he wins in a night between 10 and 100 francs, and there are nights when his winnings amount to as much as 500 francs. Naturally, it is a position which is persistently coveted, and he has to be a man who is able to defend it. Often it costs him his life! He is always partial to a few men who are his friends; this is his privilege. To one he gives the job of spreading out the blanket for the game; to this convict goes one tenth of the winnings of the money bank—on the Island this job is always the accepted right of the last man who has come from solitary confinement, simply so that he can have a few sous immediately after his release from the awful cells. Another puts cigarettes on the blanket; from the tobacco in a pack of twenty cigarettes which cost him 20 sous, he rolls forty new cigarettes, which he puts on the blanket in a box; the players have no time to roll their own, and so they drop 2 sous into the box and take out a cigarette while they play. Some other friends of the convict who holds the bank have a box or two of candy on the blanket, and the players drop 2 sous and munch one while they sit absorbed in the gambling. The game keeps the money flowing from hand to hand and creates commerce! From time to time a player goes to the privy, where he takes a bill out of his suppository and returns to play it on the blanket. Carpette, as keeper of the barrack also sells candy and cigarettes to the players, making a one hundred per cent profit; some convict down to his last sous has empty tin cans to distribute for the men to relieve themselves in, and these when full he empties in the privy, thus earning his tobacco; and, when a man makes a lucky pass, he orders a round of coffee for the whole house, or he empties the boxes of cigarettes and bonbons out on the blanket for the men who are around him.

The little lamps are put out one by one. Soon only the toothless old *fort-à-bras* is awake weaving the rug from aloes; he needs money and tomorrow the mail boat from France stops at the Islands. He will give the rug to the brawny oarsmen, who will sell it for twice the sum the old convict asks. Rolled up in their worn blankets, many of the men begin to snore. A few sitting on the edges of their hammocks whisper in the dark. This is the hour of whisperings, the hour of vice among the condemned. The other men pay no attention, for this is part of the life of the prison colony. The *forts-à-bras* are the ones who lead in all homosexual vices; they seek out and make vice slaves of the younger convicts. They are at home with prison life, for it has been their existence for years; and since they know prison life so well, they assist each other, and lack nothing whether in solitary confinement or anywhere else in the prison colony. Their self-esteem is set on a hair-trigger: over a word they will draw a knife. The Administration uses them to its advantage: they are usually appointed cooks in the camps; for if a convict makes a complaint to a chief guard about the food, he makes it at the same time against the cook; and if the cook is a *fort-à-bras* he will confront the convict and maim or kill him. Usually they do not attempt to escape: they talk about it, but do not put their hopes into effect, for their lot is better in Guiana than that of the other men.

118

They manage to get the most remunerative jobs; they have their perverts. They have neither scruples nor honor; they are the accomplices of the guards and confide to them when a prisoner has a large sum of money, so as to get their part if it is confiscated. They know that if they are surprised at any wrongdoing the guards will seldom denounce them. They become very jealous and fond of their *mômes* or young perverts. However, little by little the younger ones will grow older and more vicious themselves, and then in turn each will look for the company of a young pervert for himself. Veritable dramas turn about this phase of life at the prison colony. The young perverts are very touchy about their sexual relationships. Never does a convict permit himself to call one of them *"môme"* to his face, for this will bring on him the anger of the older man and he will have one more hatred to be on guard against. It is the older man of a pervert couple who "keeps house," so to speak—he defends his young *môme* and makes the money necessary for lavishing presents of tobacco, bonbons and other gifts on his companion.

At last it is quarter past five. *Réveillé!* The door is unlocked and the guards come in for inspection. Carpette goes to the kitchen to make the coffee. The house is cleared, and everything folded away. Knives have been hidden in the hollow bars of the hammocks, or in the rafters of the roof, and the guards do not trouble to look closely for them. The cards have disappeared, as well as the tools of the shoemaker and those of the man who was carving on the coconut. As for Carpette who, like a real smuggler, sometimes has *tafia*, or rum, to sell, he has only water now in his pot! The guards take a final look in the privy. It is at the far end of the barrack, connected with it by a narrow corridor about fifteen feet long. They are making sure, as a last measure, that a bloodstained body is not sprawled out at its end.

The privy of the Second Platoon is more bloodstained than any place of its size in the world; there, in that one spot, more murders have been done than in any place on earth of such restricted space. There, matters are settled; jealousies, vengeances and personal grudges—there, a man's money is taken from him after he has been surprised suddenly! It has happened hundreds of times. Time and again while I lived in the Crimson Barrack I have been awakened by a cry, and heard groans fade into a death gurgle. I knew where the sounds were coming from. Sometimes a victim runs back into the barrack room grasping for a support in the dim light, finally falls dead in the passageway. No one will make a move against his assailant—it is a characteristic of the convicts. But eyes flame in the darkness, those of the victim's friends, who plot the other's certain death, when he can be taken by surprise. And when, a little later, the door opens to admit the guards and turnkeys with lanterns and cocked revolvers in their hands, the guards know immediately where to look. Often, too, going to the privy in the late hours of the night, I have stumbled over a still form and have had to wipe sticky, coagulated blood from my bare feet on the sides of the corridor!

There are periods when there are two and three crimes a month in the privy of the Crimson Barrack, sometimes more than five. The guilty one? When the murderer is discovered he has nine and one half chances in ten of being acquitted. For, curiously, among the convicts the unwritten law is to place the blame on the dead man. Accuse the victim, who is dead to all suffering, and save the live one, even if he is guilty—even if he is your sworn enemy. For you can kill him later when it is convenient and safe. There is never a witness against the murderer; no one will be a *mouchard,* a blackguard informer, for he will bring upon himself the hatred of his fellow-convicts by rendering even such a service to the Administration.

Carpette comes back with diluted coffee, and passes along the hammocks with the big copper kettle. By diluting the issued coffee he accumulates beans to sell later. Each convict takes the measuring cup attached to the coffee kettle and dips into the steaming liquid, plunging the cup deep to bring it out full, but in vain, for the handle has been strangely twisted so the cup cannot be brought up full! This is another phase of Carpette's business flare. By denting the measuring cup he saves a little quantity of coffee from each man, all of which adds up to several portions, which he will sell later for 4 sous each. When he has twisted the handle too much and the men show open annoyance over his little trick, he redeems himself by having it perfectly straight for several days—thus throwing them off guard the next time he passes by, for Carpette never loiters with the kettle! He always points ahead with one impatient hand while the convict is filling his cup, grumbling that the other men are waiting! The men, including the *forts-à-bras,* are lenient with him, for he is worth keeping on the good side since they are dependent on him for the purchase of extras. He knows just how far he can go, even if he finds it necessary to distribute a gift occasionally, and he never oversteps their patience.

La case rouge! That is what the men call it. It is also the barrack of despair—for while a convict is there he has no hope of escape, and can only dream of a distant freedom while he is confined with an utterly reckless group of exiled prisoners; and while he hoards his money for liberty, he has to defend it and his life every night. Before he can return again to the mainland, he has to be promoted to the First Platoon, which is quartered on the other side of the compound. And to do this, eighteen months of good conduct are necessary; and, when a convict can see the coast on the horizon and dreams of escaping each night, this is . . . too long.

No outsiders are ever allowed on these Islands, and very few are the people who have visited them for other than official reasons. Of the bloodstained barrack of the Second Platoon, in particular, nothing has ever been

121

written. I have suffered there beyond the power of telling. I have lived nights of desperation and despair there. I kept on living while all about me blood flowed and men died.

Chapter XV

AFTER a convict has been in Guiana a few months he comes to know, from hearing them so often repeated, the names of the notorious dreaded aces of the penal colony; men who have come by their reputation through their audacity, by reason of their herculean strength or because of their easy deadliness with a knife.

In 1926 on the Islands, three men had earned the nickname of "Terror"; these three were Louis Briolat, known as *"La Brioche,"* who met with death three years later in the Second Platoon, Julien Palanco, who is still alive today and is surrounded by waiting enemies, and Muratti, called *"Le Fou"* (the Madman).

Muratti was in the Second Platoon on Royale. He was a Corsican and, although small of build, he was the most dangerous of the three men most feared on the Islands. A few months previously he had been liberated from solitary confinement, where he had done two years for his last murder. The number of men he had wounded could hardly be counted. When he needed money, he would aggressively demand it openly from some convict in the barrack, no matter whom. On several occasions he had, at night, possessed himself by force of the money bank from the man who held the game at la marseillaise! And, after emptying the contents, he would stand in defiance and cry menacingly: "Anybody who thinks he can, let him come take the money from me!" Not one would make a move, for they all knew that before the money could be reached a life would have been taken. Muratti was very clever with his knife. And thus Muratti came to be the banker who conducted the gambling game every night!

One night the six o'clock bell had just clanged for the lockup. We were lined in front of the barrack answering to the roll call, when our attention was attracted by the arrival of a newcomer to the platoon whom the turnkeys were searching under the gate before sending him into camp.

A name passed swiftly in a whisper from mouth to mouth, "Balestra! Balestra!" We all turned our heads mechanically to where Muratti stood. Time and again, after he had come out of solitary confinement, Muratti had threatened terrible menaces against another convict from Marseilles—one Balestra who, he said, attemped to poison him; for Balestra was cooking at the time for the men in solitary confinement.

"I'll kill the scum the day he puts his foot on Royale!" Muratti had sworn. And now Balestra had been brought to Royale, and had been fatefully assigned to the Second Platoon. The day for vengeance was here!

The roll call was over, we went inside. Balestra entered at the end of the line. The turnkey closed the heavy iron door, and locked the bar into place outside. Muratti did not seem to have noticed the arrival of his sworn enemy. He went over to his accustomed place in the barrack, while Balestra found himself a place at the other end among compatriots from Marseilles, who celebrated his arrival by ordering several rounds of coffee from Carpette.

I saw one of the men from Marseilles slip a freshly sharpened knife into Balestra's hand, with the warning: "Keep your eye on Muratti!"

"Right," Balestra muttered. He slipped the knife quickly into his blouse.

The darkness of night shut down on us and Carpette lit the regulation oil lamp over the center of the passageway, while the other convicts got out little ones of their own and lit them.

Soon the hour rolled around for the game to start up.

Muratti spread the blanket out, not in the usual place but, this time, near the corridor which led into the privy. He took his place at the head of the blanket and rattled the money bank. Men got up from their hammocks and before long there was a circle around the blanket, and the game got under way. Muratti, apparently, didn't have a thought for his enemy. Seeing his indifference, we thought, Well, it's not for tonight! And those who had been prepared to see blood spilled in a hand-to-hand combat reassured themselves.

The evening went along quietly, and so did the game. Balestra, who had been whispering in a group with his Marseilles friends all the time, suddenly left them and walked along through the passageway on his way to visit the privy. As he passed the circle bent over the game, he shot a furtive glance at Muratti. Muratti seemed to be watching the game with close attention. So Balestra, reassured, continued on his way and disappeared in the narrow corridor.

This was just what Muratti had been waiting for. For, while he supervised the game, he had watched his enemy like a cat watches for a mouse which it knows will come out of its hole after a while. He knew that sooner or later Balestra would go to the privy.

And, the moment Balestra disappeared into the corridor, Muratti left the game, handing the bank to his aide, and went to the privy also. The men around the blanket, engrossed in the game, paid no attention to his action. Only one or two, who, like myself, had seen Balestra enter the corridor, raised themselves up, realizing what would happen.

Suddenly there was a muffled sound, a noise of scuffling. Then there was a piercing cry, which was followed by guttural groans.

"Balestra—he's finished him!" men exclaimed, tensely.

The little lamps were quickly blown out. The players caught up their money and ran to their hammocks. The blanket disappeared, and in a few seconds the barrack was as quiet as an empty tomb in the semi-darkness of the regulation lamp.

The groans in the privy became fainter. All eyes were glued to the entrance of the little corridor, waiting for Muratti to appear—for no one doubted that the victim had been Balestra.

A few minutes later Muratti reappeared in the barrack room and went straight to the water barrel where he washed his hands and quickly wrung out the sleeve of his blouse. After this he hurried to his hammock and rapidly got out of his blouse and threw it up to dry over a bit of string. The barrack was in utter silence. There was an air of expectancy in its quietness.

Two minutes later the guards came! The bars of the door rattled and it was opened. The captain-at-arms, followed by a number of guards with revolvers in hand, rushed into the barrack room with a group of turnkeys who carried lanterns. As the convicts had expected, the turnkeys on duty had given the alarm.

"Up, on your feet, all of you!" commanded the captain-at-arms.

We pretended to be asleep, we seemed to be slowly awakened, and got up slowly.

Two of the guards went straight to the privy, with some of the turnkeys following at their heels. In a few moments they came out with Balestra's body, which they set down near the door.

"Everybody to the far end of the barrack!" commanded the captain-at-arms.

He made us file past him one by one while he examined us minutely by the light of the lanterns. He looked at our hands and clothes to see if there were any signs of blood. Muratti passed among the first, and the captain gave him a look which seemed to imply: "You're the guilty one, all right. I know it well enough! But we're both Corsicans so I'll see what I can do."

The short investigation of our hands and clothes gave no results. There seemed to be no clues. The captain barked: "Well, who's the guilty one?" There was a dead silence.

"Well! well! well!" he exclaimed. "Didn't anybody kill him? We'll see about this tomorrow." And he glowered at us.

After a few minutes he barked again: "Two of you scavengers get a stretcher and take the thing out."

Ironically enough, Muratti was one of the men who emptied the offal of the barrack. Not wishing to attract attention upon himself by hesitating, he went quickly for a stretcher to the guardhouse of the camp. And, when he returned and lifted his victim into it, he took pains to get a lot of blood on his trousers: for this would be a good alibi, should any blood be found on his blouse the next day. Then, with the other convict, he carried his victim to the hospital.

That night, Balestra died without having regained his senses. He had seven deep knife wounds in his body!

In all the prison units of the colony, the convicts who act as scavengers are the ones designated to carry the sick and wounded in and out of the hospitals, and, in addition, they also take them to the place of burial. Since there is no cemetery on the Islands in which to bury the convicts, their bodies are thrown into the sea —this sordid practice is called *le mouillage,* the "wetting."

Muratti, astute criminal that he was, had continued to get this particular job. For it required only an hour or so in the morning and he could, therefore, sleep in the daytime and be fit to watch the game all night! It so happened, then, that he was able to gloat over Balestra until the last moment. It was he who carried his lifeless body the next morning from the hospital to the mortuary slab; again, it was he who secured from Balestra's body the suppository full of money. Later, with the others in his calling, he took the body in the late afternoon to the rowboat.

A few hundred yards out at sea the oars came to rest. Muratti tilted the stretcher and watched his victim's body slide out of it and splash into the sea.

"Pull!" The guard at the tiller commanded, and the boat turned toward the landing. And, from where he stood at the stern of the boat, Muratti gazed at the great fins flashing in the sunlight as the sharks fought over Balestra's remains.

The Administration made an investigation, for it had to comply with the regulations exacted by the Ministry. The Commandant, Crucionni, was a Corsican. He had assembled about him on the Islands a group of guards who were all Corsicans: the captain-at-arms, Taddei, was a Corsican, and the assistant Commandant in the investigation was a Corsican, also! Now, Muratti was a Corsican, and these Corsicans stick up for each other; even if it is a Corsican convict vouching for a Corsican guard: for the Corsicans on Royale, at that time, were all more or less related. As a matter of fact it is not a very unusual thing for a convict to have a relative who is a guard. There was not one of the convicts on the Islands who did not know that Muratti had murdered Balestra, and most of the guards knew it also. The convict who cooked for their mess had overheard them discussing the incident, and they had spoken Muratti's name. The Commandant was in close touch with what went on in the barrack, for he had his paid informers. How then was he to be in doubt over a crime which had had seventy-five witnesses! He was in no doubt whatever about it. A few of the older convicts, whom the officials trusted not to talk about the matter, were put in prison: in two days the captain-at-arms released them, and the whole matter was forgotten. But it had permitted the Administration to make another report to the Ministry, telling that another murder had been done in a penal barrack in the presence of seventy-five other convicts of whom none was honorable enough to expose the guilty man; and in the report went another official hint of the perpetual danger the officials lived in, a suggestion that they had to be merciless with such men and they deserved better pay when they exposed their lives to watch over such dangerous criminals.

But Balestra had many friends in the Second Platoon, and these men from Marseilles decided to avenge

127

him. Maddened by the impunity which Muratti enjoyed as a Corsican, they decided to finish him.

Muratti was well aware of what was going on, and he took the necessary precautions. He gave up his place in the game, for it was one which furnished too easy a pretext for a dispute and knife blows. At night, he stayed awake: stretched out in his hammock, he kept an eye on the goings and comings of his enemies, the convicts from Marseilles, ready to spring up at the slightest suspicion with knife in hand to defend himself to the last stab. He slept only in the daytime, when the others were out of the barracks; and, even then, he kept a protégé close at hand to watch for trouble.

But at the end of a couple of weeks he had had enough of that sort of an existence. He went to see the Commandant and told him that, unless he sent him to the mainland, he would be forced to kill three or four men in the barrack so as not to be murdered himself.

The Commandant, being a Corsican, understood. In a few days, he saw to it that Muratti was transferred to Cayenne. All Royale knew that Muratti was fleeing from the Islands! But on the same boat several messages left Royale also, sent by the convicts from Marseilles to compatriots at Cayenne.

Muratti went to Cayenne "loaded"—that is to say, with a well-filled suppository. His mind was set on escaping quickly, for he knew that on the mainland he would not be much safer than he had been on the Islands. And so, a few days after he came to the penitentiary at the capital, he was out and on his way.

Was it folly? Or simply sheer bravado! For he was escaping with four men who were from Marseilles; he knew this, when he agreed to start off with them, and that they might be his enemies! Yet, perhaps he thought that in the great thrill of expected freedom they would let bygones be bygones, and think only of the future.

Two mornings later, some natives who were walking along the beach found the shark-torn bodies of two convicts and notified the guards. The convict scavengers brought the bodies to the hospital, where they were identified: one was the partly eaten corpse of Muratti, and the other the body of one of the convicts who had sneaked out of camp with him the night they escaped.

What had happened out there on the sea none has ever known, for the rest of the convicts in that *évasion* have never been caught.

So died Muratti, the Corsican murderer, who for more than twelve years had been a terror in the prison colony.

Chapter XVI

NOT having received a single fresh piece of official clothing since the day I first set foot in Guiana, I wrote a letter to the Commandant of the Islands, telling him that I was, so to speak, naked. He had me allotted a sack of effects which contained, much to my relief, a change of clothes, a blanket and a pair of wooden shoes —the last, of course were worthless as footwear, and I sold them to a man who needed the wood for a piece of carving he was doing. In my letter to the Commandant I took advantage of the occasion to ask for a writing job in one of the offices on the Islands, so I would have some work with which to pass the long days away. I was designated to help with the bookkeeping for the food supplies.

I enjoyed with this job a great deal of liberty, and almost every afternoon I would go down on the landing and spend an hour or so looking out over the sea. One day, a guard asked me if I wanted to give lessons and act as a tutor to his young daughter, who was going over to Cayenne, when the classes started, to continue her schooling. He offered me 30 francs a month! I accepted, without a moment of hesitation.

That same evening I went to his house to begin my duties. Being bookkeeper, I was free to return to the barrack at any hour providing it was before nine o'clock.

Suzanne, the guard's daughter, was sixteen years old; but raised, literally, among convicts—for from her earliest childhood she had been accustomed to seeing them in her home as servants—she knew much more about the facts of life than a girl of her tender age was supposed to know. From the very first day of my duties as her tutor, with her knowing little ways she began to turn our interest to subjects which had nothing whatever to do with mathematics and geography!

I was barely twenty-seven. For years . . . endless years . . . I had not had occasion to talk with a woman, to say nothing of seeing regularly a white girl who was young and desirable.

I was far from being unaware of the risk I was running. If her father had found out what was going on, he would have made a hole in my skull with his revolver, just as he had done to a convict who had insulted him a few months before in one of the barracks.

The element of danger, however, in a way gave spice to our affair. Two and three times in the day and sometimes it was oftener, Suzanne would come to the office where I worked, under the pretext that there were explanations needed for the assignments I had given her the day before. And she would profit by the opportunity to slip me a little love notes which, although they were discreet, were more those of a woman than a girl of sixteen.

I kept a circumspect eye open, so as not to get myself into serious trouble, and I took every precaution to keep my idyll completely under cover; and in effect no one, not even my closest fellow-convicts, were aware that I was in the middle of a romance.

Then, one night when we were having no lessons, Suzanne took it upon herself to wait for me when I came out of the office.

We had met in the dark and walked about on the island before, but the surprise of seeing her there that night when there would be no excuse if we were caught

130

together in the neighborhood of the office, made me feel extremely uneasy. But she reassured me . . . she said she would leave right away, and she added that her father was on night duty at the camp. Sure enough, she kept her promise; after she had given me a long kiss and I had returned it with another, in the shadows beyond the office, we parted.

But the next night she was waiting there again for me. And on other nights, there she was again in the same spot—just beyond the shadow of the building. I got to expect her there, every time I finished work and by a path which was little used, she would accompany me almost to the gate of the Crimson Barrack. The Islands at night are dark. On Royale, there is only a small oil lamp every hundred yards!

Then, one night . . . Our romance ended with a crash!

The Commandant happened to be strolling around in the vicinity of the barrack. He was a very quiet walker—and he heard whisperings and the unmistakable sounds of kisses in the shadow of the wall. Thinking it was some affair of a guard and his wife, a thing which is viewed in silence on the Islands, he discreetly went the other way. But—alas for me and Suzanne!— he chanced to see her running stealthily down the slope between the barrack and her house. He recognized her. Suspicious, he went to the gate of the barrack and demanded from the guard on duty at the guardhouse who the convict was who had come in last.

"Belbenoit, the bookkeeper," the guard answered.

The following morning I had orders from the Commandant to come to his office.

"I'm sending you to Saint Joseph this morning, on the ten o'clock boat," he said to me, with a penetrating look. "You are lucky it was not the guard at the landing who surprised you last night. The sharks would be eating you now!" And he continued eyeing me sternly.

I was very nervous. I had expected to be called down by the Commandant for something else, something far less serious. This was a total surprise to me, as I had not seen him the night before.

"Just what are your relations," he demanded, "with this guard's daughter?"

"We are just friendly," I replied. "I have been her tutor for several months."

"Her *tutor*, eh," he shot at me, smilingly. "Get your things ready to go across. There has been enough scandal on this island, without you convicts being mixed up in it also—tutor or no tutor."

So I left for Saint Joseph.

Chapter XVII

THE Island of Saint Joseph! the loathsome, the cursed and detestable! It is a place of punishment and repression unparalleled on earth for inflicting pain and slow death. It is here that the convict suffers most.

On Royale the convict is not under the physical torture of disciplinary confinement nor the mental strain of being completely alone. On Royale he enjoys the possibility of news from the mainland, when the boat stops off shore every week while the oarsmen go out to it to unload, and every month there is the mail boat from France which comes by. But on Saint Joseph there is nothing! One small boat of the island Administration comes out every day with supplies and with more convicts to be put in the cells; it goes back to Royale as soon as its business is over, and none of the convicts on the island are allowed to come near it or to talk with the oarsmen. And the new men are immediately searched by the turnkeys as soon as they land, to see if they carry notes for others on the island!

A road circles Saint Joseph. Another road leads to the flat hill which commands the island, and on which are ranged three rough and austere structures of solitary cells. The third of these is reserved for demented convicts. Halfway up the island, down close to the churning sea, is the camp for the men who are sent to the island but not to solitary confinement. It is surrounded by a high wall. A hundred men, including the turnkeys, are sequestered there. These are convicts who have done something the authorities on Royale didn't like and have been sent over to Saint Joseph by way of added punishment, for the Administration knows that the thing which annoys a convict most of all is to be deprived of his *débrouille*, his chance to obtain money, and on Saint Joseph a convict can make absolutely nothing, not a sou. He is unable to smoke or to do anything to better his condition. . .

Solitary confinement . . . ! Entombed in a dark cell! The convicts call it *"La guillotine sèche,"* the dry guillotine! The convicts call these three cement cell structures, The Castle. Each of these is covered with a V-shaped, corrugated iron roof, and contains forty-eight cells arranged in two blocks of twenty-four. On the cell block of each structure is an iron walk where an armed guard paces night and day. The top of each cell is a grilled network, and he can gaze down and see everything which is going on inside. The cells are about twelve feet by nine, with a height of nine feet. The roof keeps out the sun and, also, the coolness of the rain. The only light which comes in is through the barred opening above the inmate's head: he is immersed like a fish in a clammy well.

In each cell there is a narrow wooden bench for the prisoner to sleep on and, during the day, he usually sets this up on end so that he can have more space to move. A small bucket for excrement is the only furnishing in the cell. An old blanket, and sometimes a piece of rag, and the prisoner—that is all. At the bottom of this semi-obscure pit the prisoner stays twenty-three hours out of each twenty-four. Each cell has a solid door; these open onto two walled passages that lead to an enclosed court. For an hour in the morning the prisoner is taken into this silent court where he can walk around in solitude, then he is taken back to his cell. It is the only time when he can see the sky. The rest of the day he lives in dim light; from dark to dawn —blackness and silence. He is alive in a tomb.

He has no work, nothing to read, nothing to write on—nothing to occupy himself with. In the dim obscurity his mind wanders while he paces back and forth or goes round and round, and at night he dreams on his piece of board. The only sounds he hears are those of the sea breaking on the rocks and the screams of the demented crying and howling in the third structure. And these elemental sounds which faintly reach his lonely ears in the depths of the cell block are of a kind which are horribly depressing to a man . . . the monotonous noise of the sea . . . the heavy splash of tropical rains on the iron roof when the wet season is on . . . the howls and piercing screams of the demented, are the only sounds which reach him vaguely from the outside world. The cells are damp, very damp, in that region where the atmosphere is already saturated with humidity. His teeth fall out with scurvy. He watches the green mold grow and creep along in the cracks, and passes his time away making tiny patterns and designs in it with one of his long nails which he has painstakingly worn into a point on the cement.

Thoughts . . . dreams. Of what? He is alone with whatever inner self he may have. The past is dead. For many the past was so sad that they have no pleasant memories to attach themselves to: for those who have something worth while in their former lives, it is even worse, this present emptiness. Most prisoners turn to the future, where things have not yet happened, and then become lost in great dreams, in fine plans. They dream of impossibilities, they foresee happiness. Life takes on the tone of a mirage, and they are soon blissfully going crazy.

After a while a prisoner in those cells has an ungovernable desire to go to the hospital: to see somebody, to talk with someone, to smoke a cigarette. It becomes overpowering, it is stronger than he: it becomes necessary that he get out of the solitary cell no matter what the price. The one way he can get out is to go to the hospital. So he finds an excuse for the doctor's visit, when he comes to the island once in the week. He must be sick, gravely ill; he knows that, and he makes himself sick! It is a voluntary and a desperate alternative.

Some find a way to wound themselves purposely, some smoke quinine to sham fever, some breathe sulphur to sham bronchitis or rub sperm into their eyes to induce a suppuration, others put castor beans in a cut so as to get a serious infection: they try everything. They impair their health, and often pay with a part of their bodies or with their lives. But when they are in the hospital they can talk, and read and smoke; and when they are brought back to Saint Joseph again, each will have on him a suppository made with paper or bread-dough, and full of tobacco!

When a prisoner has tobacco, and has almost finished his carefully rolled cigarette, he will wait for the guard's steps to get to the far end of the walk: he then throws the lit stub, tied to a precious pebble, up through the grill above his head; the butt falls into the next cell, the inmate draws a few puffs, then throws it in his turn into the adjoining one. The guard, if he pays any attention, has a hard time finding where the cigarette came from, for the long range of cell tops all look alike!

It is a miserable life, a life of horror where beings suffer inhumanly and are cared for like beasts. They are few, those who endure five years in the cells on Saint Joseph; yet this punishment of slow rot and death is inflicted on the condemned for their *évasions,* because they attempted to flee to life out of that Hell. *La guillotine sèche!* The dry guillotine! Albert Londres has found, better than anyone else, the name for the nerve-freezing cement structures on Saint Joseph.

"Fortunate are the simple in mind." But I do not think the pitiful depraved, locked up in the third cell-block on Saint Joseph, are fortunate. When I was on Saint Joseph there were more than forty crazy men in the "Howling House,"—helpless, and treated and handled like so many rotting lumps of flesh. Their minds had been murdered but their bodies still hung together for a few more months or years. The guard in charge of them stole part of their food supply, the turnkeys stole another, and the little that was left for them was barely enough to keep them from dying of hunger. Most of them were naked, the clothes of the others were in shreds; they had nothing but part of a pair of trousers or a blouse made of old flour sack, and they chattered at night in their cells. Trembling from cold and physical exhaustion, they moaned and cried hoarsely to ears that were ever deaf; and, whenever one had a moment of lucidness and complained, a bucket of cold water thrown down on his head by a turnkey quickly calmed him—or started him off raving again.

Human derelicts prostrate in so many cages like frantic animals dirty and half-naked, their eyes bloodshot, their chins streaked with drool, they are forced to drink dirty water out of buckets that are filled whenever the turnkeys take a notion to do so. They are closed up just like the others and come out only for an hour, if at all. In the walled court some occupy themselves with their individual peculiarities. One man counted eternally, just as he had done for than a year already, "27, 28, 29—27, 28, 29—27, 28, 29 . . ." Those who are as mild as he have a chance to exist longer than others, for their folly is inoffensive and does not annoy the guards too much. There was another who, every time he came out in the morning into the walled court, would throw pebbles, or whatever he could lay his hands on, at his enemy the sun; and, in the darkness of his cell, he would burble, staring at the dim light which reached him through the grill above his head: this dim light was to him the sun's eye! Another used to have a wild fear of persecution, which was probably well founded, and would throw his food in the face of the turnkeys every time he had a chance, thinking always they came to poison him. It was not long before his cell had another inmate. There was another who scratched on his cell wall day and night, thinking his mother was in the other room, dying; in his frenzy, he thought he had to get to her. He would not stop to go out for exercise; sometimes the turnkeys, seeing his bleeding fingers, would take pity on him and drag him out into the court by force; but when they did, he would stand by the wall and scratch and mutter, without taking the time to eat his food. His fingers were worn, literally, to the bone, but this seemed not to bother him; I believe he finally bled himself to death.

Another, and he was an example of what is probably the most pitiful sort of inmate of all those locked into these rows of horror in the third cell-block, was constantly in the process of wording a letter of defense to the Director of the Administration. He was an intelligent individual, and I know for a fact that even the guards on the walk would listen, moved. He like many others who have exposed how things are in the prison colony to the press and to the high authorities in France, had been classed as demented by the Administration and was kept there in the third cell-block out of pure revenge until he actually did go crazy. The Administration had seen to that, so that there could be no come-back in the future against its action. It may seem unbelievable, but this forcing of a sane man to become insane has happened time and again. Some of the most intelligent convicts in the colony have died, reduced to raving idiots, right there in the third structure cell-block of Saint Joseph, because they took it upon themselves to tell the people of their country how things are done in the French Guiana. Forgotten martyrs, all of them! For they got no thanks for their humanistic endeavor, and the press seldom sent them money for the revealing words they smuggled out and which cost them their lives. They were individuals who were civilized, who were educated and reared in the ways of civilization— who thought their nation should know the atrocities which are done under its flag. Their names are sent back to the Ministry of Justice in France, with the citation: "gone crazy in the heat of the tropics"—that is the end to investigation, hushed efficiently by the local Administration.

Idiocy is often a pretext resorted to by the Administration to get rid of men it can't kill or silence. And proof of this lies in the fact that out of twenty convicts classed as demented there are usually ten whom the new doctors, when they arrive "for duty in the colony," humanely send back to the mainland—their professional decisions as to the mental or physical health of the men they examine on their first visit to the third structure can not be overruled, not even by the Penal Administration. But the years between the shifts of medical men are very long, and some of the doctors are not too conscientious. And many a man committed to the third cell-block when he was perfectly sane, has become demented through despair and through the howls of the crazed all around him, morning, noon, and night, before a new doctor who is sincere in his profession has arrived on the scene to take him out and to write another official report against the Director of the Administration.

Chapter XVIII

THE Commission had arrived, and although I had been on Saint Joseph Island only twenty days—in the camp compound and not in the cell houses—there were two reports against me. With others who would have to face punishment I stood before the administrators.

"Belbenoit!" a guard's voice called my name.

"Here!" I stepped forward to the desk at which the Commission sat, and stood at attention. The Commandant, M. Toutblanc (in spite of his name he was a blue-black Negro!) gathered up a few sheets of papers, my reports, and read out the first one:

"Belbenoit, 46635: Spoke impudently to a guard. To a guard's remark he answered: 'Oh stop bothering me with your damn opinions!' "

"What have you to say to this?" the Commandant asked.

"Nothing, sir," I said.

The Commandant picked out another report: "Caused his ration of bread to be weighed, asserting it did not weigh what the regulation allows. Weighed 700 grams. (24¾ ounces) Complaint unfounded."

"But I have a right to 750 grams (26 ounces), sir!" I insisted.

"Yes." The Commandant scowled—scratching his kinky head. "But you must know the bakers can not make all the round loaves of bread so they are exactly 750 grams; there may be some that weigh only 700 grams, but there are others that weigh 800 (28¼ ounces)."

"No, sir!" I said, "Out of one hundred loaves there are probably five that weigh 750 grams,—the rest will weigh less than what is prescribed by the ration—not one will weigh more!"

"Very well, that's enough!" the Commandant frowned. "Stand back!"

The injustice of the things I had been submitted to on Saint Joseph had made me foolishly lose my temper before the Negro judge.

A few moments later the Commandant announced to me: "30 days in cell for the first and 30 for the second." After a pause he added: "I am making a report against you, myself, for speaking impolitely to me—and giving your opinions out of place—30 days in the cell for that too!"

"How many, René?" asked a comrade when I returned to the camp barrack.

"Three times thirty," I retorted dryly, while I got myself ready to go to the cell blocks. My comrade filled my suppository with tightly packed tobacco, inserting some carefully folded cigarette paper and a few match heads; while he did this, I hid three 5-franc bills and a razor blade in the seams of my trousers.

"Belbenoit!" The turnkey, before I was ready, had come to take me to my cell. I was in the privy, concealing my suppository. I hastily put on my pants and went out of the barrack.

The solid door of the cell closed on me. Ninety days to do, alone . . . for nothing. Ninety days struck from the sun and the light, from the life of the living! With nothing to look at except a piece of board and a foul bucket . . . and four walls.

Little by little the darkness became clearer; I had been brought in from the bright sunlight. After a while my eyes became accustomed to the somber glow, and I could see.

I removed my suppository and made myself a cigarette. I smoked slowly, listening for the guard's steps on the walk. Then I started pacing back and forth in the cell . . . thinking.

A key rattled in the lock. It was the turnkey: he wanted to know if I wanted anything. I gave him 20 sous to bring me coffee and some bananas. And when he closed the door I started walking back and forth again.

A few thuds sounded faintly through my wall. It was my neighbor in the next cell.

After a moment, I rapped in my turn.

A telegraphic conversation now began.

The man tapped: one tap, A; two, B; three, C; and so on tapping out alphabet till they made words. I listened intently. Between each word he would stop a moment, and then he continued:

H-O-W - M-A-N-Y his telegraphic taps asked.

N-I-N-E-T-Y, I answered.

W-H-O - A-R . . .

I cut him short with three quick raps, and telegraphed my name. Then I asked his.

I listened eagerly for his name.

I-N-A-U-D-I, he answered.

Hell! It was only a stupid bestial convict for whom I had never had any use. There went my chances of having intelligent companionship near at hand when I wanted it, needed it so much!

He continued tapping for several minutes, but I

wouldn't notice him. It was better to be alone with my thoughts than to carry on a conversation with such a man!

Silence. Then the soup, at ten o'clock. The turnkey brought me the coffee and bananas with my soup.

In the afternoon I walked back and forth and thought. The air was hot under the iron roof, and it reached down into my cell. I took off my clothes and stretched on the board for a siesta. Just before dark the turnkey woke me up and told me to get out into the court with about a dozen others. We walked around for half an hour. Some asked me for tobacco, but they were not friends and I refused to give them any.

Back in the cell, rice was dumped into my plate. Then the door was closed until the next day.

Back and forth, back and forth I walked, adjusting my step so that I could push the wall with my hand for exercise as I turned.

The blackness of night shut down on me. I paced back and forth mechanically. I set the board bed up on end and steadied myself along the wall until I could grasp the grill at the top of the cell. I hung there as long as I could to exercise my arms before I finally dropped to the floor.

Thoughts. They became so clear in the darkness. I reviewed my past, my existence from day to day. I remembered men I had not thought of in months, and wondered if they were still alive on the mainland. I thought of new ways to escape. I thought of my future —my future, in which the past will not figure. Renée! She returned to my thoughts, now that I was alone with myself. I remembered every little incident of our life together. She must have found another. And why not! Why should she wait for me, who had been banished from civilization? I took her side, and thought; she is right! I took my side and was sure she was wrong. On and on my thoughts raced into the night, while I paced back and forth, back and forth in the darkness.

Then I fell asleep on the board in my cell.

In the days which followed, my thoughts toned down

and changed. I became accustomed to the isolation, and the days passed—one after another. I asked the turnkey to give me the broom: I told him I would sweep the cell myself. He gave me a frayed bundle of straw. I invented an occupation for my hands, as well as my mind: I would sweep the cell minutely, I would get down on my hands to get everything out of the cracks. Before the soup was brought to me, I would sweep the cell again. Before I ate I would cut my bread into small slices with my razor, and I would polish my spoon until it shone with a bit of earth and dust saved up in a corner with my constant sweeping. After I ate, I picked the frayed threads of my trousers and separated them out into little pieces. I would take off my trousers just to look for a fresh piece of thread and every time I found one in the darkness in which I began to see as with cat's eyes, it was a momentous discovery.

Afternoon again. Rice again. Tomorrow the ration would be dry bread, but I gave the turnkey some sous to bring me coffee to dunk the crusts in.

Night again. The cell was pitch black again. I lay down for a while. Then I got up and paced back and forth, back and forth.

My thoughts turned to the future for hope—to escape, to liberty, and I lived in essence the things which I dreamed. I would bicker over every little point that came to my mind, I would discuss with myself for half an hour the color of the suit I would buy from a tailor in New York, or in Buenos Aires, and I would calculate the price I should pay for it. I would have a date with some beautiful girl I had met in imagination, and I would be impatient waiting, in a dream world, for her to arrive—just as if it were all reality! By the mere power of thought I thus lived during long, long days of solitary darkness. Sometimes I would be on the boulevards, and I would spend many minutes deciding what the drink was to be, even deciding what tip I would give the garçon.

While I thought and imagined, I lived. It was a life of my own! A dream life! When my neighbor rapped on the wall, or when the turnkey opened the door of my cell to bring me food or tell me to go out into the court for exercise, that would annoy me. It would annoy me exceedingly, for it would break the spell, and I would have to start over again the long, detailed vision-life in which I was able to immerse myself completely.

There were days when in return for a few francs paid to the guard some of us could go down by the edge of the sea and bathe accompanied by a turnkey. I would find, by paying more francs, in a certain spot in the rocks a small package of tobacco and matches. The turnkey would pretend not to see that I had anything with me when again he locked me up.

Thirty days, 45 days, 60 days went by—30 more still, and I would be out in the sunshine.

"Belbenoit!" the voice of a guard shouted outside my cell door.

"Yes!" I yelled through the iron door. "Well, what is it now?"

The Disciplinary Commission had again summoned me. Another report, I learned, had been made against me. Fifteen days more for hanging from the bars of my grill and exercising.

Forty-five more days now instead of only 30. My cell was very damp. And the soles of my feet had softened, which caused me a lot of trouble, because I had a habit of pacing up and down continually.

I made up my mind to get out. I had had enough. My money was nearly finished. I felt myself weakening fast: two days in three with only hard bread and water to eat, the confinement, the lack of air, that bone-aching dampness were all beginning seriously to weaken me. I must go to the hospital, I concluded.

With my last few francs I persuaded the turnkey to get from the infirmary a little sulphuric acid. It was a very small amount but that was all I needed. On the day of the doctor's visit, about three hours before the time came to go before him, I began my *maquillage:* as the convicts call it when a man makes himself sick: I poured the acid into my spoon, and breathed the

143

fumes caused by its action with the metal. When I was before the doctor my lungs, through his stethoscope, wheezed excessively. I coughed and sniffed as if I had a cold. I had bronchitis, the doctor announced, and sent me to the hospital!

I left Saint Joseph for Royale, hoping to stay in the hospital long enough to spend the last one day of my 105 days there, for every day I had to lie there in bed counted on the punishment. Food! Something to read! Air and the sight of the sun!

Chapter XIX

IN THE hospital on Isle Royale I found that during my absence a scandal had broken out—a scandal far more serious than any which the guard's daughter and I might have brought about had not the Commandant sent me post-haste to Saint Joseph. This was the scandal of Maurice, Raoul, and the wife of Leclerc, the island's eldest guard.

Maurice, once a headwaiter in an exclusive restaurant on the boulevards, had during the years of his imprisonment in Guiana become a hardened, uncomplaining convict. He lived in the Second Platoon, in the Crimson Barrack, and his whole life seemed wrapped up in an intense homosexual relationship with a young convict named Raoul. The two were together every night in the farthest corner of the Crimson Barrack. While others played cards or occupied themselves with other activities Maurice and his young *môme* stayed back in the darkness—behind a blanket which Maurice habitually hung every night on a string, as a screen for their perverted orgies.

While I had been in the barrack, before being sent to the cells on Saint Joseph, Raoul had done no work. Maurice had supported him—providing Raoul with tobacco, clothes and other things in return for the satis-

144

faction of his desires. But suddenly Raoul had been commanded to work each day in the house of Leclerc the guard. The youth was about twenty years old, was handsome in spite of a very weak mouth, and had several engaging mannerisms. Leclerc was past sixty and the climate had sapped his vitality to such an extent that his wife, who was much younger—and had led undoubtedly a wayward life before she came out to marry him—decided that she would carry on an affair with a younger man.

This is not an unusual state of affairs in the Guiana settlements, barracks, and camps. Many of the wives of the guards and even of the officials are former prostitutes. I doubt that a good woman, a woman of gentle birth, education, or refinement could stand living in French Guiana for more than a month or two. It would be like throwing a rose into a vat of smelly garbage and expecting it to survive. A guard, therefore, has a hard time finding a wife—unless he sends to France and offers that compromise to some dope addict or prostitute who, at the moment, may be especially down on her luck and willing to do anything. Each time the French mail-boat arrives from France there will be a few women on board, consigned officially to various guards and under-officials who have applied for them. They are married hastily by the civil authorities—but I never knew of such a wife or of a guard who thus lived happily ever afterward.

Leclerc's wife had a voluptuous figure. She used to torment us convicts frequently by walking up and down in the island breeze clad only in a sketchy, very thin dress. It was common gossip that it had been she who engineered Raoul's transfer, during the day, to her household.

Raoul thus suddenly found himself filling a double rôle, and trying to do it to the satisfaction of two abnormally sensuous demanders. In the daytime, when Leclerc was away, he was an ardent lover. At night he had to satisfy Maurice's homosexual desires. Maurice knew what was going on, but this triangular relation-

145

ship did not bother him. Leclerc's wife, however, began to insist that Raoul keep away from Maurice. Raoul told Maurice all about it, that she was insisting she would not share him with anyone. Maurice seemed to think it was a good joke.

"Amuse yourself, but be careful!" he cautioned Raoul. "If Leclerc ever finds out you'll get a bullet in your head—and what will *I* do!"

But Leclerc's wife could see for herself each day that Raoul had given up none of his nightly activities. One day, in an overpowering burst of jealousy when she saw Maurice passing her house, she called him to her and asked him point blank to get another *môme* and leave Raoul completely to her. But Maurice told her jauntily to mind her own affair—and let him mind his.

Leclerc's wife became more and more jealous. A week later she accosted Maurice again, but this time he rudely laughed in her face. She became incensed with rage, and she determined to have Raoul all to herself at any price.

After a few days had gone by she called a sweeper, working in front of her house, and told him to find Maurice and tell him she wanted to see him. Maurice out of curiosity, and I suppose to further torment her, came to her house. When he stood in the doorway the woman called him from the top of the stairs and told him to come to the second floor.

Maurice climbed the steps and stood before her.

"It's about Raoul—finally!" she said tensely.

"Again!" Maurice said, angrily. "Well, if you don't stop bothering me about that he won't come to your house any more!" And he turned to go down the stairs. As he did so Leclerc's wife picked up a revolver and fired point blank into his back. The impact of the bullet spun him around and he fell like a sack down the steps. Instantly Leclerc's wife began tearing her dress off and screaming. "Rape!" she yelled. "Help!"

The whole island rushed to her house. Maurice was found at the bottom of the stairs. The woman said that he had entered while she was dressing and had attacked her. That she had been forced to fire in self-defense. They took Maurice to the hospital, badly wounded. But fortunately there was a good doctor in attendance and soon he was out of danger.

He became violently angry, however, when he was told by the attendant that as soon as he was well he was going to be sent to the blockhouse at Saint Laurent to await trial on the charge of violence and criminal attack against the wife of a guard. He turned over and over on his cot next to mine and swore that he would get even with her. Maurice was no fool, and he knew how to write. He sent a letter to the Prosecutor General of the colony and gave him complete details of the whole affair and charged the guard's wife with attempting premeditated murder.

Quickly the Prosecutor General made an investigation, and the scandal broke wide open. Leclerc's wife's relations with Raoul were already known to many of the men on the islands; and now previous affairs of hers with other convicts were brought to light. Finally, the sweeper she had sent to summon Maurice gave evidence which satisfied the investigating commission that Maurice's accusations were true. Briefly, her guilt was proved beyond the shadow of a doubt; but when she appeared in the civil court at Cayenne the court acquitted her. It was not seemly that the honor of an official of the Penal Administration should be publicly besmirched by a convict! She immediately left her husband and went back to France by the next boat. But while it lasted it was very exciting, and gave us all something new to talk about.

Chapter XX

IN FEBRUARY of 1927 while I was still in the hospital I had completed my island sentence, including the months accrued from additional punishments so I was ordered returned to the mainland.

Le Grande Terre, the mainland, again! Now, at last, I could once more play my chances and attempt to escape.

I was put to work during the day as bookkeeper in the workshop of the Administration at Saint Laurent. But, unfortunately, I was not able to make a single sou. This was very annoying, for I was looking for a good *débrouille*—some graft whereby I could accumulate enough money to pay my part in an escape by the sea. I gambled at night with other convicts but succeeded only in making sufficient for tobacco and cigarette paper.

In the middle of March an opportunity suddenly presented itself. The *Saint Laurent,* a freighter which brings cattle for the Administration from neighboring colonies, was to leave for Venezuela. As bookkeeper, I had charge of checking the load of firewood for its engines. In the gang of convicts assigned to the job of loading the wood into the holds were some good acquaintances of mine. While I looked on, checking off the loads, the idea flashed into my head that it would be a simple matter to hide myself in a hold with a quantity of food and water to last the trip, which was one of seven days. I revealed my intention to my comrades and, as they piled the wood down in the hold, they left an empty space in the middle. I sneaked on board in the bundles of wood several small containers of food, and these they hid for me together with a lard tin which they had filled with fresh water. The boat was to sail in the morning with the five o'clock tide, and I had decided to get into my hiding place the day before when the gangs quit work on the ship in the afternoon. As I was not checked when I went on and off the boat, not being in the gangs, the guards would go off with their full count of men and no one would be aware that I had remained on board.

But, at the last moment, a man came to me and whispered: "Don't try to do it. If the old boat gets into any bad weather the stacked wood is liable to come down on you. You'll be crushed to pieces!" That started me thinking. The man was right! Such a possibility had not once crossed my mind. I went back to camp that night, in deep dejection.

On Sunday afternoon in the first days of April, a convict asked me if I had seen the Americans who, the day before, had taken pictures of the condemned as they went into the barracks. Since I returned to the barrack at varying hours, I had not been there at the regular time and had not seen these visitors about whom he spoke.

"They must be newspaper folks," he said to me, "for they take a lot of pictures! They're staying at the house of the Commandant over in the square."

Having lost that day what little money I had, and being some 15 francs in debt, I decided to go to see the Americans next morning and propose the sale of a few stories I had written about Guiana and the life of the convicts. So, the next morning around eight, I left my desk with my bundle of papers under my arm and proceeded to the house where the strangers were staying.

It was a *relégué** who let me in; he was employed there as cook. He left me standing before the door while he went to tell the Americans that a convict was there to see them.

A man with a pleasant American face appeared and asked what it was I wanted. I explained to him, as well

*A *relégué* is a man who with four convictions of more than three months each for theft is banished to exile in Guiana for life. These *relégués* are quartered in camps in the jungle to the south of Saint Laurent and are kept separate from the convicts. Although technically they should be allowed to live freely in the colony they are restricted to the camps of the Relegation; they are guarded by the same guards who watch the convicts, are dressed like the latter and have to work and receive punishment. These men are the petty thief type the riffraff that is a nuisance to society and the Relegation is a cesspool within the Hell in Guiana. There vice reigns supreme as well as crime and stealing. Of the 20,000 *relégués* that have been sent to Guina since 1885, the year the Relegation was established, more than 17,000 have died there and not more than several hundred of them have returned to France; the others escaped. At present there are 2,500 *relégués* in Guiana. Their transportation to Guiana has been definitely suspended since July 10, 1937.

as I could, in the broken English I had learned many years previously in school, that I wished to sell him a few stories and articles which I had written about French Guiana. He took my bundle of papers and went upstairs. A few minutes later he came down accompanied by his wife. They were, they told me, Mr. and Mrs. Robert Niles of New York. Mrs. Niles,* her husband said, was a writer of travel and adventure stories.

"How much do you want for these writings?" Mrs. Niles asked me.

"Whatever you wish to give me, Madame!" I said.

She gave me a bill folded neatly. Out of politeness, I held it in my hand without looking to see whether it was large or small.

"Come again tomorrow morning," she said. "I might want to talk to you."

I thanked them for their generosity and left. When I had gone a little distance from the house I took a look at the bill to see how much I had received. I thought it might be for 25 francs. But I was mistaken. It was for 100 francs! I went straight to a Chinese trader where I bought bread, a tin of sardines and a package of tobacco, primarily to change the note; then I went to the barrack. After I had paid my gambling debt I had 80 francs left: a small fortune in the prison colony. And that afternoon I told the latheman at the workshop to make me a new suppository—one of aluminum, instead of tin.

Next morning I returned to see Mrs. Niles. She was having breakfast with her husband, and invited me to a cup of coffee and a roll. Then she asked me to sit a while and tell her the story of my life. She made many notes as I talked. She handed me a list she had written containing a number of things she wished to know, and asked me to write these things out for her and bring the work on the following morning. Then she gave me another note for 100 francs!

My fortune was beginning to turn!

*Author of *Condemned to Devil's Island*

For many days I went to see her, taking along some manuscript each morning which I had sat up most of the night writing, and after reading it she always paid me generously. One day she made me a present of a poker set, and on another occasion she presented me with a little but extremely keen pocket knife.

Then one morning she announced to me that she would be leaving soon. She and her husband were going to New York, she said, on the American freighter *Tom Gibbons,* which she would board at the Moengo aluminum mines in Dutch Guiana.

A new plan for escape appeared before me. If I could reach the Moengo mines at the same time, perhaps she would facilitate my getting a passage or a job on the outbound American freighter! The Dutch authorities I felt would show me much consideration if she were there to protect me and intervene; they would have few objections, provided they were sure I was getting out of their colony.

And so, on the eve of her departure, I went to see her for the last time; but I lost my nerve and was unable to say a thing to her about my intentions. I had once explained to her how the condemned use castor beans to sham sickness and she asked me to bring her some of these beans. I left hurriedly to get some for her so she could have them before she left Saint Laurent.

I went to the shack of a *libéré,* gave him five francs and told him to find me civilian clothes immediately. He brought me a white suit, shoes, and an old pith helmet. Then I told him he must find a *libéré* who owned a dugout, to carry me over to the Dutch side of the river. Soon we had the man, and it was agreed I would give him 25 francs to take me across the Maroni. At high noon, the hour when all the gendarmes were having their siesta, we went through Saint Laurent and got into his little dugout down by the bank. An hour later we were on the Dutch side, a few hundred yards below Albina. After I had paid him, I asked him if he wanted to earn 20 francs more. I handed him the money and told him to go to Mrs. Niles and take her a quantity of castor beans. Months later, I found out he had done so.

By a trail I reached Albina and went to a store, where I bought a bottle of beer. Not a soul bothered me; everyone took me for a mine worker. I sat around and let the afternoon drag by. When darkness settled over the jungle I left the town and began walking down the road which goes to the Moengo mines.

That was my mistake! It had been my intention to walk a few miles down the road and hide myself that night among the trees. Then when Mrs. Niles came by in a car on her way to the mines the next morning I planned to stop her and ask her to take me with her. But I had been on the road hardly more than fifteen minutes when I came face to face with two Dutch policemen, who happened around a bend with a group of prisoners being brought from road work to the prison in Albina. The presence of a white man out there in the road at that hour, headed for the interior, seemed a bit odd to them. They asked me for identification papers, my mine-registration card, and when I acknowledged that I had none, they insisted that I accompany them to Albina. There they took me to the police station. The Commissioner had no doubt at all that he had before him an *évadé!*

What a sad night that was—escape so near, and yet so far! Still another time my hopes had failed. On the following morning the Commissioner decided to send me across the river to Saint Laurent in the Magistrate's launch—the same launch which, on its return, was to bring across Mr. and Mrs. Niles. So I then took the little knife she had given me out of my pocket and asked him to please give it to her when she came over to the Dutch side a few minutes later.

I was put in the blockhouse again—but I determined to commence a struggle not to pay for this attempted *évasion*. A new regulation to the effect that for a convict to be considered an escaped man it was necessary for him to have been absent at least twelve hours, had just been passed. Now, I had left my work at ten in the morning, and that was the hour when I was reported absent, and I had been arrested in Albina at seven in the evening; therefore, I had only nine hours' absence and could not be considered an *évadé!* So I wrote a letter to the Governor, M. Juvanon, explaining my situation, and he gave me credit by filing a comment: "Belbenoit was arrested in Dutch Guiana dressed as a civilian, but he was arrested before his twelve hours' absence stipulated under the new regulation had elapsed, and he cannot therefore be considered technically an *évadé.* To be read before the Disciplinary Commission with report of illegal absence."

But in spite of his memorandum the Disciplinary Commission sentenced me to be punished with 60 days in cell, to be classed as incorrigible, and imprisoned again on the Islands. Having money and having been bookkeeper, I had no difficulty obtaining ink and paper, and before I was embarked for Royale I found an opportunity, through an intermediary who was a *libéré,* to send Mrs. Niles in New York some additional manuscript that I wrote during my two months' detention in the Saint Laurent blockhouse. Mrs. Niles made use of some of these facts and of the others I had given her before in her romantic story *Condemned to Devil's Island.*

Chapter XXI

IN THE Crimson Barrack of the incorrigibles in the disciplinary quarters on Royale, a new man was assigned to the space next to mine—a man I had not met before, Pierrot Josse. He was intelligent and had traveled far over the world as a sailor. We struck up a friendship and talked together a great deal. Brought up on sailing ships, Pierrot had later joined the Navy, but he was unruly and was sent to a disciplinary battalion in French Africa. From there he had been sent to

153

Guiana in 1923, condemned to eight years for a theft he had committed while he was a soldier. He was handsome, and also young. Furthermore, although I spent time with him only because of his keen mind, and I was attracted to him merely by intellectual ideas which we shared in common, he was a pervert. He had many admirers among the older men but he knew how to make himself more respected than the usual perverts of the prison colony and chose his intimates carefully, without being intimidated by either force or persuasion.

There is a story connected with Pierrot: a great tale of a romance such as can only exist among the condemned men in the exile colony of Guiana.

The year after Pierrot came to Guiana, there arrived a young convict who was only seventeen years old. His name was Roger Pecquet. He had been given seven years for robbery, and for firing on the police who arrested him. At Saint Martin de Ré, the island concentration port of France, Pecquet had distinguished himself by his bad conduct; ungovernable and temperamental, he was always having to be put in a cell, and it seemed that dry bread and irons meant little to him! He had drawn to himself the admiration of the *forts-à-bras,* and these had shown him respect in spite of his youth and effeminate look. A few months after he arrived in Guiana, he had earned a total of three hundred and twenty days of cell and was classed as incorrigible. And so it was that in August of 1924 Pierrot, who was in detention for attempted escape, came to know Roger Pecquet, who was also in the Saint Laurent Blockhouse en route to Royale.

Roger slept alone in a cell, while Pierrot slept among others in one of the blockhouses; but Pierrot had noticed him when they walked in the court, and he had been attracted by his youth and manner.

One day he placed himself behind him when they were walking in the court for exercise, and said: "Go to your cell, for I want to see you. I must talk to you!"

Roger turned on him, red in the face. He thought Pierrot was about to make him another proposition—

like those solicitations which had been made to him so often by older men. Pierrot perceived this, and reassured him quickly, saying, "No, it's not at all what you're thinking about! I want to talk with you!"

So Roger went to his cell. In a few moments Pierrot joined him. And, very openly and without shame Pierrot admitted his homosexual habits and asked Roger point blank if he would let him become his *môme*.

Roger who had expected the other type of proposal, such as had been made to him by other convicts, was taken off guard by this sudden and open proposal, and did not know exactly what to say. It was already time for the cells to be locked, so he merely said: "I'll let you know tomorrow." But Pierrot was a handsome youth, and Roger's vanity was flattered.

But the next day Roger left with a group of convicts for Camp Charvein. He told Pierrot, as they were saying good-bye, that if they met again the answer would be "yes." Pierrot's eyes lighted up. He promised Roger that as soon as he got out of the blockhouse he would send him whatever he could to help him. A month later Pierrot was brought up before the T. M. S. which condemned him to two additional years at hard labor for *évasion*. That same evening he was sent to Camp des Malgaches, and forty-eight hours later Pierrot was off again on another attempted escape through the jungle!

He was a fine swimmer, one of the best, probably, that had ever come to Guiana. In a few days he had got himself a canoe, two guns and a good supply of food. He stole the canoe at Albina, swimming across the river at night to get it. The guns and food supply he had stolen late at night from miners' dugouts, anchored out in mid-stream, ready to leave at dawn to carry supplies to the gold placers on the headwaters of the Maroni; sometimes there would be a Negro guarding the dugouts, but Pierrot would take whatever he needed while the fellow slept, swimming back with it to the shore or to his own dugout anchored a few yards away in the darkness. He collected a little money by secretly meeting *libérés,* and selling them the cheap pilfered supplies he did not want.

One day he met with six escaped convicts in the bush who planned to make an escape by sea, but who had as yet no dugout. Among them was one whose *môme* Pierrot had been when he first came to Guiana, but Pierrot had left him after a violent quarrel in which this convict had struck him.

"I've got everything necessary for an escape by the sea," Pierrot told them. "As you all know, I can sail; if you want to try with me we'll leave together, but only on one condition," he added. "We've got to carry with us a friend of mine who is at Charvein. I've got two guns. We can overcome the guards and get him away—then we'll dash to the sea!"

The others, eager to avail themselves of Pierrot's boat and supplies accepted, and Pierrot took them to the place where he had his dugout hidden. Night came. They sat around the fire, talking and smoking. Some stretched out. Soon when Pierrot was asleep, the others began whispering among themselves. They had no desire to go to Charvein and take a chance on being shot by the guards when a boat and their freedom lay within easy reach. That was pure just folly! They plotted together and finally decided to start immediately, carrying Pierrot along by force for he was absolutely necessary, as he alone among them knew how to sail. So they jumped on him while he slept and tied him up. Then they got things ready to be off. In the meantime, Pierrot lay trussed up by the fire, wild with anger and insulting them every way he could.

When the dugout was loaded they put Pierrot in the stern and paddled off downstream. As they paddled they tried to console him—while he continued to fume and curse with rage. They attempted to bring him to reason—telling him he could send Roger money and forged papers from Venezuela and that in less than six months Roger would also be free and could join him.

They came to the mouth of the river and paddled out into the sea. The dugout was soon rolling in the waves, and it was necessary to release Pierrot so he could show them how to raise the sail and how to steer the craft on the sea.

Without a word when free of the ropes, he took his position. It was a clear night, with the moon shining over the water. Pierrot looked at the coast: off in the distance the light on Point Galibi flickered, and he decided they must be at least five miles out to sea. For him that would be easy. It was feasible, and he made up his mind! With a sudden move he brought the helm up hard and threw all his weight on one side of the dugout. In another second it had turned completely over!

His companions cried out in surprise, but no one had time to prevent his move. In a short while they were only four, for two drowned quickly as they splashed around the dugout trying to find something to cling to. Pierrot, afire with rage, swam quietly in a circle holding his knife in his teeth; in a mood for revenge, he was looking for the convict who had once given him the blow. The other, struggling in the water, saw him coming. Relentlessly, Pierrot approached, and struck him with a sudden splash! The man screamed in the night. Now they were three. Pierrot then swam over to one of them for whom he had some esteem, a fellow named Hutin, and told him to swim easily, and that he would help him get ashore. One of the other two had found a box, which he hugged with both arms. Pierrot swam in his direction to take the box away and give it to Hutin. In the moonlight, his eye caught the gleam of a knife which the man held in one of his hands as he grasped the box. Pierrot, still smouldering with anger, was deadly in his tactics. Quietly, he slowly circled about the man, drawing nearer and nearer. His victim could not swim, but managed to kick himself around in the water to face the death that menaced him—the floating box he clutched under him was buoy of life, and he was determined to keep it at all cost.

Pierrot, however, was at home in the water. As the other twisted the box around, kicking in the sea, Pierrot circled imperceptibly nearer. His knife was no longer in his teeth. As he approached, he held it in his hand ready to strike. Slowly he circled, a fraction closer every time. Then, with a violent swirl, he changed direction and closed in on his enemy's unprotected side. Suddenly one arm arched in a flurry of spray from the water, and his knife gleamed as he brought his hand down on the other's back! Another scream shattered the stillness. Pierrot took the box over to Hutin and shoved it to him.

They swam on, side by side. When dawn broke they were close to the shore, and Pierrot spoke encouragingly to his companion, urging him not to give up. Finally they touched land. They had been in the sea more than eight hours! Worn out, they lay down and slept. Before noon, however, they woke up. They were being shaken roughly.

"Hey, you! What are you doing here?"

It was a turnkey; and a guard stood near with his revolver cocked. Unfortunately, they had reached land near Camp des Haltes. That night they were back in the blockhouse.

It was Hutin, himself, who told me the details of this story of Pierrot's vengeance.

From the blockhouse, Pierrot, in detention again for *évasion*, corresponded with Roger as often as he could by means of notes carried by convicts going to Charvein or brought from the camp of the incorrigibles to the blockhouses; and, whenever he had an opportunity, he sent Roger some tobacco and, now and then, a 5-franc bill. When he appeared before the T. M. S. Pierrot was punished with six months in solitary confinement, and was taken to the cell blocks on Saint Joseph. The new regulation had just come into effect, punishing *évasion* with solitary confinement instead of adding additional years of hard labor.

But this new regulation suppressed at the same time, temporarily, the dread camp of Charvein, and the *incos* there were removed and taken to Royale. And so it happened that Roger, also, was embarked for the

Islands. Now they were nearer, only the distance between Royale and Saint Joseph separated Pierrot and Roger. Roger worked as water carrier on Royale, and from this he made a little money. Now, in his turn, he assisted Pierrot, who was still buried in the cell blocks, by sending to him by guards or turnkeys tobacco and money. Then Pierrot was freed from the solitary confinement cells on Saint Joseph and brought to Isle Royale—and to the Second Platoon. At last, after two years of trying, they were united! Since the time they had become acquainted, they were now together in a barrack for the first time!

But their ecstasy did not last long, Roger had been classed as an invalid by the doctor on the Islands, for he had become subject to spells of epilepsy; he was to be sent again to the mainland—to the Nouveau Camp. He tried in vain to be removed from the list. He gained a few more weeks with Pierrot by paying the bookkeeper every week to leave him out of the current list of those going to the mainland!

Finally Roger had to leave Royale. Pierrot promised him he would try by every means to join him as soon as possible. He set about doing it; he began smoking quinine incessantly, to make himself ill.

It was at this juncture that, sentenced to Isle Royale and the Crimson Barrack, again an Incorrigible, I found Pierrot and came to know him—and watched with interest his attempt to gain his freedom from the Islands and join the youth Roger for whose company he pined incessantly.

He would talk with me for hours, about the sea, about the world he had known—but all the time he was smoking quinine and getting physically weaker and weaker. Finally, he actually became very ill, almost an epileptic himself. He was at last able to maneuver the doctor into issuing an order for him to be sent to a mainland camp. But the doctor ordered his transfer not to Nouveau Camp but to another camp— the dreaded Camp Kourou, one hundred and fifty

159

miles away from the camp he had hoped he would be sent to so he could be with his friend Roger!

I never saw Pierrot again, and was certain he had died of fever or dysentery. Kourou was the deadliest camp in all the penal colony. Four thousand convicts died there in three years. This Camp of Death has always been the Administration's "regulating camp." It is opened for six to eight months every year, when the convicts are put to work on that notorious Route O, for every yard of which there is a convict corpse. This death camp is opened every time the number of convicts passes the normal total which the penal colony is prepared to take care of; the work they are sent to do on the road is a mere sham, for since 1907 it has not passed beyond the 25-kilometer mark. The road is in the heart of swamp and jungle along the coast; the men work up to their waist in mud and water, their food ration is the minimum allotted in any camp in the penal colony, and day after day they are at the mercy of mosquitoes and tropical sun and rain. They are sent to Kourou to stay until malaria or dysentery ends their days. Convicts sent to Camp Kourou will do amazing things to get away. I knew one, named Coupleux, who pushed a guard into the mud, rifle and all, and fled through the jungle to the penitentiary at Cayenne. They sent him back, however, and he died there. When I met Coupleux he had only four fingers and three toes; he was a fat fellow who cringed at the sight of a knife, but he had discovered that it was painless to lop off a finger or toe. The guard confiscated all the meat for the convicts; he would take it to the black mistress he had in Cayenne, who would sell it and split the profits with him. Even Albert Londres, in his book on the penal colony, referred to this matter; for this guard, half crazed from the rum he drank every day, tried to shoot him and wounded a convict who was standing beside him when he made a visit to Camp Kourou.

The story of Pierrot's adventures, however, came back to me. It became, actually, a legend of the prison colony.

When he had been at Kourou six days, Pierrot escaped with four other convicts and headed in the direction of the Nouveau camp to find Roger and organize an escape by sea. But on the second day after they left Kourou he and his companions were caught in the vicinity of Sinnamarie. Pierrot, alone, escaped in the night. He continued on his way by himself, following the cut made for telephone wires through the wild jungle. At the end of ten days he was at the edge of Camp Nouveau, and got word to Roger that he was hiding near at hand in the jungle.

Now, again, these two men were once more united. In a hut which Pierrot built a short distance from the camp, they saw each other almost every day. Roger, as though hunting butterflies, would visit him in the afternoon. Again, life was bliss to them. Roger brought Pierrot tobacco and food. Alone, there, in the deep solitude of the jungle they found together the kind of happiness they both desired.

Then, they started getting ready for the escape. Pierrot soon found a good dugout down the river, and brought it back into a creek. In the meantime, several convicts at the camp to whom Roger had talked had decided to go with them. One of these convicts was Big Marcel—the same convict who accompanied me on my bloody second escape. On a clear night they left, eight men altogether, with as much food as they could buy or steal.

Pierrot was at the helm. Roger sat next to him. They gained the mouth of the river. The sea was calm and Pierrot was an excellent sailor. Nine days later they were entering the Orinoco. They were in Venezuela; they were, they thought, at last *free!*

A few months earlier they would have had their freedom, but now the authorities of Venezuela, which had always been a land of liberty to men fleeing from the death and starvation in French Guiana, had begun rounding up and arresting all the escaped French convicts in the country. And these eight, who had come thinking they had sailed to freedom, walked right into prison!

Arrested by the Venezuela police, they were thrown into the citadel of Puerto Cabello. Soon they were taken to work on the highway between Ciudad Bolivar and Caracas—a highway which for many years has been constructed almost entirely by the labor of men who escaped from the French Guiana. Life, laboring on that highway, was trying; bad food, hard work, and rough treatment. All that after they had risked their lives and thought they would be free! It was not long before Roger, with his rebellious nature, had his temper and patience at the cracking point. One day, when one of the guards struck him across the back with the flat of a machete, Roger leaped at his throat. That cost him his life, for he was brought to the ground riddled with bullets! Pierrot had witnessed the murder of his friend. Maddened by grief, a few days later, he attempted to stab one of Roger's murderers. And Pierrot fell, in his turn, under a volley of bullets. Big Marcel, finally brought back to the Isle Royale, told me of Pierrot's and Roger's last adventure and of the end of these two inseparables.

Chapter XXII

THERE are some men whose audacity surpasses the imagination. Launay—we called him La Pomme—was beyond doubt one of the most strong-hearted and daring convicts ever in the penal colony. The story of his last effort to escape is a fantastic tale.

Launay, punished with three years in the dark cells of solitary confinement for his last *évasion,* was aboard the *Mana* with a group of other convicts being shipped to Saint Joseph. The hatch had been left open. During the night of the crossing he proposed to one of his comrades that they slip into the sea on one of the life buoys which hung at the side of the boat. His friend refused, feeling no fancy for struggling in the black waters some twenty miles from shore and being a prey to the sharks. So, twenty-four hours later, Launay was confined in one of the solitary cells of the "Castle."

But when he found himself in the cell blocks, in the semi-obscurity where he could hardly pace six short steps and where he was sentenced to exist three long, unbroken years, he had but one idea, which soon became a fixed obsession—to escape.

A fortnight later he had tapped out his intention to his neighbor in the next cell, Marcel Mazet, a Parisian like himself, whom he knew had similar ideas. Marcel agreed to join him in the attempt, and Launay revealed his project to him, which consisted in getting over to Royale and escaping from there. And they set about doing this.

Neither one of them was sick. But for the convicts in the cell blocks, helpless as tigers in a pit, there is only one way to get off the island of Saint Joseph, and that is to get themselves sent to the hospital—which is on Royale. The condemned have innumerable ways of shamming sickness, tricks which in the convict slang are known as *maquillages;* and they are so clever at it that they will often fool an able doctor. For four or five days Marcel smoked cigarettes in which he had mixed quinine copiously with the tobacco, and in this way he was able to show the doctor on Saint Joseph that he was running a high temperature.

Launay also made himself appear ill and simulated erysipelas; he stuck a needle through his cheek and, holding his hand over his mouth, he would blow constantly and hard until soon he had the side of his head inflamed and very swollen. And so, when the doctor came on his weekly tour of inspection, he sent them both to the hospital. The next day they were in the rowboat which is the only link between the two islands. The first step in their scheme had succeeded! But, as they knew, it was the easiest one of all.

Stretched on their hospital beds, they both mused incessantly over one idea. How and with what were they going to get away from Royale?

Launay, at first, had thought of stealing the operating table. But he discovered this would be impossible. For the hospital guard slept in the operating room. The best thing to do, then, would be to make a raft with trunks of banana trees lashed together; it was on such a raft that Dieudonné had gotten away from the island several years before, and had succeeded in reaching the coast.

Marcel, also, was thinking of the same thing, when his eyes fell on a pile of boards in a corner of the long ward. There were about twenty of them, stacked along the floor. These boards are used to replace those on the beds of the sick, which consist of two iron supports across which three boards are placed to hold up the mattress. A brilliant idea came to Marcel. Their raft! Their raft was right there before their eyes. And he disclosed the possibility to Launay.

The next morning, under the pretext of changing the boards of their beds because these were full of lice, they fooled with the stack over in the corner of the ward until they had sorted out the largest and lightest ones.

The problem now was to get the boards out of the hospital and get themselves out also. The situation was a difficult one. The ward they were in was on the second floor, and Launay proceeded, in an indirect manner, to find out from the attendant what was below on the ground floor. He learned that it was a room in which old mattresses were stored. So, in the night, kneeling under his bed, he patiently cut a small hole in the decayed wood with the metal saw he carried in his *plan d' évasion.** Before dawn, he had finished, and he closed the hole neatly and got back into his bed. The other convicts could be trusted, of course; they knew what they were doing, and followed every move with interest. That afternoon Launay bribed the attendant

*This is a special escape "suppository" which contains a key for regulation handcuffs, a screw driver and a small metal saw; the compact outfit being made and sold by convicts working in the shops at Cayenne. Carried in addition to the regular money *plan*.

to take a note to a friend in the camp, and that night he received a ball of stout cord which he and Marcel used to tie into bundles, the boards they had selected.

Eleven! It was the hour of the rising tide.

All was quiet in the hospital. At six that night, when the bell tolled for turning in, they had lain down quietly. They had decided to make the attempt that night, when the rising tide would drift them straight to the mainland. They had no clothes to wear, for these had been taken from them when they entered the hospital. But they had 800 francs in their suppositories between them and they knew they could buy clothes later. For food, they had no need; they expected to spend only one night on the sea, and were confident they would find something to eat on the coast next day.

Launay was the first to descend through the hole. Deftly, Marcel passed him the bundles of boards. Then he dropped him a blanket and a sheet, and let himself down. Soon they were in the court of the hospital. They had not made a sound!

They threw the blanket, folded, over the wall which surrounds the building, encrusted at the top with sharp pieces of broken bottles. Marcel climbed up. Launay handed him the bundles of boards which, cautiously, he slithered down upright on the other side of the wall. Soon they were by the edge of the sea.

The raft was easy to put together: four bundles of two boards, across which at each end they secured, at right angles, a board on top and another below. Quickly, they lashed it tightly with the cord. Then Launay stripped the sheet which he had carried wrapped around his waist, and tied an end of the strip to the raft and the other to his left wrist.

Marcel, amazed at this, asked what he was doing.

"I'm tying myself to the raft, so it can't get away from me," Launay answered. "I don't know how to swim."

It was true. This man who had the courage to face the sea at night on a flimsy raft and venture among

165

sharks which were fat from feeding on human bodies could not swim!

When all was ready, he muttered to Marcel, "Let's go!"

Royale has a rocky shoreline, and the sea breaks over the rocks with a great commotion. There is always a surge of waves. The night was dark and without a moon, and, as they advanced into the water, each one holding up an end of the raft, they could see barely a few yards ahead. Soon they were waist deep in surf, and the noise of the waves kept them from hearing the warnings they gave each other. They struggled out with the raft, trying to get it through the waves and away from the rocks.

They were lost in the darkness. They faltered in the swirls. Suddenly a big wave lifted the raft. Marcel, carried off balance, lost his footing and let go. The waves boiled him over the rocks and he felt a violent pain. Then he lost consciousness.

He came to his senses a few moments later, and floundered to a sitting position in the water. His head throbbed sickeningly and, when he put his hand to it, he felt a deep cut; warm blood flowed down the side of his face. Then he remembered Launay! He struggled to his feet and shouted for him in the darkness. But there was no answer.

Marcel then decided to get back into the hospital, and slowly climbed the slope toward the building. But he was so weakened from loss of blood that he couldn't scale the wall. Blood from the wound in his head covered his face and neck. He sat down on the ground and asked himself what he should do. Give himself up at the guardhouse? But then the alarm would be out and the guards would be after his friend! He doubted that Launay had gotten through the surf, but made up his mind to wait until dawn. Yes, he would stand the pain and wait until then. If Launay was alive, that would give him a better chance.

When the guard at the gate saw Marcel stagger up that morning all blotched with blood, he gave the alarm immediately. A check was made, and Launay was found missing from the hospital! None of the convicts were sent out to work that morning. While they were held behind bars, the guards and turnkeys combed the island. But they found no trace of Launay! And there was no raft on the horizon.

The news of his *évasion* got beyond Royale. There were rumors of all descriptions, and every convict had his theory. The audacity of Launay's escape rapidly became a byword among the men! Then word came that the wreck of the raft had been identified on Devil's Island. Later a message was relayed from Sinnamarie that Launay's partly eaten body had drifted up there on the beach!

But all that was not true. The following is what really happened. It was not known until four months later, when Launay returned to Royale and told me about his adventure.

The wave which had nearly drowned Marcel on the rocks had carried the raft out as it retreated. Launay, clinging to it and safe, had called for his comrade but had received no answer. The raft was dragged into open water by the current, and drifted toward the shore.

When day broke, the Islands were out of sight, and Launay found himself barely a few miles from the mainland. He was still moving toward the coast, and his heart pounded with joy. At last he had gained that freedom for which he had worked and thought so hard!

In a few minutes . . . He saw himself free in Brazil, in Paris! Free! The raft drifted slowly to the coast. Nearer . . . nearer! Soon he was less than a hundred yards away. He watched the beach, every yard counted. Then he noticed he was no longer drifting toward the shore. The raft had come to a standstill! Then slowly it began going out to sea! Launay understood. The low tide which had set in, took him out and out until he had lost sight of the mainland.

The next morning he drifted back to within a few hundred feet of the coast. If he could only swim!

It would be an easy stretch, and in a few minutes he would be on the shore! But he did not know how to swim, and that short distance was an immensity to him. Maddened by rage. and in despair, he felt the raft come to a standstill and then start drifting slowly back to sea again with the changing tide. He loosened a board and paddled, but the strong tide overcame him mercilessly. A few hundred feet, only, separated him from liberty, but even to him, as strong and as desperate as he was, they were an abyss, which with all his courage he could not cross! That night, again, he was far out on the open sea.

He was hungry. But the thing from which he suffered most was thirst. Naked—at night he was cold, and during the day he was parched and blistered by the hot sun. Each day was an eternity. His malaria came over him and, to keep from falling off the raft in his spasms of chill and shivering, he tied himself down on it.

Soon he was in a state of delirium. Four days passed. Sharks followed around the raft, and when he was conscious he watched them in terror.

He endured seven days of it.

It was in this state that a party of Indians who were fishing off the coast of Dutch Guiana found him. The drifting raft attracted them and, when they saw a naked white man lying on it, they took him into their canoe. Launay was still alive, and they brought him to their village, where he pulled through, thanks to the attentions of the old women who worked over him.

In eight days he was well and on his feet. He decided to cross the Maroni River and while hiding out look up some friends in the camps around Saint Laurent. He had money, and with them he hoped to organize an *évasion* by sea. But a detachment of soldiers came through the Indian village on a round of inspection and discovered him, and two days later he was back in the blockhouse in Saint Laurent. He was sentenced by the T. M. S. and, within four months, he had been taken back to Saint Joseph. Four more years had been added to his previous sentence of soul-blasting solitary confinement!

But, more than ever, he was decided not to stay in his dark cell on Saint Joseph!

"Launay, 39,875. Suspected shammer. Not to be sent to the hospital except in case of extreme urgency." These words, in the shape of a boldfaced sign, had been put on the door of his cell by order of the chief guard. Every time Launay came out for his half hour of sunshine in the court he would read that sign to himself. He was thinking more than ever of *évasion,* dreaming about it every night. He knew it would be a difficult matter to get himself back in the hospital, but he had hope. Constantly, he schemed and thought.

Months went by, and Launay was very quiet in the depths of the Castle. He seemed to be beaten. Then one night, the guard, as he paced the iron walk along the top of the still cells, heard groans coming up from one of them. He plunged his flashlight ray into the darkness below, and saw it was Launay who was twitching spasmodically on the floor and groaning miserably. After a while he got the attendant, and the two entered the cell to see what was wrong.

Launay was clutching his abdomen and there was foam on his lips. The attendant questioned him, but he continued to writhe and groan and made no answer. The attendant told the guard it looked as though Launay had a severe attack of colic, so they gave him a few spoonfuls of paregoric and left him there.

The next morning was the day for the doctor's visit to the cell blocks. Launay, of course, knew that. He acted as though he were dreadfully sick. He told the doctor he had had an attack of appendicitis in the night, and it was the second one he had suffered in two months. And he begged the doctor to take him to the hospital and operate on him! The attendant and the guard said that Launay had been in great pain all night, and the doctor considered this a confirmation of what Launay claimed to be the matter with him. The doctor, in spite of the warning sign on Launay's cell door, ordered him sent immediately to Royale. The chief guard of Saint Joseph protested, assuring him Launay was a dangerous individual, a suspected shammer, and had had absolutely nothing wrong with him.

"Him again? You ought to throw him back in the cell!" exclaimed Morelli, the hospital guard, when he saw Launay arriving at the hospital. He had not yet forgotten the thirty days without pay that Launay's last escape had cost him!

Launay was locked up inside a barred room which is reserved for those men who must be attended to with caution. The next morning, Wednesday, the doctor came in to see him, and ordered two days of diet. He said, "I'll operate on you day after tomorrow. You must eat nothing, absolutely nothing, understand? Stick strictly to the diet."

Morelli was standing by the doctor. "Have no fear, sir," he commented. He was going to take personal care of Launay, in his own way.

Friday I'll be far away! thought Launay to himself. For he had a good friend in the chief attendant at the hospital, Pelissier, who that morning had taken a note for him to one of his friends over in the barracks. The note read:

My dear Toto: I came to the hospital yesterday afternoon. Let me know if you are still decided to escape with me. If you are, let me know by Pelissier the attendant, who is bringing this note. Slip me a metal saw in a package of tobacco, but don't send me anything to eat for I am on a diet and the turnkey won't let anything pass except the tobacco. Give me an answer right away, and by tonight I'll send you another note telling you what is to be done. Your good friend, La Pomme.

Toto wrote him in the afternoon that he was ready to escape. Launay quickly sent him another note, which read:

Dear Toto: We will leave tomorrow night when it is dark. When you are free in the day, hide everything in the Flat Rock. We need a machete, extra clothes and strong string. Leave the platoon at 11 o'clock, and meet me on the rock. I'll get away from the hospital at the same time. Thanks for this good saw. La Pomme.

And on Thursday morning Launay woke up secure in his mind that that evening he would not be sleeping there!

That same morning Morelli was airing his views to Pelissier. He was still very suspicious about Launay. "Do you believe Launay's going to have himself operated on?" he demanded.

"Sure," Pelissier replied. "Why not?"

"Well, I, for one, am absolutely sure he has nothing wrong with him. He's here in the hospital just to do what he did that last time—he's going to try to escape!" Morelli scowled as he walked up and down.

"Maybe this time you can stop him," Pelissier chuckled.

"I'll bet you three bottles of champagne Launay won't be operated on tomorrow morning!" Morelli snapped.

"Good!" said Pelissier. "An easy way to get champagne! I accept!" And they shook hands on it.

The value at stake in this bet is something which should not astonish the reader. For Pelissier, convict attendant, received extra pay for giving quinine injections to the guards and their familes and for other attendance as well, and he also had his *débrouille* from the food rations for the sick; so that he made as much money, if not more, than the guard Morelli.

Late in the afternoon of that day Launay received a note from Toto. It read:

Comrade: I am sending you 250 francs which were collected for you among our comrades here in the Second Platoon. They think this time you will get away, and are wishing us both good luck, I have

everything hidden and ready in a spot on the rock:
there's a machete, some good string, and trousers.
But we can't go tonight, because Gros Mouton is the
guard on duty, and you know how he is. I can't do
anything with him, and know I can't get out tonight.
I can manage it tomorrow night. We will go then
tomorrow night, Friday. Don't fail me. Be patient,
and tomorrow LIBERTY!!! Toto.

Tomorrow night! Launay knew he was going to be
operated on in the morning!

How would he manage to delay the doctor? He
thought a long time. If he ate something the doctor
might have to delay the operation.

Later, Pelissier came into his grilled room. He asked
Launay how he felt. "Not so good," said Launay and
this time he meant it!

"Do you know that I've just bet with Morelli?" said
Pelissier.

"No idea," Launay replied absently, his mind absorbed in his problems.

"Three bottles of champagne, of the best champagne! He bet me you won't go to the operation tomorrow, and I took him up on it."

Launay sat up, and looked Pelissier squarely in the
eye. "Then, my friend, you've lost your bet," he confided.

"You're not going to let the doctor operate?" Pelissier exclaimed in surprise.

"No! I'm supposed to make my *escape* tomorrow
night," Launay answered. The attendant was an old
friend of Launay's, and he had absolute confidence in
him. For Pelissier had attempted an *évasion,* himself;
in 1920 he escaped from the Islands with Dieudonné.
Caught, he had paid dearly for the attempt.

"Listen to me," Pelissier replied. "If you intend to
escape, do it tonight. For what are you going to tell
the doctor tomorrow? You know Morelli is sure there
is nothing wrong with you, and for two days now he's
been repeating it to the doctor. If tomorrow morning
you refuse the operation, the doctor'll think you've

deceived him. He'll send you immediately to Saint Joseph, and you'll have one devil of a time getting to the hospital again."

"But the agreement is for tomorrow night! And I don't know where the things are hid," said Launay.

"Well, then, you'd better let him carve," Pelissier advised.

"Thanks!" Launay exclaimed.

"Sure," Pelissier continued. "The doctor will see you have nothing wrong, and he'll stop the operation. Then you'll have ten days here in the hospital, when you'll have lots of time to prepare an *évasion*. I'll help you! It's the advice of a friend I'm giving you. I wouldn't say it just to get three bottle of champagne, you know that!"

Launay understood—it was his best course.

"I guess you're right," Launay said. "Get word to Toto, and tell him what's happened." And, as Pelissier was about to go, he said smiling, "Maybe you'll give me a glass of champagne?"

"Two!" Pelissier laughed. His trick had worked!

It was early in the morning, Friday. The doctor had finished his rounds, and was in the operating room. "Is everything ready for that operation on Launay?" he asked Pelissier.

"Yes, sir," answered the attendant.

"Well, bring him in," said the doctor.

Morelli went with Pelissier, and unlocked the grill, himself. A few minutes later Launay was in the operating room, stretched full length on the table.

"You haven't eaten anything these last two days?" the doctor questioned while he cleaned his instruments.

"No, sir," said Launay.

"How about your heart—has it ever given you any trouble?" asked the doctor.

"No," replied Launay.

All this while, Morelli looked on, a bit disgusted at the turn of events. He had never believed, for once, he would ever see Launay on that table! Now he would be out the price of three bottles of champagne.

The doctor had no chloroform, so he put Launay under ether. Pelissier smiled as Launay became unconscious—and smacked his lips thinking how much champagne he would soon be able to drink.

Fifteen minutes later, the news spread like wildfire through the wards and barracks. Launay was dead! An accident? Certainly! Possibly orders. At any rate, so died one of the convicts whom the Administration couldn't beat or cower into subjugation and cell death.

That afternoon, at dusk, Launay's body was flung into the sea a few hundred yards off the rocks of Royale. He who had had the courage to balk the sharks at the expense of so much suffering, in the end became their dead prey. We made a large wreath for him with flowers and palm fronds which grow on the islands (a rare homage on the Islands), and the oarsmen pitched it into the sea over his body.

And at night, Morelli the guard and Pelissier the attendant sat with their glasses and three bottles of champagne.

Yet in the hospital, it had only been another accident!

"Of course there was nothing the matter with him!" said Morelli. "The autopsy showed he had no appendicitis!"

"Sure," Pelissier replied. "But the bet was whether he'd let himself be operated on, or not!" He smiled to himself as he raised his glass to the dead man in the sea who had been his friend.

Chapter XXIII

DURING my long months in the isolation of the Islands, I wrote a manuscript in the many hours of idleness which were weighing heavily on my mind. I managed to get this manuscript off the Islands by secret means, and sent it to Governor Juvanon in Cayenne.

It was a heartfelt work, in which I described in detail the sufferings and trials of the condemned and revealed fully their side of the lax conditions which exist in the penal colony. I sent it to the Governor with an humble request that he read it.

I wrote in it this dedication:

> *"To his Honor, Governor Juvanon, who saved me from solitary confinement by his leniency and thereby caused me to appear before the Disciplinary Commission for my third escape and not before the T.M.S. In recognition,*
>
> 46,635, René Belbenoit."

The Governor received my manuscript a few weeks before he left Cayenne on a tour of inspection of the Islands; and, when he reached the quarters of the incorrigibles on Isle Royale, he had me brought to him. As I stood at attention, he thanked me for the manuscript, and then told me: "If you have a record of good behavior for three months, I shall see to it that you're *déclassé*." Grateful again for his interest in me, I assured him I would do my best.

The weeks passed; they were trying ones, when my heart ached with suspense as I did everything humanly possible to avoid having one single report given against me by the cut throat guards. When, at last, I had three months of good behavior, I sent a letter to the Governor, reminding him of his promise. His reply came immediately by the next boat, instructing the Commandant to take me out of the incorrigibles, and adding that I was to be disinterned from the Islands and sent to the penitentiary at Cayenne on the first boat to the capital city.

And so, in November of 1927, I went to the mainland again and saw Cayenne for the first time. I had been in the penal colony almost six years. At last, I was in the favorite penitentiary of the condemned— at last I had come to the capital, the center of the penal and civil activities of French Guiana. But Governor Juvanon, whose much-needed protection I had enjoyed, was called to France, and I was unable to see him again before he departed.

To see Cayenne is to see the depths of human degeneration. It is the sort of capital which should be expected in a colony which, after more than three hundred years as a French possession, and the only French possession on the continent of South America had only butterfly wings and stuffed monkeys to send to the Colonial Exposition of 1931 in Paris. Cayenne! The convicts call it Tafiatown—Rumtown! Although it is the main city of one of the oldest possessions under the French flag, it is the capital of a colony without colonists. For who would establish himself in a region where, at every moment, he comes face to face with none but convicts?

Founded in 1626, French Guiana flourished for two hundred years until, in 1848, slavery was abolished. Then the large plantations collapsed, for the freed African natives scattered into the South American jungle and refused to work. The Colonial authorities thought they had found an expedient to relieve the situation: four boatloads of orientals from French Indo-China were imported. But these men, instead of working the plantations for the colonists, set up small stores and exploited the commerce of the possession. So that failed. There was no one to work the large plantations, and things went from bad to worse.

Followed then the idea of white labor, under the regime of Napoleon the Third. Convicts were sent out in 1852 and the Penal Colony was planted. Since then French Guiana, as a colony, has simmered down to nothing, and is in complete ruin.

In 1852 three hundred and fifty-four convicts were brought to the possession and since then the total number has passed fifty-six thousand.

At first, for many years, they served their term and then were taken back to France after they had worked at forced labor in the colony. In those days there was much interest in the colony; so the idea was propagated that, if the convicts were made to stay on, being already there anyway, they would marry with the colonists and have children, make their lives over, and the colony would thus become settled by hard, strong men. For this reason, the accessory penalty of *doublage* (doubling) was pinned to the statutes of the penal code. A freed convict had to serve as a *libéré* a period of exile equal to his original sentence.

But nobody wanted to have anything to do with the convicts when they became free men forced to stay in the colony as colonists. Not even the black women would marry them. The people accustomed to having seen them chained and ordered around in gangs, shunned them and began to be afraid of their increasing numbers. This all gave the colony a bad name in France and citizens in search of new fields went elsewhere; and so, since the days when the penal system was established the possession has gradually dwindled into a place where there is no progress: where lawlessness, degeneration, poverty and misery surpass that of any other colony in the world.

Today, ruined, French Guiana is the camping ground of futility. It has less than fifty miles of road, including the tragic "Route de la Mort" which Albert Londres christened "Route Zero" because built in the jungle by convict labor it goes from nowhere to nowhere. There is not a mile of pavement. There isn't one industry, one single factory, one railroad. Once a month a cargo steamer comes in with supplies and returns empty. The only development there today is the penal system planted eighty-five years ago. A quantity of Negroes are concentrated in villages. A number of Chinese carry on the meagre commerce. Indians shuffle along the path sidewalks. And the adjacent prospering colonies of Dutch and British Guiana struggle frantically to keep the wave of penniless convict would-be colonizers out of their inviting boundaries.

France has long realized that the plan is a failure. Once famous for its Cayenne pepper, which takes its name from the capital, producing spices, sugar, and precious woods, the colony now exports only raw gold and has become nothing more than a depot for criminals. Each Governor who arrives tries to develop something or other; one tries coffee, another cattle, another cocoa. But there is no element of population to sustain an interest in exploitation, and all efforts fail completely. Even cattle for beef have to be purchased in other lands.

Unattractive and ugly Cayenne, the capital of the colony, is representative of the complete failure which France's experiment in her American colony has come to, and even in France the name Cayenne is a synonym of prison; it brings to every Frenchman's mind the thought of assassins, thieves, and outcasts.

The town stretches along the sea-shore for about a mile and is choked to the south, east and west by the great equatorial rain-forest of the northern South American coast. Five dirt roads, paralleling the sea, leave from the market-place and pier and cross the town, to end at the wireless station, where the jungle begins and where, also, is situated the penitentiary.

These roads are the capital's main streets, and they are kept fairly clean, although they are not paved. But the small crossroads, traversing the town in the opposite direction, are a deplorable sight. These present an utterly abandoned aspect; all of them choked with weeds and grass. From time to time a gang of convicts is set to work pulling up the weeds and grass, but a week later the place where they worked will look no better cared for than it did before. The drains and ditches are choked with mud and more obnoxious refuse, and there millions of mosquitoes and flies swarm and breed.

The houses are low, usually not more than one story high, and they are built of wood; their architecture is indiscriminate, and they are painted without taste in shades of green and faded rose or whatever colored paint may be at hand.

In this town, where rain water runs through the streets in great abundance, water in the houses is at a premium. For it flows through the pipes of the householders only twice a day, for about an hour in all, and it is just too bad for the housekeeper who didn't draw enough for her daily needs while she could. She will have to wait until the next day! Electricity is also insufficient; the small power plant runs only at night, from six until four in the morning. There, also, the convicts are the ones who run the machinery, and when there is an attempt at escape by night they will cut off the current and put the whole town in darkness at the moment of the escape—for only 20 francs. *Débrouille,* rackets and combinations to procure the precious money—they are everywhere!

The disposal of sewage is handled by convicts also. At night they go all through the town on wagons which are drawn by oxen, and they go in under the houses and take away the filled buckets which they replace with empty ones. Whenever these convicts are in need of money they will not hesitate to work this simple racket: The regulation specifies that the sewage buckets of Cayenne must not be entirely full—they must have at least a space of five fingers width left empty at the top, so the men can pick them up without soiling their hands; so the convicts drop a large stone into the bucket, and after that they wake up the civilian and show him that his bucket is too full! They refuse to empty it. The civilian is then forced to give the convicts 40 sous to take the thing away. Sometimes a civilian who has forgotten some article of clothing outside his house on a line, or in the court, finds, next morning, that it has disappeared, and the men doing the sewage collecting are the ones immediately suspected. The position of sewage collector is a sought-for job; there are always a few francs to be had from the naive practice of the convicts in the late hours of the night. There is often a pair of trousers to be had from one clothes line or another and, maybe, even a silk nightgown which can be used to sleep in when they return to the penitentiary. The morning garbage service is likewise handled by the condemned. Every morning six of them drive through the town hanging onto a truck. As they empty the garbage it is the job of one of the men to set aside everything which might possibly be of use or which can be sold or repaired: old rags, pieces of lead, broken plates and glasses, and all sorts of other things; these all find their way into the penitentiary where they are made into something or are repaired to be sold later to the Negroes or to other convicts for a small sum. *Débrouille* again!

The only interesting monument in the town is the statue of Schelcher, who caused actual slavery to be abolished in early Guiana; and this statue, strangely enough, is of a nature which is ironically symbolical. Schelcher has his arm around the waist of a small Negro, and with his hand he is pointing to something. And when there is a gang of convicts pulling weeds around the statue, he seems to say to the little black boy—in actual words, almost: "Do you see them? You are free—these are the slaves now!"

The only attractive thing in Cayenne is the Place des Palmistes, a square which is probably unique in the world. It is a squared-off park some two hundred yards wide from which soar two hundred and fifty giant traveller's palms. These rise to a height of more than eighty feet, and are crowned with huge, sweeping fronds which stir dreamily and deliciously in the afternoon breeze.

The population of the capital is about 11,000 souls; more explicitly stated, it is of 10,000 souls and 1,000 bodies, for there are 700 convicts and 300 *libérés* in Cayenne. The others, the civilians, may be divided into four classes. There are the officials, mostly white, who live off the budget and the graft of the colony, and if one adds here the few white merchants who do business in the colony, one has the total white population of the capital, which amounts to about 1,500. The Oriental element in the capital comes to about 1,000 people, mostly retail merchants who have small stores from and in which they exploit the convicts as well as the civilians. Finally, there are the Negroes who are in the capital in large numbers just as they are everywhere else in the colony. Most of them have small plantations in the outskirts of the town, which suffice to keep them alive. Some of them have the energy to go off to the gold mines for a few months, where they make money; but they come back to the capital to eat it up or, more commonly, to drink it up in the dives kept by the Orientals.

In the market place down by the water one sees the population of Cayenne meet and melt into one. There, in the corrugated iron structure, all paths come together in the early morning. *Doudous,* as the Creoles call the black women, stand in groups, chatting and laughing in a loud voice. Bedraggled and penniless *libérés*—men free of prison but still exiled to French Guiana—wander hungrily among the booths, looking for cheap bargains, picking up vegetables that have fallen on the ground. Convicts are there in their wide straw hats and red striped clothes buying something to take off to eat with their regulation ration. A few white women pass here and there through the crowd, often followed by some admiring convict, making their own purchases because they are too poor to hire a servant. And there are also the cooks of the Governor, of the General Prosecutor, of the Mayor—these servants are convicts, but they are dressed as civilians except for the wide straw hats.

The cost of living is high. Three string beans are worth all of 2 sous, two small carrots are 2 sous also, and a tomato costs 10 sous. True enough a sou is not much; but it is to be remembered that money is at a premium in Guiana, and that a sou is the relative equivalent of a dollar to many of these miserable and destitute souls. Among the venders in the market, there are more convicts: the chief butcher, for instance, is none other than the former leader of the famous Villette gang, and is a man who was sent out to Guiana for life for a triple murder. Buying from him may be seen Metge, of that famous Bonnot gang which terrorized France, and who, condemned for life for a double murder, was cook for three Governors in Guiana.

The convict is everywhere; he overruns the town.

At the far end of the town, near the sea and with its back to the great rain-forest, is the penitentiary. There are no walls around it—for of what use would these be, when a convict wanders alone and freely in the town all day long! This penitentiary is encircled only by a few iron fences which enclose a garden. There are three large barracks in the penitentiary, one for the Orientals, another for the Arabs, and the last for the European convicts. Many of the convicts sleep in town at night, at the houses of their employers.

This is the penitentiary which the condemned dream of, for here, in all Guiana, they have the most liberty, the most chances to make money. For the high civil authorities are right at hand and the condemned are better treated and are not subjected to as much abuse as in other penal units. At six in the morning the gangs of prisoners leave the barracks, accompanied by only one turnkey, and the first thing the men do is to stop by an Oriental's store and have a glass of *tafia* and buy tobacco. At ten they return for the food ration. Then they go out at two, work again, and come back at five in the afternoon.

When a man is at Cayenne he can have his *doudou,* and he can find an opportunity to sleep with her almost any afternoon he likes—all he needs is the 40 sous to give her, and a little more money to buy her one or two glasses of *tafia. Tafia* is the drink of the town, and it is part of the pay the many prostitutes demand; it can be had straight, adulterated with various drugs which the Orientals know how to mix with it to make it sweet, also weakened with water to which pepper has been added—so the unsuspecting customer will not realize he is being cheated. The stores are prohibited to sell any drink to the prisoners, but each day a convict will drink from two to three glasses of his favorite *tafia;* while he is inside a store drinking with others, a convict friend lolls at the door watching out for a passing guard, and the Orientals who sell *tafia* are all accomplices, for they have no scruples.

Without the convicts, Cayenne would perish, and it

is for this reason that, whenever anything is said in France about suppressing the penal colony, a cable is sent in protest by the Mayor at Cayenne on the instigation of the populace, for the civilians are at a loss to know how the town can live if the convicts are taken away. They are the slaves of the colony today. They are its necessity, though evil spirit, and the civilian populace of Guiana is too ignorant to realize that it is this spirit of the condemned, this taint of degeneration, which will perpetually constitute the check and ruin of Cayenne as a city until the day comes when it is blotted out.

Everything is fantastic in Cayenne, in this colony where so much lawlessness, degeneration, poverty and misery exist and flourish more than in any other possession or colony anywhere in the world. Here are a few incidents which could not have taken place anywhere else except in this colony where nothing is normal.

There is a remarkable little incident which is very characteristic. It is the story of a convict who played Governor!

His name was Leffay. The Governor of the colony at that time was Thaly, a very black Negro from French Africa. He had gone to the Islands on a tour of inspection and had taken along with him his butler, Leffay. He returned to Cayenne on the *Biskra,* which had stopped by for him on its way from Martinique to the capital. The captain of the ship had invited the Governor to dine on the ship, so, when it arrived at Cayenne, the Governor entrusted his brief-case, which contained all the reports and other documents that he had collected on the Islands, to his butler. And he said to Leffay, "Take this to the Government house, and when the postman brings the mail you will have him put it on my desk, and you stay there until I come."

Leffay went to the Governor's house. A few hours later the postman came with the official mail which had arrived from Paris on the same ship. This mail was, of course, strictly official; there were registered dispatches, sealed instructions from the various Ministries, and other papers of that sort.

"Put it all on the Governor's desk," said Leffay to the postman.

The postman did as the man sitting in the Governor's chair instructed, but he demanded a receipt. So Leffay then calmly took the post-office record book and signed on the dotted line: "Received for His Honor, the Governor of Guiana.

The convict and butler,
Leffay."

It was only a few days after this that the Inspector General of the Colony noticed that there was not the Governor's but a convict's signature affixed to the receipt which announced the safe arrival of all the official mail from France. It was necessary to destroy that page which Leffay had signed, for the Administration could not allow that signature to go back to France. So the whole record book had to be copied over because its pages were in numbered sequence. The incident cost Leffay his job, the fine job of butler to the Governor, but, since he had been prompted merely by a desire to be of service to the high official of the colony and had signed the receipt in pure ignorance of the consequences which might arise, he was transferred to a similar job in the employ of a minor official.

Another incident, a tragic thing which was a veritable drama, occurred later. It had an international repercussion but, more than that, it is typical of the degenerate and lax ways of things in Guiana. Eight miles out to sea beyond Cayenne, on a rock which is only some forty-five yards in circumference, is the beacon of *L'Enfant Perdu,* which guides ships into the harbor and which is one of the main lights along that part of the coast of South America. This beacon is always tended by three convicts.

In the middle of March one of the convicts at the beacon became sick. The distress signal was raised, and on the following day the port launch came for him. According to the regulations, this man should have been replaced right away. It was not done, however, and the other two convicts at the lonely watchtower on the rock didn't insist that a third man be sent out, for they hoped the port authorities would give them the pay of this other man which would mean 30 additional francs they would share between them.

The days passed. April came. Habitually, the food supplies were brought to the rock between the first and the fifth of the month. The fifteenth of April came, and still nothing had been sent out to them! Since they had the ration of their absent comrade they concluded they had not been restocked because back on the mainland this had been taken into account. In the meantime, however, they had been feasting well, and now on the morning of the fifteenth of April they had enough food for only two days more. They raised the distress signal, so that Cayenne would think of them. But the launch failed to put out for the rock—neither did it come on the next nor on the second day after the flag went up! The distress signal was kept flying, and they watched anxiously for the launch. Since they now had nothing to eat, they had to resort to the shellfish which, fortunately, abounded on the desolate and sea-beaten rock. The twenty-third passed, the twenty-fourth . . .

The twenty-sixth passed, and they were still marooned. Then the gasoline for the beacon gave out, and they also had no more matches for the light! On the twenty-seventh they failed in their efforts to keep the flame going. That night *L'Enfant Perdu* was shrouded in darkness! And it is one of the main navigation lights on that part of the South American coast! Two more days passed while they continued in that predicament, and still the port launch didn't come from Cayenne. What could be the trouble? In the town they could not have failed to notice that *L'Enfant Perdu* had been dark for the past three nights, and they couldn't have missed spotting the distress signal which had been flying all day long for more than fifteen days! Then, on the thirtieth of April, the launch finally came out to the rock. It approached to within a short distance of the famished men, but the sea was so bad that it turned back.

The first and second of May passed, while the two stranded men groped in the foam of the receding surf for shellfish and gambled their lives against the hissing swells. They knew they had been left to die. The dark beacon no longer made any difference to them. They were helpless to do anything with it, anyway, and the only thing which concerned them now was to save themselves, for it was a question of only a few days before they would be dead of hunger. They made a heroic decision; heroic because one of them couldn't swim, and in that wild sea it took courage to do what they proposed to try. Rather than die there on the rock of *L'Enfant Perdu,* they decided to try for the mainland on a raft, which they put together with the wood of the tiny hut in which they lived at the foot of the tower. The sea was running dangerously high. On the sixth of May, after they had waited all day clinging to the hope that they would be given succor, they finally realized they must either make the mainland or die where they were, and they took the raft to the water when the last brief glints of sunlight faded. The sea was so rough that it overturned their raft twice, and they barely escaped drowning in the surf.

In the middle of the night, after struggling for hours in the lashing, vicious waves they reached the mainland. They were naked for they had left their clothes behind so as to lessen the danger of drowning. They spent that night on the beach, not knowing where they were, bitten and tormented beyond endurance by the mosquitoes. When dawn broke, they started fighting their way into the jungle tangle; at the end of a few hours they finally broke through into the Colonial Road, the futile "Route Zero" on which convicts have been at work for twenty years, near a gendarme post. They told their story to the gendarmes there, who, after giving them food, took them on to Cayenne, where they were sent immediately to the hospital, under arrest for deserting their post! One of these two convicts, who was named Job, had the audacity to report this incident to the International Lighthouse Commission, thus causing an investigation and an international complication for French Guiana. Job was sent to camp Kourou to do the four months which remained of his sentence and he was kept there for additional punishment until he died. The other convict was freed of the remainder of his term and also of his *doublage* and was allowed to return to France. His pardon was given him because he had not exposed the matter to civilization!

In a certain room in the hospital at Cayenne there are seven large bottles side by side on a wide shelf: in them are the seven heads preserved in alcohol of criminals who were executed on the guillotine! Seven heads —but among these seven there is one which is not the head of a man who died on the guillotine and who was never condemned to death in the penal colony!

These seven heads are a horrid sight. The jars containing them are filled with clear alcohol, and one can examine them minutely at close range. The hair on their heads, their beards and mustaches are massed in abundance inside the large jars, for, as most people know, hair grows for a long time after a man's head has been severed from his body. Among the six human heads which, true enough, were sliced clean by the guillotine, are some of men who created something of a stir in the penal colony; there is that of Pstate and also that of his accomplice, both of whom butchered an entire family of Indians in Dutch Guiana merely to rob them of some gold—but unfortunately, they left a little child alive, who later identified them and caused them to die on the guillotine; in another of the jars there is the head of the convict who killed a doctor at camp Kourou, and who, because of this murder he committed at the medical inspection, brought into effect the practice whereby all convicts coming before doctors on their medical visits must be completely naked so as to avoid the possibility of having a weapon concealed on their persons. As for the rest of the heads, all pale, macabre, and diabolical-looking, they are those of convicts who killed some official or civilian.

But it is the seventh one in this row of horror, that head of a man who never walked up to the guillotine and who was never condemned to death, which is the most macabre of all. This head has a sad and an atrocious history; it belonged to a man who was accused, and convicted, of a horrible crime of which he was innocent. His name was Brière: he was accused of having murdered his five children, whom he had gathered together at a family feast. He had a sixth child, a little girl, whom he had also invited for the gathering; but she had not come in time, and the prosecutor declared she had thus escaped being murdered by a miracle, for, he said, her father would have killed her also. Brière defended himself as best he could protesting that he was innocent. But, nevertheless, he was condemned for life. Fifteen years later a half-crazed tramp confessed on his death-bed to a priest that he had been the author of this mass murder, and he gave such a detailed description that justice had no doubt about the truth of his confession. Brière was recognized to be an innocent man, but French law waited until he died before rehabilitating him, and for two long years, his innocence acknowledged, he clung to life in the penal colony waiting for a re-trial which would give him back his freedom. And there he died. The poor man passed away in the hospital at Cayenne, still a convict branded with the ignoble stripes, two years after he had learned the name of the man who killed his five children and after the people of France had realized his innocence and French justice had been brought face to face with its error. French justice, which will never admit a mistake, withheld its verdict on the revision of this unfortunate's case month after month and kept him unnecessarily in the penal colony, and let him die there!

But that is not all. Someone among the officials of the bloated and corrupt Administration of the penal colony, decided that the innocent man's head should be cut from his body and lined up in an alcohol jar in the midst of those of the executed criminals. Who could be so base in mind to allow that such a thing be done? Why was it done? No one knows, and no one ever will know. I do not know, myself, although my curiosity prompted me to try to find out through various channels; but I never found even a doctor or an attendant or a guard who could tell me. Not even in the records in the archives of the Administration could I find the slightest clue as to what made the authorities of Cayenne exhibit an innocent man's head. It is shameful, even for Guiana!

Chapter XXIV

MORE than three fourths of the condemned in Guiana have but one thought: to escape as soon as they can!

There are four types of *évasion* or escape from the penal colony; through the jungle; by way of Dutch Guiana; as supercargo of the Brazilian contrabandists; and, lastly, by way of the sea. There is also a fifth method which is rarely practiced—although it has a one hundred per cent chance of success. This last is an *évasion* prepared by a free individual, a relation or friend, who comes after the convict with papers in order, sends word to him to join him at a designated spot and then takes him away with forged papers. This has happened, strangely enough, very rarely, but every time it has been tried it has been successful. I know two citizens of the United States, the only two from that country who have been in the prison colony in the last twenty years, who escaped in this fashion. They were brothers, and had been soldiers in France during the War, and were condemned for life for murdering a cabaret girl in Montmartre. Soon after they arrived in Guiana the elder one escaped by sea in a pirogue and managed to reach the United States.

He then took it upon himself to free his brother who had been left behind. He went to Baltimore and talked with the sailors of a freighter which made a trip every two months to load bauxite at the Moengo mines in Dutch Guiana, thirty-one miles from Saint Laurent. One day an Indian appeared in Saint Laurent and asked a convict if he knew where C.C. was located. The convict asked the Indian what he wanted. He was handed a note which instructed him to follow the Indian. He did so, and was never seen again in Guiana. These two brothers, Americans, condemned for life, remained in the French prison colony less than a year! It is, as I have said, a rare type of *escape* perhaps because the relations and friends on the outside do not know just how it is to be arranged.

Escape through the jungle is almost an impossibility. No one has ever gone from French Guiana across into Brazil through the jungle: there are large rivers to cross which back their waters miles and miles into the rain-forest; it is impossible to proceed on foot, and a pirogue cannot be pushed upstream by white men. It would be a long wearying expedition, which would require the right equipment, and this the men in Guiana do not have. Only monkeys, leaping through the trees, could flee without preparation in that direction. The convicts, although they are changed into beasts by the life and regime under which they exist, have no chance to learn how to overcome the privations and natural barriers of the jungle—they become its prey when they expose themselves to it, and they perish.

Escape by way of Dutch Guiana? Before 1923, the *évadés* were well received by the Dutch. They were tolerated in the colony, where they easily found work, and in the capital there were at least a hundred of them. Then one day one of them—Coutancot—committed an atrocious crime. He was sentenced to death and hanged at Paramaribo, and after that incident all the *évadés* have been consistently hunted down and arrested in the Dutch colony, and sent back on the first launch to Saint Laurent. Only the German convicts get by Dutch Guiana now. The German consul at Paramaribo has special funds for helping out his nationals and facilitating their passage through the Dutch colony. They have only to get across the Maroni. The police commissioner in Albina verifies that they are German, and then gives them a pass to proceed to Paramaribo, where their consul shelters them and embarks them on the first steamer for Hamburg. This is a tacit international situation which is, in some ways, remarkable. Hitler does not forget to save his subjects condemned to hell and death by another government. However, the Administration has become aware of all this, and puts the German convicts on the Islands or in the penitentiary at Cayenne—one hundred and twenty miles away from the river! But, all the same, this does not keep a few of them from getting through the jungle between Cayenne and Saint Laurent and crossing the river. And when they do, they are never heard of again. They are free!

There is the *escape* as stowaway. It often happens that a convict, escaping from a camp, hides himself in the freight on a vessel out in the river at Saint Laurent; he mingles with the gang of convicts working at the unloading of the cargo, and hides himself on board. When the gang has finished for the day the guard counts the men and, since he is not one of them, the vessel goes away and he is not discovered. Some succeed that way. But it is rare, for most are taken in Martinique, as they come out for food and water. Convicts who try for liberty as supercargo of the Brazilian contrabandists or "pirates," as these are called in Guiana, take a greater gamble. These "pirates" demand 1,000 francs per head to carry a man from Guiana to liberty, but nine times out of ten they throw their passengers overboard . . . after having searched them and cut them open to see if they carry a suppository full of money. It is especially true at the present time, since the Brazilian Government, which formerly closed its eyes to this passenger traffic, now seizes the contrabandist's boat and makes him pay a heavy fine if he is caught bringing an *évadé* from French Guiana into the country.

There is, last of all, the great and magnificent adventurous *escape*—by way of the sea. This is the most dangerous of all, yet the one which offers the best chance of success. Every year there are at least six or seven such escapes attempted, out of which one or two succeed: which is to say liberty for eight or sixteen men. Four of the attempts result in capture and return from the neighboring colonies or from Venezuela and Colombia, and the rest disappear forever, swallowed up in the silence of the sea.

It is no easy matter to go several hundred miles through the turbulent and treacherous waters of the Gulf in a slender Indian pirogue only twenty feet long and less than three feet beam. To gain the republics of Central America, and even to reach Venezuela, requires a voyage of some 2,500 miles, sailing well offshore at a distance of a hundred miles. One if forced to remain sitting down and bent over in the narrow craft for a fortnight without being able to move—or for more than three weeks sometimes—suffering from thirst and often from hunger also, drenched constantly by waves and by the heavy dew at night and scorched by a fiery sun during the day. And there are the heavy squalls to ride and the sharks which haunt the wake. Yet it is this venture which every year tempts from forty to sixty convicts! The chances are eight to one they will be brought back, unless they manage to get beyond Venezuela, or that they will sail into disaster; they know all that but, nevertheless, it does not stop them. For always existence in the prison colony holds up to them the two alternatives: escape or die.

In the middle of February of 1928 I received an answer to a letter I had written Mrs. Niles. She advised me not to try to escape again, and to finish my term, which now lacked only eighteen months. But, since even after finishing my sentence of eight years I would be forced to live all my life as an exile in Guiana, and it would, therefore, be necessary for me to escape later anyway, I decided to make another attempt as soon as possible.

I started thinking of attempting an escape in a dug-out by way of the sea. But in Cayenne, where the men who are ready to take the risks of *évasion* are few, I was unable to find a sailor to do the navigating.

Now I was firmly decided, just as I had been on previous occasions, to get away, particularly as I had such a sum of money in my possession, and I had a restless urge to get out of Guiana before any of this money which meant salvation for me got out of my hands. I had to go as soon as possible, while I still had it! So I thought up a scheme. It was a good one: I made up my mind to embark as a passenger on a French coastal ship which was going to the colony's Brazilian frontier and, there, I would get on a Brazilian mail-boat and go on down the coast of South America. To do this, however, I would need papers; they were an indispensable requirement. To obtain these necessary papers I found, after looking around, would not be difficult. The most important thing of all was to obtain a Brazilian passport, and this I got without trouble: the employee who acted as secretary for that country's consul in Cayenne was a convict, and he was able to find me a passport to which he had affixed all the required seals and stamps . . . for a price of 100 francs. I needed, also, *libéré* papers in order to ride on the coastal boat. The *libérés* are so miserably destitute in Guiana that they will sell their papers for even as little as 5 francs when an occasional opportunity presents itself, and I was able to buy the papers I needed from one who had finished his term of exile and was, therefore, free to take any ship and leave the colony. He would have gone back to France long ago, no doubt, poor fellow, but he had never been able to get together enough money to buy a passage. I sent this same man to buy my ticket, himself, with his papers and in his own name. It was a passage to Saint Georges, on the Brazilian frontier, and I planned, when time for sailing arrived that I would pass on board the ship with the passport and papers of a freed exile.

The ship was scheduled to leave at five o'clock on the following Saturday afternoon and, by Thursday, I had everything ready: I had my civilian suit hidden in the hut of a *libéré* friend down on the waterfront; I had my officially stamped passport to re-embark at the frontier on the Brazilian mail-boat. I expected to get myself in readiness for the *évasion* at three o'clock that Saturday afternoon—I would leave my gang at that hour, and then go dress myself and walk on board. But, at two o'clock that Saturday afternoon, as I emerged from the penitentiary to work with the gang, my heart filled with hope and joy, I heard the town-crier drumming through the town that the ship *Oyapoc* had been delayed, and would not leave until eight o'clock Sunday morning! That was the French coaster, *my ship,* on which I had banked all my hopes of freedom, and this delay troubled me greatly. If I left my gang at two o'clock in the afternoon, as I had intended, and were then arrested before the ship sailed, I wouldn't have more than three or four hours of absence and could not be considered attempting an escape! But, the ship leaving on Monday morning, it would be necessary for me to start preparing my *évasion* on Saturday after-noon all the same, because on Sunday I wouldn't go out from the penitentiary to work; I would have to spend the night outside, in hiding therefore, and, if anything happened when I tried to get on the ship and I were caught then, I would have more than twelve hours' absence and would be considered a convict in the act of trying to escape!

But there was always the cheering thought inside me that everything would be all right. I had a certain amount of confidence in my predicament; I told my-self, reassuringly, over and over again that, if I was not arrested at the moment the ship sailed from Cay-enne I could consider myself as having attained my freedom; for, at Saint Georges, that diminutive village of eight hundred inhabitants on the Brazilian frontier, there would be only one black gendarme, who would have nothing to say to me, since I was completely in correct form as a *libéré* who had finished his exile and could go anywhere he liked. Oh, I had it all planned in my feverish mind! Once landed in Saint Georges, I would after night came pay a Negro 25 francs to row me across the river to the frontier village in Brazil, known as Demonti; I would throw my *libéré* papers into the water while I crossed the river and, when I found myself in the Brazilian village, I would show the authorities, if they asked for it, my official and valid passport which was visa'd and in order for entry in Para! Yes. It would all work out just as I planned, I told myself, over and over again. It would be silly to falter, when I had the whole thing so clear in my mind. The only hitch was the delay in the sailing of the ship. Still, that was no reason to change my plans and be afraid to take the chance—the opportunity was one in a thousand, since I had all the papers which I required in my pocket and in order. Few were the convicts, who, in the history of the penal colony, ever had the good luck and opportunity which was now in the palm of my hand! I decided to take the chance, and followed it out step by step.

At three o'clock that momentous Saturday afternoon, I left my gang as we worked on the weeds along the edge of one of the streets, saying to the guard in charge I was going over to a store to get something to eat. I entrusted my weeding tool to the convict who worked at my side, giving him 19 sous to take it back to the camp that night, to avoid suspicion. I went straight to the hut of my *libéré* friend, where I had my civilian clothes hidden, and there I hid myself. I spent the night pacing the floor, too restless to sleep. Would I gain my liberty this time? *Would I!* As soon as dawn flooded the village the *libéré* went to the pier to find out the exact hour the ship would sail. He seemed to be gone hours. Then he came back, advising me to get myself ready right away, for the hour of sailing had not been changed, and telling me it would be best for me to get aboard the ship then, as soon as I could, when there were fewer guards about in the streets.

I dressed myself rapidly. In a few minutes I was ready. Clothed in a neat, white suit, with a pith helmet set at a smart angle on my head, and wearing a pair of green sun-glasses over my eyes, I left the hut, accompanied by my freind, and together we crossed the town, picking out least frequented streets. After a while we arrived at the pier—nothing had gone amiss so far.

We were in front of the gate. Beyond it jutted the long narrow pier and there, at its end, was the ship. I took my comrade's hand and shook it warmly, squeezing it so hard that he flinched. Then I turned and, without batting an eyelash, I passed by the gendarme on duty at the pier's gate. Once by him, I broke into a cold sweat. I was on the pier now! It was like a long runway to freedom, with the ship, resting languidly at its end under the morning sun, as my goal. Slowly, embued with a deadly calm, I walked on—the pier seemed to have no end. It was interminable. I counted every step, I remember them today—it was five hundred and sixteen steps that I took slowly and calmly, with my heart in my throat, before I came to the ship's side. I walked up the gangplank, presented my ticket, and a steward showed me to my cabin.

"Ouf!" I breathed, when he had taken his tip and closed the door. Now I was alone, and could think—check over everything and see if I had made any mistake. Everything was perfect—this time it was freedom at last!

Standing in the center of my cabin, behind the locked door, my heart brimmed with joy. "It worked," I murmured over and over to myself, the tears in my eyes. "It worked!" Soon, however, my restlessness returned to me. I wanted the ship to start moving, to get going. I peeked out of the porthole; the river glided by beneath my eyes, and the little eddies in the water glinted in the sunlight as they passed my line of vision. The Dutch bank lay directly in front of me. As I stared at it, as I had done before countless, endless times for hours on end, it seemed a cursed mirage. "Good-bye!" I breathed, as I stared at it shadow-etched outline under the early morning sun—"Good-bye! Never again, so help me God, will I ever have to look at you any more." Then I turned back into the cabin with a deep sigh of relief, and began pacing back and forth. I had no watch. I yearned for the ship to start, to feel it moving—moving, and taking me with it, out of that Hell on earth. I was getting very nervous. "It must be time, now! Why are they waiting?" I kept asking myself.

Then the whistle blew. The first signal! Soon the ropes would be cast off! Mad with joy, I slipped up on deck and found a secluded spot from where I watched the last passengers coming on board—I was safe on deck, as there are no penitentiaries or jungle camps in the region of Oyapoc on the Brazilian frontier, for which the ship was destined, and so there would be no guards or convicts coming on the ship.

The whistle blew again. It was the second signal. In a few more minutes, now, we would be free of the pier, and I would be free of the penal colony and French Guiana for the rest of my life.

Then, just at this moment, when my heart was pounding with elation, I saw a gendarme running full speed down the pier. He was waving at the ship with his right hand as he ran at top speed! My eyes became glued on his form while I reasoned with myself to allay my feeling of terror. How could he be coming for me? But he *was* coming for me—I knew it, suddenly, and my heart thumped with excitement.

I remained standing, motionless in the seclusion of the spot where I was while he rapidly approached the ship. He hailed the ship's officer in charge, who was at the top of the gang-plank, and came up into the ship with great strides. I overheard him ask the officer if there was a man named Ormières on board. "At all events, his name is on this passenger list," the gendarme was saying, pointing to a sailing register blank which he had brought with him.

197

Ormières! I stood against the rail, thunderstruck. Ormières was the name of the *libéré* from whom I had bought my papers. But why was this gendarme looking for Ormières? He was a freed man, and there would be nothing wrong with his being on the ship. I was thinking very fast, and all my senses were riveted on the conversation going on near me.

The officer had called the steward by this time, and the steward told the gendarme that there was an Ormières on board and said he was most probably down in his cabin.

They went below. I decided in a flash that there was no time to lose, and, as they went down the stairs which led to the deck where my cabin was, I went down the gangplank. My feet once on the pier, I started walking down its length at a rapid stride. Once more, that pier seemed an eternity; but this time there was terror in my heart, where less than an hour before there had been bursting, overpowering hope! Rapidly I walked on, my goal the little gate at the far end of the four-hundred-yard pier.

"Ep! Ep! Ep!" It was the gendarme, somewhere behind me. He must still be on the boat, I concluded. I had gone almost one hundred yards by then. I wanted to break into a run, to race with all my might for that gate. But I didn't dare. The jig would be up, if I did. He might even shoot! So I walked on, without even turning my head, at the same rapid pace.

"Ep! Ep!" He was closer now. I could distinguish the sound of his footsteps. They were like thuds pounding in my head like blows. I was the only soul on the long pier—and the only thing I could see was that gate far in front of me. There was not a sound, except the feet behind me drawing nearer every second. It was all I could do to stay my impulse to run. He was after *me,* all right! There was not the slightest doubt about that. But perhaps he might let me go—he was looking for Ormières and I was not Ormières. I had no other saving thought to cling to.

I walked on, the steps behind me grew louder . . .

louder . . . louder. I knew I would look very pale in spite of all my efforts to control myself, when that gendarme caught up with me and looked into my face.

"Ep! Ep! Ep!" This time it was at my very ear, and I stopped. I had to face him.

"Where are you going?" he demanded.

"To the town," I said calmly.

The moment he took a look at me, amazement seemed to spread over his face. The people on the ship were pointing and making signs at me.

I played my last trump then. I tried to take advantage of his apparent perplexity. "I forgot something in town, and must get it in a hurry," I said simply. "The ship's about to leave." I feigned an anxious voice, as if I feared I would be left, and looked back and forth from the ship to the gate at the end of the pier.

He didn't seem to know what to do. I merely stood and waited, while the split seconds dragged. If he would only tell me he'd made a mistake, I could give him a rapid "It's perfectly all right!" and dash at a mad run down the long pier. . . .

But the people back on the deck of the ship continued making signs, insisting I was the right man. The gendarme looked at them, then at me. I shifted on my feet and stared impatiently at the gate. He pulled at his mustache, undecided what to do. Then, since the people on the ship were so insistent, he asked to see my papers. So I calmly tendered him the only ones I had, which were those of the man he sought!

He opened them hurriedly and examined them at a rapid glance.

"But you," he exclaimed, "you are not Ormières!"

"Yes! These are *my* papers," I said emphatically, as if surprised that he shouldn't think so.

"But I arrested Ormières yesterday, dead drunk in the street! He's in prison!" the guard said.

In a flash I realized what had happened—Ormières had become drunk with the money I had paid him and had had a set-to with this gendarme!

"But I am Ormières, also," I said to the gendarme.

"The same name evidently; but you can see I'm not the man you arrested." It was a possible loophole through which I might still squeeze.

It might have worked. He might have given back my papers and passport which were strictly in order and let me go my way, if it hadn't been for that cursed Ormières' first name—Gabriel—which was written down in both! For, when he arrested Ormières, he had taken down his whole name—and there it was, Gabriel Ormières, on both my fine documents to freedom.

That was what finished my chances. He insisted that I come along to the gendarmerie where things could be investigated properly. There I was quickly identified and taken to the penitentiary, where I was thrown into the blockhouse!

What a fatal curse coincidences can sometimes be. Ormières had, true enough, insulted this particular gendarme in one of the streets of the town, being dead drunk from rum bought with the money I had paid him for my freedom, and the gendarme had slapped him into the civil prison (for Ormières was a civilian, since he had ended his term of exile); the gendarme had then happened to see his name on the passenger list. Ormières had been set to work in the market place, and the gendarme had concluded he had intentions of running away. Fatality, it seemed, dogged my every step. Had the ship sailed Saturday as it was supposed to do, everything would have been all right. I would have sailed down the coast to certain liberty!

Chapter XXV

I STILL had in my possession almost all of the large sum of money which I had received from Mrs. Blair Niles, and I made up my mind to make every effort to leave not one thing undone to avoid being given additional years of hard labor as a convict for this fourth attempt to escape. There remained only eleven more months for me to do to finish my term. If I were punished with two or three more years as a convict, all my money would then be dissipated in the vicious circle of my lengthened misery, and I would have none to finance another attempt.

My predicament was extremely bad, however, and the chances were all against me. At the Gendarmerie they had found and confiscated my false passport, and the fact that I had in my possession one which was officially stamped and in form made my incrimination all the stronger; there were, also, my false *libéré* papers, which they had caught me in the act of using. It looked bad for me: in addition to being guilty of *évasion,* I had been caught red-handed with false identification papers. But by now I knew the way of things in the penal colony thoroughly, and I realized there was one means of getting myself out of my difficult situation which had fair chances of working and thus saving me from disaster.

This possibility lay in the former deputy of French Guiana, Monsieur Jean Galmot, with whom I had had dealings several weeks earlier. Jean Galmot was running for deputy again, in the elections which would soon take place in the capital. Being certain he would be elected, he had asked me to write him a revealing and smashing exposé against the Administration and its penal system, which he expected to use to back up his demands for the abolition of the penal colony. I had written for him a thorough and detailed treatise of more than two hundred and fifty pages, and, when he had asked me how much I wanted for it, I had told him, "Nothing! I am glad to contribute what little I can to help put an end to this Hell." He insisted, however, and gave me 100 francs and he promised me that he would always be interested in me, and assured me he would be glad to aid me should I at any time need his services. It was now the time, I concluded, if ever, and so I wrote him a letter in which I explained the difficulty of my situation. In a few days I received his answer.

"I give you my word," he wrote, "that, as soon as these elections are over, I will have you set at liberty for your attempt to escape, no matter what the results of the elections are. Therefore, have patience for a few weeks."

And, in his note, he enclosed 25 francs attached to a slip of paper on which he had written "For cigarettes!"

One month later Jean Galmot died a mysterious death, allegedly poisoned, and the entire black population of the capital was in an uproar, suspicious of foul play against their "Papa" as they called their demi-god. The morning after his death the Negroes of Cayenne rioted. They burned to death, in revenge, the six councillors of the town; the Governor was forced to flee in haste to the Islands for safety, while the director of the Bank of Guiana had himself locked into the blockhouse, dressed as a convict, to escape being massacred! And in that way ended my first and, as I saw it then, my only hope of escaping punishment.

I turned now to another possible chance to save myself. Leonce was, at this time, at Cayenne. I had learned through him, and through other convicts who knew him at Saint Laurent when he worked as cook for the Director of Administration, that he had great influence over this highest official of the Administration. The convicts had confided to me that this influence was the result of a sexual relationship existing between the two. I had never spoken on the subject with Leonce, but he had told me that the Director had repeatedly begged him to return to cook for him at his headquarters in Saint Laurent, and that he had consistently refused. I now wrote a long letter to Leonce, thinking he might be able to influence the Director in my behalf, in some way or another. I sent it to him by a turnkey, and in a few days he answered me:

"I am going to write to the Director and ask him to employ me in his house again," he wrote. "I promise you I will do everything to get you out, and I think I will succeed."

Before a month had gone by, Leonce left for Saint Laurent to be cook for the Director. A few weeks later, I received the following:

"*René—I can do nothing with the Director. You have too many évasions against you, and, in addition, he remembers only too well that manuscript you wrote for Juvanon. But there is a possible help for you from another source, which is unexpected: an officer of the Salvation Army who has been visiting the penal colony and making an investigation of the conditions here, lived here at the Director's for a week, and I cooked for him; I told him all about your case, and obtained his interest in your behalf. He has talked to the President of the T. M. S. and to the Prosecutor, and he took your side very strongly. They promised him to treat your case with due consideration, and I feel sure they will, for they are in touch with him and wish to please him, because he is an important personage, sent here by the Ministry to see what can be done to better the conditions for the libérés in the colony. I think that what he said to them about you will be of great importance in helping you out when you go up for trial, for I explained to him how your attempt lasted only six hours, that you did not steal any money or food or a boat in order to escape. I told him how you had money of your own which you had earned. Leonce.*"

This letter reassured me.

After a long detention of seven months in the Cayenne blockhouse, I was taken to Saint Laurent to appear before the T. M. S. The public prosecutor at Cayenne had predicted to me that I would not get less than three years in solitary confinement, at best. He was one man who did not have the slightest use for me!

I appeared before the T. M. S. on the third day it sat, in November of 1928. From the punishments which had been inflicted by the court during the previous days I had reached the conclusion that the President was not an unreasonably hard individual, for he had given the minimum punishment to most of the convicts who had appeared ahead of me.

I was given six months in prison, only! When I might have been given five years in solitary confinement. I had gotten out of the dangerous situation better than I had ever hoped.

In a few weeks, they sent me to Saint Joseph to do my term of imprisonment there. I kept myself under strict control, and did nothing which could be put down against me as bad conduct, for I hoped to obtain a conditional liberation from my term of imprisonment by the middle of my punishment.

One day I was called over to Royale. I was wanted in the office of the Commandant.

"I've just received a letter from the new Governor," the Commandant said to me as I stood at attention before him. "He wants to know if you have a copy of the manuscript you wrote for Governor Juvanon, Belbenoit?"

"No, sir," I answered. "But in a few weeks I could make him one, sir."

"Good!" replied the Commandant. "I am going to give you paper and writing material, and I will instruct the chief guard at Saint Joseph. You will start on this immediately for the Governor. Apparently, he expects the matter to be attended to with haste, and you must do it as quickly as you can for he is very exacting in his demands."

The new administrator was Governor Siadous. I got to work on the manuscript the very next day, hoping earnestly that it was going to help me obtain the conditional liberation which I was so anxious to get.

While I worked feverishly at this manuscript in the barracks on Saint Joseph, racking my memory and thoughts for the least details which could interest or be of use to the new Governor, the chief guard there, aware of what I was engaged in, began to look unfavorably on what I was doing. He got it into his head that I would use this opportunity to expose the ways of the Island Administration to the new Governor—and, if I did that, both he, as well as all the other guards, would be represented as cutthroats to the new head of the colony. This was exactly what I had wanted to do, and was doing; and this was exactly what Governor Siadous expected me to do, for he had read, I learned, parts of the manuscript I had sent to Governor Juvanon, and he wanted complete information to help him see through and combat the corrupt ways of the Penal Administration, from the Director right down to the turn-keys!

At this time on the Islands laxness and immorality were rampant. The doctor was an insatiable pervert and slept with convicts who were his patients in the wards —he would keep his favorites in the hospital for weeks, when space was needed for other men who were dying and needed attention. When he made his rounds of the solitary confinement cells on Saint Joseph he would pick out the young convicts who seemed to him likely ones, and would have them sent over to the hospital. Matters on the Islands were a scandalous mess: the guards, who despised the doctor because of his partiality for the convicts who were his favorites, were at constant war with him; and they were also united in a deep enmity against the Commandant, who was trying to please and gain the favor of the new Governor, and bore down on their laxness and underhand practices with both fists. They finally won in their struggle against him, and were instrumental in having him recalled to France.

I worked at the manuscript like a demon. The chief guard persisted in his attitude of disapproval: he decided he would do what he could to get even with me, and gave orders that I was not to be given my breakfast coffee in the morning, under the pretext that, since I did not go to work, I had no right to it! I lost no time in complaining to the Commandant. In a few days I had my coffee in the morning. After that, the chief guard insisted on examining what I was writing. But I refused to let him look at it; it was a private work, I said, asked for by the Governor. He then refused to allow my writing to go off the island sealed, under the pretext that in the envelope there might be letters being sent to the Governor by convicts, for the Governor seemed to be taking his task seriously and to wish to suppress the abuses of the guards of the Administration. At last, one day, I succeeded in sending my manuscript without the knowledge of the chief guard; it reached the Governor, and the results were felt very quickly. Without warning, an order came for the chief guard to be demoted from his position on Saint Joseph and sent to Devil's Island! The other guards clubbed against me, and wrote to the Governor, saying that his action had been unjust. But he did not even answer them. What he did was to send a dispatch to the Director of the Administration, instructing him to have me taken from the Islands and sent immediately to Cayenne. In the meantime, the Governor gave me my conditional release, as his thanks for the revelations I had made to him in the manuscript, and I was transferred to Royale, where I waited with relief for the next boat from Saint Laurent, which would take me off the Islands and again to Cayenne.

Chapter XXVI

I HAD a well-stuffed sack of clean fresh clothes, my suppository was full of money, my health had been improved by the salt air and breezes, and the dysentery and fever had worked out of my system. As I watched the Islands fall away behind me, from the deck of the *Mana,* I was overflowing with courage and decision.

I arrived on the mainland as night fell. I walked up to the penitentiary and was put in the barracks reserved for convicts of the Third Class, and there I found most of the convicts with whom I had been confined the previous year. They were astonished to see me off the Islands so soon; I had quantities of notes for them from their comrades on Royale and Saint Joseph, and these I distributed around as soon as I was locked in. Most of that night I played at *belotte* (one of the favorite gambling games of the condemned), while I drank a stiff measure of rum which the keeper of the barrack gave me by way of celebrating my return. I was at Cayenne, where most of the convicts managed to get what they need and have enough money for tobacco and rum!

The next morning I answered the roll call with the others. The chief guard told me that I was to go to the office of the Commandant. So I remained in the barrack, and at eight o'clock I left the camp alone and proceeded to the Commandant's office, which is at the other side of town. As I passed through the Place des Palmistes I stopped in at the Sisters of Charity, and the Mother Superior had a letter for me from the French writer, Francis Carco; he enclosed 300 francs for some articles I had sent him which he had published in *Gringoire*.

"Good morning, Belbenoit!" the Commandant greeted me affably. "So here you are, back in Cayenne!"

"Yes, Monsieur the Commandant," I answered.

"Well, I hope you will conduct yourself properly this time. No more *évasions*, understand! Governor Siadous has taken an interest in you. He wishes to talk to you." The Commandant looked at me quizzically. He then took the receiver from his phone and rang Government House. After a brief interchange of words he turned to me and said: "Governor Siadous will see you now. Go immediately to Government House. I am going to see what I can do to find you a good job here in Cayenne," he added, smiling at me benignly.

"Thank you, Monsieur the Commandant," I said quietly. Then I left his office. This time I was in a hurry. I got to the Government House in a state of profuse perspiration. It may have been the warmth of the morning, but I think it was really due to my excitement. The Governor's messenger boy went upstairs to announce me. Finally, he came back to where I stood by the door, holding my wide straw hat in my hands, and said the Governor was ready to see me.

I climbed the steps, wiping my face on my sleeve so I would look my best. The door of the Governor's office was open, and I held myself at attention as I stood in it.

"Come in, Belbenoit," said a sharp voice.

I dropped my straw hat in the hallway and went in. The Governor was busy with some papers, and merely looked at me for a split second. "Sit down," he said.

The Governor was a middle-aged man, with gray hair about his temples. One could read on his face that he was an energetic man as well as a serious thinker, and that he was an individual who had tremendous will-power.

After a few minutes, he pushed the papers on his desk aside and turned to me. Before he spoke, his penetrating eyes studied me from head to foot.

"I wish to thank you for the manuscript you sent me from the Islands," he said. "What you wrote interests me very much because it seems written with frankness and, I believe, impartiality. How much more is there left for you to do of your term, Belbenoit?"

"Only ten months, your Excellency," I replied.

"You are not going to attempt to escape again?" he asked looking at me sharply.

"No, your Excellency!" I replied. Two minutes earlier that would have been the last thing I would have said. For, when I set foot on the mainland and proceeded to the penitentiary at Cayenne a quick escape was the thing uppermost in my mind!

"What kind of work can you do, Belbenoit?"

"Any sort of job will do, your Excellency," I replied, "So long as the guards will leave me alone and not molest me."

"I understand that, readily," Governor Siadous replied quickly.

He got the Commandant on the phone. There was a slight pause while he listened, then I heard him say, "Very well! That will be all right." He hung up the receiver.

"Well, Belbenoit, you will try that," he said. "You will go to work with the *Antares,* the gunboat which is here to map the coast. You will sleep on the pier. The work is very light. How is that?" It was thus that I now became connected with the hydrographical work which the gunboat, *Antares,* was doing along the coast. My job was very simple: it consisted in measuring the height of the tide, every fifteen minutes, in the port of Cayenne. A marked scale had been set in the water and, at the specified minute, I would read off the depth and write it on the chart. I worked with Bayard, an old convict, and with another prisoner; between the three of us we read the soundings for the twenty-four hours, in eight-hour shifts.

One night a boatload of sailors from the gunboat, who were working far up-shore, did not come back until late in the night. They were lodged in the soldiers' barrack-house, which was situated at some distance from the pier, and that night they were all so tired when they landed that they put the sail and rudder in our little hut by the water and went off to sleep. Usually they took everything along with them, but this night they waved aside the precaution; they had become accustomed to us, seeing us every day on the pier and talking with us frequently there, and that, I imagine, had given them a certain amount of confidence in us.

About ten in the night Bayard said suddenly: "This is a chance we'll never get again, comrade." And he looked at me: "René, are you coming?"

"Coming . . . where?"

"Why, with the boat of the *Antares!* Everything's right here in our hut." Bayard's sunken eyes blazed, overflowing with excitement. "All we need is food!"

"No," I replied. There was no hesitation in my voice. "I'm going to be liberated soon, and I promised the Governor I would not try to escape."

"*Eh bien,* comrade, *we* are on our way!" the old convict replied, jerking his head at the other. His voice trembled, such was his emotion.

"You have only to give the alarm tomorrow morning at *réveillé*. Say that you were asleep and heard nothing. When you awoke we were gone, and the boat too!"

In a few minutes they had filled five empty cans with fresh water. It took them no time to adjust the rudder and the sail. Without a sound they pushed off into the quiet water and, while I watched, the night engulfed them.

Alone by the water's edge, I turned this suddenly arisen departure over in my mind while I smoked several cigarettes. The darkness was a velvet stillness, and in it I felt dismally lonely. What I yearned for with heart and soul was to be in that boat. It was such a good one for escape. But my common sense had said, "No!" Perhaps it wasn't my common sense—perhaps it was a vestige of honor which I still had in me. I had never once dreamed of a beautiful opportunity such as this when I told Governor Siadous that I would not try to escape! Had I said it to the double-dealing Commandant, I would now have been in that boat—and free in twelve days! But with Governor Siadous it was, somehow, different. For the first time in years a man had asked me a question and made me feel that he would accept my answer as the truth.

Dawn came. Nervously, I paced back and forth waiting for the guards to get out of their houses and for the life of the prison to start stirring. I went to the camp and told the guards that I had awakened to find my two comrades and the boat gone.

There was a big stir. The sailors were immediately summoned to the gunboat to explain their carelessness. In less than an hour one of the vessel's high-speed launches had left in pursuit; but it came back that night without having sighted the fugitives.

Just as I expected, I was summoned to the Government House. Governor Siadous looked at me—through me—with that same penetration. "And so, now tell me what happened, Belbenoit," he said, his fingers rapping the desk.

I told him the truth; exactly what had taken place, giving him each detail.

"I'm glad to know that you, you did not go also," he said. "You are dismissed."

That was all. I left the Governor's office not quite decided in my mind just how I stood with him; whether I was promoted or demoted in his estimation.

But I remained on the job just as though nothing had happened, except that now I was doing the job of three. But I didn't mind this; it was more work and an alarm clock woke me up every hour during the night, but to me this was not a rebuke for having been an accomplice in an *évasion*—I felt I was being trusted that much more in being left alone to do the job. It is hard to convey how much that feeling meant to me. For, in the degeneration of the penal colony I had at last found an official in whose sincerity I could have faith.

The work, however, in the long run proved too much for me. I needed to sleep, at least for a few hours, but I couldn't on that job where the height of the tide had to be set down on a chart so frequently. I did my best to stick it out, for, in addition to having the Governor's confidence, I was getting the pay of the other two convicts, and for me that was a valuable little fortune which I meant to add to my hoard against the day when I became a *libéré*. At the end of a week the gunboat finished its work, slipped anchor and went on to Saint Laurent. I had stuck to the end, fighting blindly against exhaustion, but my frail body had been so taxed by fatigue that I developed carbuncles and had to go to the hospital where the doctor lanced them for me.

The morning after my operation I was put on the outgoing list of the hospital. The bandages were still fresh and bloodstained and when I left my bed I was very tired, and was suffering with pain. But the Governor had phoned the camp and given orders that I be sent immediately to work at Government House, not knowing that I was in the hospital and having an operation. And the stupid chief guard phoned the hospital,

saying I was to be sent out as soon as I could walk—
adding that the orders came from the Governor.

The Governor had sent for me, I discovered, to set
me at a task which was a very special one and full of
interest to me. The archives of the colony were in a
great disorder; they were in a state of abandon and
needed straightening out, for the papers and records
had been stacked in piles for years and were moldering
where they lay. Many of the files were unnumbered,
and there were many documents which needed to be
classified and filed away. It was impossible to find anything in the archives of the colony without spending
hours rummaging around, and it was this lack of system and order which irked the Governor and gave him
the idea that here was a useful job for me. And so,
with his characteristic energy and impatience, he had
called the camp as soon as the thought came to him
and had instructed the chief guard to send me over
immediately. I took up my duties that same day, without letting the Governor know I was suffering pain from
an operation. This was a position I had never dreamed
I would ever get! And, from the very first day, my
task as archivist became the most interesting thing I
ever did as a convict. For, also in the same rooms,
were the complete archives of the Administration and
I was free to read them as much as I chose!

Sometimes the Governor would come see how my
work was progressing. He would usually find something
to say to me, and would talk with me for a few minutes. And more often than not I would have some
question to ask him about how to classify or arrange
this and that; he realized I took an interest in my task
and was always ready to give me helpful suggestions.

I admired Governor Siadous very much. His face
was hard, but he was fair and kind. He was a strong
man, the very spirit of energy. He was a conscientious
person with a keen insight into things, and saw them
just as they were. He investigated a problem thoroughly
before he came to a decision; he was a man of action,
whose working hours would have broken the health of

the average man in that climate. I remember occasions when he slaved eighteen hours a day, working incessantly in the interests of the colony, when he could have accepted, philosophically, the existing conditions, as others before him had done, and taken no action to try to remedy them. But he had no support whatsoever; and throughout his entire term in office he met with no coöperation from either the Administration or the civil population of the colony. He was particularly impressed by the miserable lot of the *libérés* and tried to do something about it. He saw how the civilians took the convicts for their various house jobs because they could get them from the Administration for next to nothing. Realizing this was one of the principal causes behind the helpless misery of the *libérés,* he passed a decree saying that convicts were not to be let out to civilians for work, except for cultivation jobs, when large numbers of condemned men might be used to advantage in exploiting the agricultural possibilities of the colony. His purpose was to force the civilians to employ the *libérés* in their houses as cooks, servants, paying them enough to live on, instead of the pittance which they had paid the convicts who had their food and quarters provided by the Administration. The first thing the Governor knew, the civilians came to him asking permission to hire a convict here, two there, to do the jobs he had reserved for the *libérés.* He stuck to his idea for rehabilitating the *libérés* but soon he realized that in Cayenne there was no such thing as a social sense or desire for progress and organization; for the civilians laid their complaints before the General Council of the colony, and went so far as to pepper the Ministry in Paris with petitions demanding that the Governor be replaced.

In the two years he was in office, Governor Siadous tried first one thing then another in an effort to better conditions in the colony. His efforts did not stop with the civilian element; the convicts absorbed his interest and were just as much his particular concern. But the corrupt Penal Administration, instead of putting into

213

effect the improvements he proposed, refused to coöp-
erate with him and met his constructive energy with
the force of inertia. The officials of the Administration
more than hated him; they actually feared him, for he
took a delight in uncovering their abuses and laxness
and in showing up their inefficiency. One of his favorite
tricks was to order a convict in his employ to snip the
main telephone wire late at night; the next morning,
bright and early, he would be off down the road to
the camps; as he came to one camp, there was no way
to pass the word along that the Governor was out on an
inspection, and at each camp he came to he saw things
just as they would be on any ordinary day! The first
time he did this out of a clear sky the officials had a fit.
The chief guard was missing from one camp; in another, he found a guard drunk, lying in his house in his
hammock after an orgy of rum which had begun the
night before and lasted on until noon; he found convicts working naked in the blistering sun, their tongues
were hanging out for water which they couldn't have
because the gang had done something which had an-
gered a guard. He was good at catching the officials in
their finer shades of cruelty, also; and it did not take
him long to make himself familiar with the many forms
of graft and with the rackets they practised continuously, bleeding the treasury and preying on the helpless
prisoners in their hands. And it was from the convicts
whom he picked and used in his employ, like myself,
that he gained most of his information and thorough
knowledge of the ways of things in the penal colony!
He revoked the appointments of many officials and sent
them back to France; among these was the Commandant of the Islands. Several guards were guilty of gross
murders and he saw to it that they paid for their bar-
barity. The Administration joined in with the civilian
populace, and sent demands of its own to have a better
Governor sent out. But he remained to the end of his
term, and by the time he came to the end of it he had
dug up so much dirt in the colony that, back in France,
they were constantly on edge lest he should bring to

light some deadly scandal which would give the colony an even worse reputation than it already had.

One day, as he stood thumbing some documents in the archives he asked me, "What are you going to do when you're liberated, Belbenoit?"

I gave him the true answer—the only one there could be: "I'm going to attempt to escape," I said, "for it's the only way I can remake my life. Here in Guiana it is impossible."

He was silent for a few moments, then he said: "You won't have to escape! I will give you your passport to leave the colony."

Such a thing had never been done in the history of the penal colony. Tears filled my eyes at the sound of his words, and I could only say, hoarsely, in a choked murmur: "Thank you, sir, thank you!"

After that I spent many months arranging and working on the archives of the colony. Governor Siadous never spoke again on the subject, but I was as sure of his word as I was of the sun, and I knew that when the day of my liberation came I would be free to go. I could work at the task he had assigned to me all day long as long as I pleased; there were days when I remained in the archives all morning and afternoon, stopping only to eat; at night I returned to the barrack when I pleased, as late as ten o'clock some nights, for I always had the good excuse that the Governor had kept me working late. I accomplished much in arranging and putting into working order the material I had been entrusted with; but at least half of the time I spent in the archives was devoted to my own particular interests and investigations. In those musty and moldy old rooms, where I sat at a desk alone all day long, I combed the shelves and stacks of papers for the things which interested me to read. The reports and files of the Administration, from the day the penal colony began, were there; also, I found in the archives all the books and articles which had been written in many languages about the notorious prison, all sent in—often with notes or letters attached—by the diplomats and consuls of

France from many parts of the world. I read there the first book ever written about the horrors of the penal colony—by General Pichegru who, after winning the battle of Jemmapes, betrayed the Revolution and was sent to Guiana from which he finally escaped to the United States. I read and examined everything: books, articles, reports on convicts, accounts of the Administration, lists of food, supplies, clothing, materials. I took down notes and figures. And it was during these many long months when I sat doing this in those dingy rooms that I got the knowledge and documentation, and the facts and figures, which have enabled me since then to fight efficiently for the abolition of that hell and expose irrefutably the corruptness of its Administration. Many of these chapters were first written at that desk, in the heart of that criminal colony and while I was still clothed in the infamous red and white stripes. For once, after so many years of stagnation, I had found something which absorbed my whole being; for once I had found something to *do*.

Then, one morning, Governor Siadous called me into his office and said: "I am sending you back to the barrack, Belbenoit. I find it's necessary for me to economize as much as I can on the budget, but I'll arrange for you to have a good job for the last months that remain of your term."

I was amazed. However, there was nothing for me to say one way or the other. "There's something else here," I told myself. "It's not because of any economy on the budget that the Governor is sending me back to the barrack."

When I appeared in the office of the Commandant, the latter exclaimed jestingly, "So, you have left the Government, Belbenoit!"

"Governor Siadous has sent me back to camp," I replied levelly, "and I suspect, sir, that the Administration is mixed up in all this."

"How? Now, now—you're always imagining the Administration has it in for you, Belbenoit!" The Commandant pretended to be innocently amused.

"But I think I can prove it this time, sir," I retorted. My smouldering anger had mounted to my head, and was fast doing away with my caution and good sense. "It's been six months now that I've been in Cayenne," I said to the Commandant, "six months of good conduct, for I have not been given one punishment. But nevertheless, during these six months, I've had the lowest marks in the whole penitentiary; I'm the only convict here who's been given a mark of 0 for six consecutive months." The convicts are marked or graded by the chief guard of each barrack from 0 to 10 according to the guard's report of their conduct, and my last eighteen marks had been eighteen 0's. I was the only convict in the whole colony to have such a set of marks!"

The Commandant was at a loss what to answer. But he said, waiving the matter aside: "Well here! You're going to the barracks to take over the bookkeeping for the penitentiary, as the present bookkeeper is making a quantity of errors and his books are a jumble. It'll be lots of work for you, but you'll also have a great deal of freedom. I'm going to let you go into the town whenever you wish; also, you will sleep in the office, by the gate of the camp. You can earn some money, and I don't think the job will be too hard for your strength."

"Well, that's that!" I said to myself as I made my way to Government House to collect my few belongings and fetch them all to the barrack.

The Governor saw me when I went by the door of his office and called me over to him. It was to tell me that he had sent a note over to the barrack, instructing the chief guard that he had designated me a convict of the Second Class.

I thanked him. But I was still disappointed and bitter over the turn of events which had taken me away from my all-absorbing work in the archives, and I said: "Not once in the years I've been a convict, Monsieur the Governor, have I been able to get to the Second Class, and I believe I might just as well have ended my term in the third."

The Governor saw what I meant—he knew that he was the only thing that stood between me and the Administration. "But I know it will be of use to you," he said. "Now go, and mind what you do and watch your step!" he exclaimed as a parting admonition.

I learned later that I had been removed from the archives because of statements made by the Commandant about the serious risks which existed in my being at the task, since he had proof that I knew people in the United States and might send information which, if published, would do harm to the prestige of France abroad. Governor Siadous hadn't known I had these contacts; and the Commandant, by pressing the issue to the Governor, had been keen enough to take advantage of the latter's conscientiousness and sense of duty as a servant of his country. What really interested the Administration was to get me away from its records. But I had worked double time and had remained in the archives enough months to find out far more than the Administration ever imagined.

Not long after I assumed my duties as bookkeeper in the barrack I got my comeback at the Commandant. There had been, in connection with the hydrographical work which the gunboat *Antares* had been doing along the coast of the colony, a party of six convicts sent off to an island near Cayenne to do some part or other of the survey; they were accompanied by a guard and were gone two weeks. This guard, being in absolute charge of the group, made out the list of food they would require to take along, but once they had set out, he gave the six men only a third of the food supplies to eat, and he brought the rest back and later sold it to the Negroes in Cayenne. When I assumed the bookkeeper and accountant job for the penitentiary, these convicts, knowing I stood well with the Governor, came to me with their complaint; I took the matter to the Commandant, who in turn called the guard in and reprimanded him for his action. The Commandant decided that the guard had done the Administration out of 15 francs. At the time he was conducting his investigation and bawling out the guard, I, as bookkeeper, was in the office. Now, the Commandant at the time owed me 15 francs for an inlay box I had made for him; so he calmly told the guard to pay the 15 francs over to me! Instead of paying me out of his own pocket, he decided he would just let it come out of the Administration's budget.

Here was my chance. In less than an hour's time I was in the Government House. I knew the Governor would be interested in the incident, for it was just the sort of thing which was a constant chip on his shoulder. He was! The Commandant was heavily fined.

Before long I had another altercation with the Penal Administration. It was rather humorous in some ways.

At this time I had a little cat. I was very fond of it! One day the captain-at-arms caught sight of my cat chasing his chickens, and he warned me if he saw my cat after his chickens again he would kill it. I answered him that if he killed my cat it would cost him several thousand francs. But, he merely laughed at my words.

Well, a week later my cat disappeared. There was no doubt in my mind where it had gone, so I found the captain and said to him "I told you if you killed my cat it would cost you several thousand francs. You'll see, two or three days from now, if what I say isn't true!"

I then went back to the bookkeeping office at the camp and wrote two reports, one for the Governor and the other for the Prosecutor General of the colony. This is what they contained: "For more than three years the cook for the guards' mess has figured in the accounts of the penitentiary of Cayenne under the entry of messenger-boy. On the budget, the guards have no right to cooks; if they use a convict as such, they must pay the Administration 4 francs a day to employ him. The cook for the mess at Cayenne, being entered as messenger-boy in the books, has not been paid for; in the three years the guards eating there have mulcted the treasury in a sum which approaches 4,000 francs. An investigation should be made into this."

The next morning the Governor sent his secretary to

the penitentiary to look into the truth of my report. The chief guard had been at the camp only three months, so the situation put him very ill at ease, although he had nothing to do with it. He came to me and demanded why I had taken it upon myself to do what I had done.

"This has nothing to do with you," I said to him, "for you have been here just a short time. It is not meant for you. It's to punish the captain-at-arms for killing my cat!"

"But this is going to call for a tremendous amount of work!" replied the chief guard. And he went on to tell me how my meddling had caused the Governor to order all the names of the guards who had eaten at the mess in the last three years to be listed, with the number of months they had eaten there, and a bill was to be made out for each of them, which they were to pay as a refund for the money owing by them.

Every word the chief guard said filled me with exultation. "I will do all the work at night," I replied. "Leave the whole job up to me!"

And every time I saw that captain-at-arms I would repeat in answer to his sallies: "When I told you my cat would cost you dear, I meant it!"

After that he left me alone and never troubled himself to meddle with anything I did. In that merciless penal colony one has to use all his wits in order to get the treatment due a human being and to be shown a shadow of respect.

I enjoyed a great many advantages as bookkeeper and accountant of the penitentiary at Cayenne. The guards were afraid I'd report something else. It is, in every penitentiary and camp in the jungle, a position of much favor, for the bookkeeper is the man, really, who directs the camp and he has his fingers in everything. If he knows how to work his job he can make a lot of money through the endless forms of *débrouille* which fall within his sphere of activities.

It is far more valuable to the condemned to have the favor of the bookkeeper than that of ten of the chief guards. It is the bookkeeper's job to set down names, to fill out vacancies here and there, to send men to this camp or that when the names are turned in to the Commandant on the lists; and to him fall countless other matters which are of vital concern in the existence of the convicts from day to day.

The bookkeeper's principal source of income lies in the sale of the various jobs which are to be had in the camp. When a convict wants some particular job or favor, that is, one which gives him a chance to make some money for himself, he goes to the bookkeeper and offers him a substantial consideration; if he can offer more than anyone else has for the job, he may be sure of getting it.

The bookkeeper of the penitentiary at Cayenne has to work an average of sixteen hours a day. That is a lot of work, but for it the Administration only gives him a *gratification,* or tip, of several quarts of coffee every week. The chief guard at the camp doesn't examine and verify the correctness of the books and accounts, which are complicated and would absorb an enormous number of his hours which he would rather spend in his hammock or drinking rum with his colleagues; but, however, it is he who is responsible for everything the bookkeeper does. He has to sign all the reports and accounts rendered, and all the other lists and papers which are written up by the bookkeeper, and if anything goes wrong he has to answer for it. So it is very important and even vital to his ease of body and mind to have a convict on the job who does the work efficiently. But, if the bookkeeper is getting nothing out of this exacting task for himself, he would much prefer to work eight hours a day in some other job than twice that long in an office where he makes nothing for himself; and if he is intelligent enough to hold down the hard job of accounting and bookkeeping he will have no trouble at all getting some other job where he can make a little money for himself. Since the chief guard, of course, has no desire to tip him out of his own pocket he allows him a great amount of latitude. The bookkeeper, therefore, has no end of chances to make up through favors to the convicts for the long hours he has to slave at his task. If a convict, for instance, wants to be assigned to work in some gang, he goes to the bookkeeper and promises him ten francs. At the first vacancy in the gang he will get in—unless another convict in the meanwhile should offer the bookkeeper 15 francs for the same place.

In the larger penitentiaries, like the one at Cayenne and Saint Laurent, this *débrouille* or graft of the bookkeeper nets him a substantial sum; so the chief guard extracts a share of these profits for himself as a tribute for leaving the bookkeeper's hands free!

The most successful *débrouillard* or grafter-bookkeeper I knew in the long years I was in Guiana was a certain Bébert Abavent, who handled the barracks at Saint Laurent for many years. Once when he and I were on Saint Joseph he told me he used to average 50 francs a day; sometimes this was more, particularly at the time when Vilsouet was captain-at-arms at the camp. This Vilsouet was a rare character. Bébert told me that he gave him his bottle of rum every morning in order to have a free hand with the books! If a convict wanted to go to some camp, or come to Saint Laurent from a camp in the jungle, Bébert's charge was ten francs. If one of the men wanted to change barracks, that was two francs. The job as street-sweeper in the town cost five francs. The position of keeper of the barracks was worth 50 francs. Whenever the captain-at-arms, Vilsouet, was in need of several hundred francs he would resort to any one of various rackets.

One fine morning he came to Bébert's office with a list of some thirty names and instructed him to change those convicts to other barracks that same afternoon. After the captain had left the office, Bébert, who knew every man in the camp, perceived that all the ones on the list were young convicts. He thought at first to himself some new regulation must have been passed to check the dissolute homosexuality abounding in every barracks; but before long he saw that this was just another new racket the captain had invented. He followed the captain's orders and that afternoon he instructed the men whose names were on the list that they were to change barracks, and told them which they were to move to that very afternoon. The next morning there was a regular waiting line outside the door of Bébert's office! The older men were all there to ask him why their young *mômes* had been taken out of their barracks, and each offered him something if he would have the transfer cancelled. Bébert couldn't do anything in the face of the captain's orders, so he went to him and told him how things were, hoping he would allow him to juggle things properly. "That's good!" the captain replied when he heard the news. "You send them all back to the barracks, but you know the tariff! And," he added, "make allowance for *my* share!" That little racket brought 300 francs.

Bébert told me another little trick of the captain's. When the end of the month arrived he had invariably spent his pay, so he would come to the office and tell Bébert, "Tomorrow convict X will go to Camp des Malgaches. Put him on the list." Invariably convict X would be a man who had a good and lucrative job, such as keeper of a barracks or a man who held the money-box for the nightly game of *la marseillaise*. Bébert would tell the man he was going off to slave or die in that horrible camp, and the other, amazed at this sudden piece of news, would want to know why. "The captain's orders," Bébert would say. "Go see him if you like!" So the convict would go to Vilsouet and arrange the matter with him—that is to say, he would hand him 50 or 75 francs! And the next morning the captain would come to Bébert and tell him to cross out convict X and send an Arab to Malgaches in his place.

In all the camps and barracks that sort of thing went on continuously.

One afternoon the chief guard sent me to the hospital to register a death. Boppé, the dead man, had been one of the celebrities of the penal colony. The previous afternoon he had drowned while taking a

223

swim. He had been in Guiana only a few months, where he had arrived on the *La Martinière* condemned to five years of hard labor for attempting to poison his wife in his beautiful chateau in the neighborhood of the town of Nancy, where he lived luxuriously as Inspector General of Forests and Streams for the East of France; a family council gathered in one of the lavish saloons of the chateau to decide what measures were to be taken. Should he be turned over to the authorities? If that were done the honor of one of the greatest writers of the nation would be spoiled and his career might be affected. The family decided the matter should not be made public; but this would be done only on one condition—that Boppé provide a suitable income for his wife, who refused to live with him any more. Boppé was told that unless he agreed to this condition he would be turned over to the law, and would receive no protection or support from the family; and he readily acquiesced. But he failed to carry out what they demanded; for he was certain in his mind the family would not dare bring a scandal to light which would cast a shadow on their name. Seeing he had his mind made up not to keep the agreement, however, they exposed him, and the courts gave him five years in Guiana.

When he got to Guiana, Boppé decided that he'd spend all the money necessary to get an easy life. He had become fascinated by the jungle; he determined to devote himself for a while to the study of tropical flora. Possessing a substantial fortune, he had no trouble in winning all sorts of favors from the Penal Administration. They had even gone to the absurdity of appointing him "convict botanist" of the colony! He caused all his scientific apparatus to be sent out from France, as well as twelve fine hunting dogs.

But death robbed him of his purchased advantages. Less than a fortnight later, a full pardon for him arrived from France. It had been signed by the President, at the request undoubtedly of influential Parisian friends, eight days before he drowned. But it came too late!

My term drew tranquilly to a close. The eve of my liberation had now arrived—the twenty-first of September, 1930! I had had to do two punishments of six months each which had added a year to my eight-year sentence. Yet I had been lucky: luck, added to my keeping of my wits about me, kept me alive through those nine endless years of suffering and restlessness. For many had been given two or three years for their first *évasion* and five for the next, while I, with my four desperate attempts to escape, had only had to do an extra six months. I knew full well that with my nervous temperament and bad health I would never have been alive on the twenty-first of September of 1930 had I been made to stay three straight years in the cells of horror on Saint Joseph!

Chapter XXVII

I PLAYED at *la marseillaise* with my comrades in the barracks until past midnight. I would have played all night long until *réveillé,* just to greet wide awake my happiest dawn, if they had not been too tired and left me to get some sleep. For they were not, as I, going to be set free the next morning; their prison grind would begin again at six.

The moths flitted about the regulation lamp; criss-crossing under the dim pale light: mosquitoes hummed and bit incessantly. In the breathless stagnation of the rain-drenched night the gloomy barracks seemed like a weird vault, in which the only sound was that of men snoring, moaning, and mumbling in their restless sleep. That dim regulation lamp flickering uncertainly was to me a symbol of Guiana, where men live pale and half extinguished.

Five A. M. The *réveillé!* The keeper of the barracks

handed me a cup with the remark: "You have no right to it, and tomorrow you'll have to earn this coffee!"

My comrades in the barracks gathered around me for a moment to say good-bye!

For the last time I watched the line of gangs go out to labor, and then I went to the clothes commissary to turn in my convict suit. I was given the customary package which is handed to all convicts when they become *libérés*. It contained a blue suit of coarse material, a black felt hat, a white shirt, and a pair of wooden shoes. The suit was too large and hung on me. As for the regulation shoes, I hated the feel and weight of them, so I sold them on the spot to one of the kitchen men for forty sous.

The captain-at-arms gave me a paper to take to the cashier of the Administration to claim my convict pay.

I entered the town and took my pay slip round. The cashier counted out eighty-five francs and ten sous and handed them to me. Noticing the look of stunned amazement on my face, he proffered me a sheet of paper which bore the following account:

769 days of labor at 0.50 francs a day ....f. 384.50		
stamps ....f. 12.50		
Charge, Dept. of Justice ....f. 30.00		
¾ held against voyage back to France ....f. 256.50		
	f. 299.00	f. 299.00
	Balance	f. 85.50

"Three fourths held against voyage back!" I cried. "I was sentenced to eight years—that means perpetual exile! . . . They'll never let me go back to France!"

"I know it," he said. "But it's the regulation. Three fourths of every prisoner's pay must be held out."

There was nothing I could do about it. Again, even in the last instant of my convict life, injustice was to assert itself—to rob me of two hundred fifty-six and a half francs! I pocketed the money with an oath and went to the Commissary of Police to obtain my freed-convict *Libéré* certificate.

There I was officially informed that, by law, I would have to remain in French Guiana for the rest of my life. If I tried to escape I would be sentenced to the Islands for five years.

After he had announced the above regulation to me, the Police Commissioner added: "Furthermore, for ten years, you will not be permitted to reside in Cayenne, you must leave the city limits by tomorrow morning or you will be arrested and punished!" I had hardly been freed an hour when I found myself threatened with being locked up again!

Eighty-five francs and ten sous! That was all I had coming to me, after I had been kept like an animal and worked like an animal for nine years. And an ordinary pair of shoes would cost all of one hundred and twenty francs! I bought a cheap pair to cover my bare feet. I also bought a pair of socks. My food for the day . . . a room . . . a few little purchases, and by the next morning the entire sum had disappeared. I went to the Government House to see Governor Siadous in his private office.

He greeted me with a smile. "Belbenoit, you are now a *libéré*, eh?"

"Yes, your Excellency!" I replied, my voice tense with emotion. "But the penal authorities say I must get out of Cayenne immediately. I must live in the jungle like a baboon!"

"Good! I am very glad. And now—have you by any chance enough money—enough cash to buy a passage away from Guiana?" he asked.

"Yes, your Excellency," I said, remembering his promise and trembling in uncertainty as to whether now he would keep it or not. "I've received money from Mrs. Blair Niles. But the penal authorities say that if I try to leave the colony they'll arrest me—and give me five years solitary confinement in the Islands!"

He scowled and searched in a drawer of his desk for a few seconds. Then he drew out a typewritten sheet which he handed to me. "Here," he said, "take this. You will address me a formal petition to leave the colony for one year, basing your demand on what you read on this sheet. Send it to me as quickly as possible. You can leave on the next boat!"

"You mean . . . really, on the next boat, Sir?" I repeated.

"Yes, Belbenoit. I am presenting you with this year of freedom no matter what the penal authorities say!" the Governor replied with a gleam of humor in his eye. "Petition me formally that, since there is no way for a self-respecting man to earn a living as a *libéré* in Guiana you want to be allowed to go somewhere else for a year where you can find a job and save up some money."

That same night I wrote out my petition. Two days later Governor Siadous called together his colonial Privy Council to submit my request to its members, which formality was readily granted, since it was the personal wish of the chief of the colony. On the following Saturday the decision of the Council appeared in the official publication of French Guiana as follows:

DECREE OF THE GOVERNOR OF GUIANA
The Governor of Guiana and the Privy Council of the Colony, in the session of the 27th of September, 1930, Decided: That libéré *René Belbenoit,* Libéré *Number 16,444, is authorized and given a passport to leave the colony for one year.*
Given in Cayenne on the 27th day of September, 1930.

SIADOUS *Governor*

I needed, however, a visa from the consul of Venezuela, to which I planned to go, so I now went to see him to ask him to visa my passport papers. To my great disappointment, he refused to do this. He told me he had strict orders from his government, which in the past year had arrested all the men escaped from the penal colony found in the country, and was determined not to have any French convicts or *libérés* in the country. He told me that, furthermore, he had received just that morning a report from the penal Administration which did not seem commendable or a recommendation in any sense. Upon my asking to see it, he let me read this paper, which read:

Belbenoit, René: 46,635. *Libéré*: 16,444

1. Condemned to eight years at hard labor for theft   in 1921
2. Condemned to six months of prison for insult   in 1925
3. Condemned to six months of prison for escape   in 1928
4. Classed as Incorrigible   in 1925
5. Classed as Incorrigible   in 1927
6. Interned on the Islands as a measure of precaution in 1925
   1927 and 1928. Conduct Mark, when liberated, Zero.

Although it was the last one it could possibly make, this was in every sense a truly typical back-slap of the Penal Administration! It could not prevent the Governor from doing what he wanted to do, but it took this underhanded method of getting back at me—and foiling my chance of actually leaving the colony. It was actually a stalemate of the Governor's decree.

I now told the representative of the Venezuelan nation that it wasn't my intention to reside in the country, and that I wished to go to Panama; but since that republic had no representative in the colony, I had come to him to give me a visa to pass through Venezuela en route, and in that way I could get my Panamanian visa at the port of last call. To support what I said to him, I showed him a letter I had from Mrs. Blair Niles in which she wrote advising me to go to Panama, where she would help me find work in the American Canal Zone.

This he now consented to do, and stamped on my passport: "In transit for Panama." This was all I needed! Now I was free to go! The penal authorities were furious.

It was a double day of celebration and joy for me for, in addition to the fact that at last I was going away from that land of torture and torment, it was the day of my saint, Saint René.

The *Biskra* was scheduled to leave at two o'clock in the afternoon on November 12th. I was dressed for the occasion, and my small amount of baggage was ready. My ticket was safely tucked away in the bottom of my pocket!

I went to the Government House. I wanted to thank the Governor again for what he had done for me. Would that Guiana had had other Governors like him!

He took my hand and wished me good luck. He exacted a promise that I would present myself to the French Consul in Panama, that I would not overstep the time of leave he had given me, and above all that I would not write anything that could affect the prestige of France. At this final opportunity of speaking with Governor Siadous, I was able to do a favor for one of the few friends I had in the penal colony. Richard was his name and he was interned on the Islands: He had sent me a petition of release from the Islands which he asked me to put in the hands of the Governor with a good word for him. The moment to do the favor had come.

"You have confidence in my word, sir," I said to Governor Siadous, "and I feel that now, before going away, I'd like to do something for another convict who I know is unjustly treated." And I handed him the petition Richard had sent to me.

When he had read it he asked me, "Is this true, Belbenoit?"

"Yes, your Excellency," I said, "I know the man well, and you can be sure of that."

"Very well, then," he replied. "You can write him that his release from the Islands has been granted and that he'll be brought to the mainland within a month's time."

I thanked Governor Siadous again, but this time for another man. And my heart was glad as I left the Government House.

At two o'clock the *Biskra's* whistle sounded. I was off! Going into the future, into the great world—Free at least for one whole year! I was the first *libéré* in the history of the penal colony ever to be given such a furlough. Many convicts and *libérés* heard the whistle blow and must have watched us go and thought of me —and—envied my opportunity of going away for a year with a legal status in the wide open world.

When we stopped off the Islands, Richard was among the oarsmen in the Island boat. I called down to him and gave him the good news of his own transfer to the mainland.

"But I want your word that you won't try to escape while Governor Siadous is still in office," I said to him. "He's being recalled to France soon, so you haven't long to wait!"

Richard promised. And he added, "Once he's gone through, I'll join you in Panama, comrade!"

We arrived at the long pier at Saint Laurent. This time I walked at ease and happy, not worrying at all about the evil-eyed Corsican guards. I mailed some letters Richard had entrusted to me. I met some of my *libéré* acquaintances. I treated them to a meal at the best Chinese store. They were glad of my good luck, but sad because of their own unyielding fate.

In a few hours the *Biskra* was on its way down the Maroni River. From the rail I watched the jungle slip by. When we reached the mouth of the river night had come. Soon the coast had faded in the stern, lost in darkness. I stood at the rail looking out over the dark sea thinking of the future, where I knew there would be another struggle for me—but this time the struggle would be for life and success and not just a struggle against death.

Chapter XXVIII

AS though I suddenly saw the world through a kaleidoscope, as the ship turned over the horizon of the earth after my years of captivity, Paramaribo the capital of

Dutch Guiana, Georgetown the capital of British Guiana, and Port of Spain, the capital of Trinidad came up out of the sea—and went down into the sea behind me. Then Guadeloupe and Martinique, the French islands, were left to sink in my wake. I was, at last, a free soul on a boat carrying me farther and farther away from French Guiana.

I paced the deck all day long. I felt constantly in my pocket to make sure my passport was still there. I talked to the passengers. With them I sang songs and played games. At night I left my cabin after only a few hours of sleep and paced the deck to greet the new dawn. Each day I saw born, from black night into a golden-hued sunrise. I was free!

I walked down the gangplank at Cristobal Colon, at the Atlantic entrance to the Panama Canal, and hastened to the French quarter where I secured a cheap room. Then I went out job hunting. After a few hours I secured a job at the Gorgas Memorial Hospital as a gardener. For eight months I worked and lived happily. I put some savings into establishing a small hand laundry with a native partner. I was now a man busily earning a living—and respect. One thing only began preying on my mind: Time was fleeing behind me. Month after month was expiring—and leaving me with less and less of the year of freedom which Governor Siadous had presented to me. I sent a cable to him, followed it with a letter enclosing my excellent conduct and earnings card of the Canal Commission, and asking him to grant me permanent freedom. But I learned that he had left the prison colony. Another Governor had taken his place.

Though free physically I now became a mental prisoner—fighting daily against the thought of returning to Guiana for life. As the days and weeks and months went by I became frantic. I didn't want to break my promise to Governor Siadous—but I didn't want to return to French Guiana. I counted my savings. I had enough money to buy a steerage passage to Paris. Suddenly I made up my mind to go to France as quickly as possible, find some authority who would grant me a permanent passport. My leave of absence would expire on November 12, 1931.

On October 19th, a month before my year of freedom was up, I took passage on a ship to France. On November 2nd the police of Havre, on coming out to the ship in a launch of the Public Health Service, looked at my papers and placed me under arrest. I was kept incommunicado in a jail during the entire months of November and December, I spent Christmas Day and New Year's Day in jail. The little money I had left went in an attempt to get messages delivered to people who might help me, but I never received any answers. It seemed as though some unusually stringent orders had gone out from the seats of the mighty to keep me locked up—my jailer almost told me this by the way he looked at me—and by his unctuous politeness. But no one came to see me and day after day passed, until, on January fifteenth, I was suddenly taken from the jail late at night and sent, in an automobile guarded by three gendarmes, to the embarkation wharf for the island of Ré.

There I was placed in a solitary cell to await the convict ship. For eight months I stayed on the Island of Ré, while prisoners were collected from various parts of the French empire. Then, on September 20th, the Guiana prison guards marched into the fortress to escort the condemned to the anchored vessel.

"Well, Belbenoit!" a big Corsican said when he came to my cell door to take me from the jailer, "A round-trip ticket, eh? We've been talking about you!"

He shoved me along the alleyway with his bayonet, only taking it from my back when we came out into the open courtyard and I took my place with the other men. Down the wharf, across the intervening water, up the gangplank of the convict ship they marched us. To me it was an old, dim story. A voyage to Hell, to be sure, but I had already made that trip. The cages in the filthy hold were familiar. I had already suffered in them. I was better off than the men who were shoved

233

for the first time like frightened rats through the narrow grill.

We stopped six times during the fifteen days to drop corpses overboard with a mock funeral. On October 7th we anchored in the mouth of the Maroni River to await high tide. The men in the cage with me strained to get their heads to the portholes to look at the moonlit jungle, but I sat far back. That jungle was something I had gazed at many a time and much too long. My mind was ablaze with anger—an anger so intense that it was silent and inactive. Nowhere on French soil had I found any justice save from one lone man—and he had gone to the other side of the world. Tomorrow I would step ashore and be under the heel of the Guiana Penal Administration again! Governor Siadous could do nothing for me. Nobody could do anything for me—except myself.

All night long I did not sleep. The mosquitoes from shore came out and tormented the prisoners, but my thoughts tormented me so much more that I didn't notice the physical pain. At dawn we were landed on the wharf of Saint Laurent. I had but one thought in my head. It pulsed as though it were an animated heart deep in my brain. No matter what was in store for me, I would bide my time. Now I had no more promises to keep. Now I was a man at bay. I'd promise nothing to anyone. I'd await my time—and I would escape.

I was singled out by a corporal of the blockhouse guards, taken from the other seven hundred convicts and locked up in a solitary cell.

Thus went my year of freedom. Now again I was just another man in the battalion of the condemned. I had tried very hard to orient myself, to work, to behave, to break no law, no rule. I had lived frugally. I had won, from the Americans in the Canal Zone, an excellent behavior certificate. "Work . . . Excellent. Deportment . . . Excellent," the pay-off card stated. But I had gone to France to seek justice, an extension of my passport and perhaps a pardon; that was my real mistake. I should have stayed in Panama. I *would* have stayed—had I not promised Governor Siadous that I would honor his parole and report to the French authorities before the year he had granted me was up. All right! I had kept my word. Now let the prison authorities do what they wanted to. I owed nobody anything now. I'd take whatever punishment they gave me and, as soon as I became a *libéré* again, I'd escape.

I was sent to Royale. The island had not changed a bit in four years. But the guards were meaner and the men fought back at them more madly than ever before. But I managed to hold my peace week after week. One month passed, then two, then three, then four. The cell in which I paced all day long, and sometimes for many hours in the dark night, was like a living tomb. Food was shoved through a hole to me. I had no money to buy cigarettes from the guards. They completely ignored me. I walked back and forth, back and forth. I jumped up, gripped the overhead bars and chinned myself—to keep the muscles in my arms alive. Day after day I fought there alone just to keep from rotting, rotting in mind and body. Five months, six months, and in long-drawn-out loneliness finally a year closed in back of me. September, 1934, passed—I marked each day with my fingernail on the wall—and then on November 3rd, three years after I had been taken from the ship at Havre, a key turned in the lock of the rusty door, the door opened and a guard handed me a paper. My eyes were dimmed by so much twilight and I had to squint to read the document. It said that, having served three years for entering France while a *libéré* I was now, again, a *libéré*. I could go to the mainland of Guiana, and take up where I left off—a free convict!

A *free* convict! I burst out laughing. Free to live like a homeless, mongrel dog. Free to live in the jungles around Cayenne or Saint Laurent like a monkey, but prohibited from making a living in the town. Free to live—but nothing to live with, or on. Free to be a prisoner for life, in Guiana! But the poor dumb guard thought I was laughing only because I was so happy to be liberated from my solitary cell! He escorted me down to the wharf. The little coastal steamer was there, but the sunlight was so bright that I could hardly open my eyes. I stumbled over the rough dock and climbed on board.

I had stayed alive. That was the song that sang in my mind, as the little boat ploughed through the coastal waves toward Saint Laurent. I had stayed alive. I had continued to exist, not died, not gone stark raving crazy. I felt my body. None of it was numb. I was as thin as a skeleton, but my body was all there. No part of me was gangrened, no part paralyzed from confinement. I thanked God that I had had the strength of mind to make myself walk back and forth each day, to exercise in the darkness, just to keep my body in working condition. It had, verily, been a battle of mind over matter—and it seemed that I had won.

The guards all saluted me, as I walked off the wharf at Saint Laurent, with wry faces and cat-calls. It was evident that all through the colony word had passed that, having been befriended by the old Governor, I was to be—I had been, and was to be at every opportunity—tormented. Yes, that was evident. I was now a *libéré*—a *libéré* marked out for special meannesses. I no longer had to stay behind bars. I could forage for myself. I could eat garbage or whatever other food I could obtain. I could sleep in the jungle, like hundreds of other *libérés*. I could die, the sooner the better. No guard missed a chance to snicker at me.

I hunted up a *libéré* I had known four years before, miraculously found him still alive. Friends in France had sent him a few francs a month. He had a small grass hut and offered to share it with me.

"You're in wrong with the administration, Belbenoit," he said. "They say you made it possible for Governor Siadous to close down their profitable grafts. The penal authorities have it in for you! They'll take it out on me when they find I've befriended you. But to hell with them. I won't be alive much longer for the beasts to play with!"

"Eat!" he exclaimed setting down a gourd bowl of

236

coconut meat boiled with rice and sugar cane in front of me.

Let me repeat once more what it means to be a *libéré* in French Guiana. It means that you have served your time. You have stayed in the prisons for the sentence that was imposed upon you. You have served three years, five years, or ten years in the Camp of Death, or in the Crimson Barrack, or in the dark cells, and now, still alive, you are free. Free, but free only to stay in Guiana. Not free to go where you want, to take up human life again, to see your friends, to start all over again to build something from the wreckage. Not free to pull yourself up out of the mud and disgrace and begin a new life. Free only of the cells, of the punishment camps, of the vile barracks. Free to live in Guiana—where there is no means of living!

A man can't climb through the trees, like the sloths do, and live on leaves. He can't fly over the jungle, as the parrots do, and live on nuts. He can't swim in the muddy rivers, as the fish do, and live on weeds and molluscs. He has no fur or feathers; he must have clothes.

A man needs work to do, a job to accomplish each day, a task of some sort which repays him with cash. With cash he lives. But in the whole of Guiana there is no way for a *libéré* to earn honest cash. He cannot get a job sweeping the streets, for that is done by convicts. It costs nothing. He cannot get a job sweeping out private homes, for that is also done by convicts rented out by grafting guards for practically nothing. He cannot even get a job cleaning up the garbage, for that job must be bought from the administration. There is only one honest chance for a *libéré* who has no friends to keep him in funds. He can catch butterflies and sell the wings to the officials at a bargain, or he can make various objects by hand and sell them at minute prices. Both butterflies and these hand-made articles fetch high prices in France and in the West Indian tourist hotels—but the *libéré* doesn't get more than ten per cent of their price.

I caught butterflies, I made odds and ends and toys out of rubber which I collected in the forest. I managed to have a parrot to roast for Christmas—shot with a bow and arrow. I celebrated New Year's Eve over a boiled armadillo, dug out of its hole with a broken pickaxe which I had salvaged from an old dump. I celebrated Easter with a stew made from boiling the cores of palms and adding lizards. I bought a package of the cheapest cigarettes, tore them up and made three new cigarettes out of each original wad of tobacco. I hauled water out of the river. Unlike most *libérés* I boiled it before drinking. I picked ticks out of my body, worms out of my toes. I had no teeth left but that did not bother me, for I had nothing that needed chewing.

Other *libérés* fared a little better. At night they crept into the town and stole things. But I did not want to steal anything. I tried to use my wits, to concoct things out of the jungle, but the jungle does not give to man— man has to take whatever he can, with expensive tools and organization. I searched my mind for some way to get together enough money to finance another escape, but I had nothing to grab hold of. I was like a man swimming in a turbulent, sucking whirlpool, searching the water for a rock to catch hold of, or a floating log. But nothing came my way. Several times I thought that I would walk up to some penal official in broad daylight and hit him in the face. That would bring about my arrest. That would cause me to be sentenced to another six months or a year in the barrack or cells, where the authorities would have to feed me and give me prison clothes.

Money! Money was what I needed, needed more than any man ever needed it before—to buy an escape from a living Hell. A hundred francs would buy an old Indian canoe. Fifty francs would buy food for a fortnight at sea. Another fifty francs would buy the material to patch together a makeshift sail. Suddenly I made up my mind that I'd go and visit an aged *libéré* whom the years had made so wily he was almost like a human fox. He had a small canoe. On dark nights he

238

paddled across the Maroni River to the Dutch bank and smuggled back things, free of duty, for the penal guards. Often he brought packages of cocaine, sometimes a new girl, a young mulatto, for the bachelors of the administration.

Yes, drive a man into the deep corner of despair, and he may do anything!

Chapter XXIX

I LIMPED down the hot roadway along the outskirts of Saint Laurent, the village of the condemned, thinking that I would have to do something quickly to get funds to finance an escape before I went crazy. To escape through the jungle, I had learned by three terrible experiences, was impossible. To escape by sea required the assistance of seamen partners. I would have to obtain a boat. I would have to seek companions who, like myself, preferred death at sea to life in Cayenne—men whom I could trust not to whisper my plan to any Corsican guard. To escape by sea required, in addition to a good boat and good companions, a substantial amount of food and supplies. It would require at least ten days of favorable weather and wind before we could reach a safe landing place. These three requirements seemed impossible to satisfy.

A man in freshly washed and ironed linens and a white sun helmet, which marked him immediately as being some sort of a tourist, stopping for a moment or passing thrugh the penal colony, crossed the sunbaked roadway and beckoned to me.

"Where can I find a prisoner who speaks English?" he asked in schoolboy French.

"I speak a little English," I said. Perhaps this stranger would give me a tip for some chore.

"I want to find a prisoner named Belbenoit," he said in English. "The man about whom Blair Niles wrote

239

her book, *Condemned*. I want to talk to him. Guide me to him, or bring him to me and I will give you five dollars!"

I looked around hastily. No guard was in sight. "Give me the money," I said. He peeled a bill from a fat bundle of big notes and handed it to me. "Which way?" he asked.

"Right here!" I said laughing for the first time in years. "I am Belbenoit!"

"You!" he asked looking down at me disparagingly. "Are you the prisoner who has escaped four times?"

"Who are you?" I asked.

He seemed a little taken aback, but finally announced that he was an executive of an American motion picture company. His company, he explained, was going to make a motion picture based on Blair Niles' book—a film story about Devil's Island—one that would feature a dramatic escape. He had flown down to French Guiana to study the convict colony at first hand. He wanted the picture to be accurate, he said, a true-to-life portrayal of a man's sufferings in the worst prison in the world. Would I be interested in giving him information, supplying him with additional factual material which could be used in his forthcoming picture? If a prisoner tried to escape, how would he do it?

"He'd escape by the sea—in a sailing boat," I said, voicing the thought which had been racing through my head for many long days. "He'd . . ."

"No," he interrupted me. "This must be an escape through the jungles . . . combat with fierce animals, snakes, swamps . . ."

"Nobody has ever escaped through the jungles!" I insisted. "I tried it three times. I ought to know!"

"Maybe so!" he said. "But it makes a better picture. In our picture the hero has to escape through the jungle. I've heard that you've had more dramatic escapes than any other convict," he added. "If you answer all my questions I'll make it worth your while!"

Well, Fate for the first time in my life was offering

me a helping hand. It was not for me to quibble over a motion picture hero's ability to escape through the jungle! I spent the whole night sitting at a table answering his questions, making rough drawings of prison cells, punishment racks, describing in detail my three attempts to escape through the jungle, giving him details of horrible backgrounds, answering every question while he took a bookful of notes. By dawn he said that he had enough. He peeled some bills from his money roll and handed them to me. The aeroplane in which he had arrived soon was but a speck in the Caribbean sky. I would have given my soul to have been so free as he—privileged to soar through the heavens to pleasant lands. A lump was in my throat as I realized how casually this man had landed, asked questions, and flown away—as though he hadn't a moment's thought to waste on me as a brother man. To him I was but an information bureau, something he could pump dry, transmit profitably into continuity and impersonal celluloid.

But in my hands he had left two hundred dollars! With so much money—I knew a Chinese who would get me a boat and package together food—and with such an outfit I knew I could find other penniless *libérés* who would join me. I made up my mind that this time I must not fail. There was to be no recapture. I must make my way first to temporary freedom, some West Indian island that would give us temporary sanctuary, and then to the United States. Thousands of miles lay between French Guiana and New York, but with each mile gained I felt that I should escape that much farther from inhuman, atrocious existence and should gain that much toward civilization—and Liberty. The people of the United States, I'd heard, would not deport a *libéré* who had gained its shores—from Devil's Island.

"This time I'll make it!" I whispered over and over again to myself as I set about organizing my expedition.

I searched through the penal colony like a hawk—

241

for men whose plight was most terrible, for companions I thought would be of greatest physical aid for my escape. At last I selected four convicts: Dadar, a young *libéré* whom I had known for a year, who had served a five-year sentence for a first offense robbery; Casquette, who had served fifteen years for killing his mistress; Bébert, who had struck a cruel Corsican guard in the face and nearly had his head blown off by a blast from the guard's gun—after release from the hospital he had served an additional four years of solitary confinement; and "Panama," a convict whose name none of us knew, but who had once escaped and lived happily for twelve years in Colombia only to be apprehended at last by a new French consul and returned for Devil's Island punishment. Four men who promised me that they preferred freedom or death.

But none of us had any knowledge of navigation. None of us were seamen. So I looked farther and finally selected Chifflot, who had been sentenced to five years at hard labor for killing, in self-defense, the son of a powerful Negro chief of a Congo protectorate tribe, who, subjected to the influences of modern civilization, had become a procurer of white women in Montmartre. Chifflot had been a sailor. If I furnished the boat and food, all he'd need, he promised, was the sun and the stars to guide us to safety over the horizon of the Caribbean Sea.

"We are going to Trinidad first," I said. The people of that British island I knew loathed the existence of the French Hell, and would allow escaped men a safe resting place.

At six o'clock on the night of May 2, 1935, we six men met stealthily at a Chinese shop in the penal colony village of Saint Laurent. The night grew black. Noiselessly we glided into the forest and made our way to Serpent Creek. The boat which the Chinese had promised to hire for us proved to be only half the size of the craft bargained for—a dugout canoe barely three feet wide. In disgust I examined the packages of provisions, found them to be less than half of the things agreed upon before I had passed my cash to him. I had a terrible sinking feeling as though my escape had failed before it had begun. My companions talked about postponing the attempt. Even a little shark, they said, could overturn such a craft—we would all die at sea.

But something told me not to let myself turn back. I got into the canoe, urged them to take their places—and soon we were out of the creek and paddling noiselessly down the center of the night-shrouded Maroni River. The tide was with us, and we moved swiftly. Now and then we passed a canoe manned by Negroes or Indians. They called to us but we did not answer. The Chinese had supplied us with a water keg, but to make sure the water hadn't been poisoned we stopped at a fresh water creek and filled it with water that I knew would be safe.

At the mouth of the Maroni we hoisted our patchwork sail. Chifflot took the home-made tiller. The long slender canoe began to dance upon the water, like an eighteen-foot cigar. Chifflot pointed out a star which he said would guide us due north. Waves began coming over the side of the canoe. Two men sat close to Chifflot, to keep him company at the tiller—and to make sure he didn't fall asleep. Others began bailing.

Men in their right senses would never have gone out on the merciless Caribbean Sea in such a craft—but we were driven by a quite insane desire to put Devil's Island and the Penal Colony behind us—to seek freedom at any price. The night passed all too quickly as we looked over our shoulders constantly to make sure that a power boat was not coming out into the night after us. When the dawn came we were far out at sea, and there was nothing save a querulous gull to spy on us.

We complimented Chifflot, and Casquette took his place at the tiller. I volunteered to be the expedition's cook. Charcoal was lighted in a kerosene tin, and strong tea soon revived us. The Chinese had cheated me thoroughly on the food supply—I would have to stretch it out very thin during the coming days. But no one, during the first day, grumbled. We all talked with nervous gaiety—we were, at last, free of French Guiana! The fiery red of the setting sun made us work carefully to tie down all our supplies. Chifflot warned us that following such a sunset we could expect rough weather.

At eight o'clock the wind began to blow, helping us forward as it came from the continent behind us. The stars disappeared. I crept to the stern and sat beside Chifflot, with a little compass in my hand. The canoe went faster and faster over the waves. I judged that we must be racing over the sea at about 15 miles an hour. The other men became frightened as waves wet us— but to me every mile we gained ahead of the growing storm took us that much nearer freedom. Casquette was supposed to relieve Chifflot at the tiller, but to do this would have been too dangerous. We were precariously riding foaming waves—the least false move with the tiller would have caused us to capsize. Chifflot sang songs all night, his voice rising louder and louder in competition with wind. Then, shortly before dawn the wind miraculously died down, the brassy sun rose over the horizon—and we set about removing our clothes and hanging them up on paddles to dry.

We had to repair the sail. A mattress cover and several old shirts had been used to make it. The cloth was so old that many of the patches had been torn apart. Not a sign of a ship was seen all day. The sun and glare of the sea burnt our flesh. The wounds on our legs, inflicted first by the iron bands that were welded about our bare ankles during our early prison days, and aggravated by constant rubbing of our shackles, began to open and run—and burn under the intermittent soaking of salt spray.

The third night found us not such good friends. Each of the six men, cramped for fifty long hours against his neighbor, had first talked himself out of joviality— and then everyone began to find fault with something or someone. Chifflot's hands were so blistered with holding on to the tiller that Casquette had to relieve him. Clinging desperately to the tiller in the darkness, and on a sea more turbulent than it had been the previous night, Casquette had all he could do to keep us from being swamped in the deep sea trough. We did not attempt to keep a course. The sea washed the compass from my hands in one mighty wave, and not a single star was to be seen.

When dawn came at last we were drenched, stiff, hungry, thirsty, and sick at heart. I dipped some water out of the water keg—and discovered that the sea water had got in and turned it salty. I mixed it with condensed milk and passed it around to my companions, they said it tasted terrible.

"We'd better turn and try to reach the mainland!" said Bébert. "We'll get fresh drinking water and put out again."

"We are probably off Demarara," Dadar guessed. "That's less than half way to Trinidad. I'd rather take a chance on the jungle—there's at least plenty of water to drink!"

"We've only been gone three days!" I said, "and you speak already of turning in toward the coast. I told you when we started that I would not turn back. If we reach Trinidad we are safe. If we land anywhere on the mainland coast we will be turned over to a French consul. I know! I've tried it!" Thus we quarrelled all day long.

The fourth night was increasingly cruel. The fifth, sixth, seventh, eighth nights were nightmares, we became like six beasts. Eight more days we lived—how I do not know. Many times I thought the canoe would be buried in a black wave but, as though some kind power lent it at the last moment a charm, the frail craft magically came up over the foaming crests, quivered for a moment and then plunged into another wave.

"Trinidad! Bah!" Dadar growled. "We'll never make it! And if we do—what surety have you, Belbenoit, that we won't be arrested? There's a French Consul in Trinidad, isn't there?"

"Yes, but the British people, I believe, won't turn us over to him," I insisted. "They'll allow us to rest a few days, replenish our food; those Britishers—they're sportsmen. They'll grant us a few days' refuge! Stop worrying and I'll show you!" I was at the tiller, and kept the bow pointed steadily northwest.

"Bah!" Bébert in the bow of the canoe snarled. "Change the course! I've had enough of this. I'm going to land on the coast and take my chance—with my feet on the ground!"

"Stop!" I yelled at Dadar who began crawling toward the sheet of the sail. I reached into my shirt and drew out a small pistol which I carried next to my skin, wrapped in oil cloth. I aimed the pistol at Bébert and then at Dadar. I am a very little man. I should have been no match for any of my companions in physical strength. But I had made up my mind to turn neither to the right nor left—but keep heading toward the British island of real security. The five big men glowered at me but even a mouse can become brave when his freedom is at stake.

"Rush me if you like," I said, looking over the muzzle at my companions. "Here are six bullets—and I will kill each one of you if you insist!"

Chapter XXX

I DID not want to kill my five companions. As I looked at them over the barrel of my stubby pistol I realized that, like myself, they had swallowed much salt water from the angry sea; that they were hungry, and scared of the shark-infested water. Their insistence on my shifting the tiller, altering our course, and heading in for land was born of desperation and not of personal animosity.

"You are mad!" I said to them. "The coast is Venezuelan territory. You will surely be arrested and returned to Devil's Island. We cannot be far from Trinidad. There we'll be safe. I promise you, in Trinidad we will be safe to rest, eat good food, revive our strength, before taking to the sea again."

"Put the sail over!" Bébert shouted to Chifflot. I aimed my pistol at Chifflot, but at the same instant Dadar jumped up, tried to spring past him and snatch my gun. Before I could fire Dadar had slipped and fallen against Chifflot, and both of them tumbled against the half-submerged gunwale.

"Beasts!" yelled Casquette. "You're going to capsize us all!" He seized Dadar by the ankle, hit him behind the ear with his bony fist.

"Better tie him up!" Panama cautioned, throwing Casquette some wet cord. The unconscious man was securely tied, hands and feet together so he couldn't move. Then Casquette put his hand to his forehead and looked over the horizon.

"Look over there!" he yelled. "It's land!"

The others stood up and looked, but I, thinking it was a trick to get me away from the tiller and off my guard, didn't budge.

"It's Trinidad!" shouted Chifflot. "Come, Belbenoit, and see for yourself!" The sail obscured my vision of the horizon to which they pointed. Cautiously I tried to get a clear view without risking a sudden onslaught. I turned the tiller sharply to swing the bow over a big wave, and as we crested the foaming whitecap I saw that they were not trying to outwit me. There, against the horizon, were high, green mountains outlined against the blue sky.

The sight of those mountains wiped out all animosity, all evil talk, all quarrelling, from our minds and voices. We all shouted joyously, smiles replaced anger-drawn scowls. I pulled the tiller back and set the course again. The wind grew stronger behind us. We had been at sea fourteen days in a canoe that needed constant bailing, but now each of my companions except Dadar bailed happily as the sail bulged under the pressure of the breeze.

A few hours later we were riding the swells off shore. A thatched house set in a grove of coconut palms seemed deserted. I turned the tiller and steered the bow through the waves until the canoe, like a surf board, was shot up on the glistening white beach. My companions tried to leap ashore eagerly, but they were so weak that they stumbled and fell sprawled out on the dry sand like men suddenly robbed of all strength.

"Now do as you please!" I said. And I cast my pistol far out into the sea.

Some Negroes, fishing along the beach with nets, passed us, circling us warily; but I called to them, begged them to climb the trees and get us some water coconuts to drink and eat. They put down their nets, climbed the trees, and secured the nuts. But they would not approach nearer than fifty feet. They rolled the nuts down the beach to us and then went off hurriedly.

I hacked off the tops of five nuts, passed one to each of my companions. I cut the cords that bound Dadar and lifted him out of the slimy canoe, held the cool sweet liquid to his mouth as he drank. We drank the water of two nuts apiece, ate the white meat, then started to wobble across the sand like drunken scarecrows. The earth seemed to dance under my feet— to ebb and flow as the sea for such long terrible nights and days had done. In the hut there was a big black kettle full of rice and salt fish. We dug our hands into it and ate like wolves until, stuffed and drugged with relief, we rolled over on the floor of the hut and fell into a drunken sleep.

When we awoke I suggested that we go immediately to the nearest town and announce our arrival. At first my companions didn't like the idea at all. They insisted that we'd probably be arrested. It would be better, they said, to spend a few days here, eating coconuts and foraging for other food and supplies without the authorities knowing about us. But I insisted that this would not be as good for us as going to the authorities immediately—before they had heard indirectly of our arrival.

"I'm going to report myself!" I said, starting into the coconut grove—"You can stay here if you like." But they fell in behind me and soon we were walking over a narrow road. We saw no one but Negroes—very black and big Negroes speaking English in broad accents, who looked suspiciously at us with big eyes, and gave us most of the road when they passed. After two hours we reached the little hamlet of Moruga, which, I learned, was the administrative center for the southeast coast of Trinidad.

I went directly to the police station. The constable of Moruga sat behind an old table. He was a tremendous Negro with the face and neck of an ape. He was dressed in a military uniform spotlessly clean. We stood before him while he summoned two policemen who towered over us like ebony giants.

"Where do you come from?"

"From French Guiana," I said.

"Where are you going?"

"To the United States."

"For what reason have you landed in Trinidad?" he asked as soon as he had laboriously penciled the previous information on his blotter.

"Because we have been at sea in a conoe for fourteen days. We were half-drowned. We had no fresh water. No food."

The constable stood up, went to the telephone nailed on the wall above our heads, turned the handle. "Six French fugitives landed here last night," he said. He listened to instructions from some superior, then hung up the earpiece.

"Get eighteen loaves of bread," he said to his policeman. "Get six pounds of rice, six pounds of sugar, six pounds of coffee, six pounds of codfish, twelve packages of cigarettes." He made out an order of some kind and signed it with a rubber stamp. "Give this to the storekeeper," he ordered, and when the two policemen had left he turned to us and began reading from a notebook.

"Hear ye the law of Trinidad and be guided accordingly!" he said. "No French convict escaping from Devil's Island and reaching the shore of Trinidad will

249

be arrested by any authority—unless after landing on Trinidad he breaks a law, regulation, or disturbs the peace. If the fugitive arrives by a boat which is still seaworthy he will be given food and allowed to embark again. If the boat is not seaworthy he will be given transportation to Port of Spain, accompanied by a police officer who will escort him directly to the Controller of the Port. Is your boat seaworthy?" he asked.

"No!" I almost shouted.

"I will have to inspect it and make sure," the Constable said. When the food had arrived he took us down the road in an old car, then we walked down the path to the sea. He looked at the canoe.

"Would you like to go to sea in a thing like that?" I asked. "Look, the hull is already splitting open!"

The giant Negro scratched his head, looked for a few moments out over the wave-chopped sea and then shook his head. "I'll take you to Port of Spain!" he said.

Back at the police station he gave us each a bottle of beer. A Negro woman prepared a meal for us—rice and baked plantains, fresh fish, steaming coffee, preserved mangoes, salt beef. She would accept no payment.

We drove during the afternoon through the island, passing a constant stream of Negroes on donkeys, until we reached Port of Spain. Here we were taken to the military prison. Our things were searched, our names taken, and we were locked up in one of the guard rooms.

"This is to notify you," said the sergeant in charge, "that you are not under arrest. But you must stay here —where the French Consul can't get you—until the Controller looks into your case." A large meal was served to us in the guard room and after eating it we all fell asleep, and slept soundly until nine o'clock next morning.

Shortly after ten o'clock a man in civilian clothes was admitted to the guard room.

I nicknamed this man, after a short while, "My Friend."

"Where are you going, my friend. . . . What can we do for you, my friend. . . . I will see what I can do for you, my friend," he said, asking endless questions all of which I answered frankly.

"Follow me, my friend," he said at last, knocking on the door. It was opened immediately. He led us out of the military prison, walked with us down the street until we came to a place where a sign with "Salvation Army" painted on it hung over the sidewalk. We apparently had been expected, because a dining-room table had been set with six plates. A Captain Heap and his wife introduced themselves to us. Mrs. Heap, in spite of our insistence that she should not do so, began waiting on us, serving us with better food than we had tasted in many cruel years. Neither Casquette nor Bébert had eaten at a table for fifteen years, and all of us, accustomed to being treated like beasts, had tears in our eyes.

"This is where you will stay, my friend," said the plain clothes officer. "I will return to talk with you tomorrow, my friend," he added as he took his departure. Captain Heap told us that he was an intelligence officer assigned to the special supervision of administering to the needs and fate of fugitives from Devil's Island. Before 1931, he said, fugitives were not allowed freedom on Trinidad. Up to that time Venezuela welcomed escaped prisoners, and let them live in freedom. But now Venezuela had passed a law ordering the arrest and imprisonment—at hard labor—of all French Guiana fugitives, and Trinidad and its people, who had continually criticized the existence of the French penal colony and the methods used there, had passed a law under which French Guiana fugitives would be given a twenty-four day permission to reside, and a means of continuing their flight to some other country.

We lived in the Salvation Army's depot, now, without a care in the world for our present safety, free to come and go as we pleased, to visit the cinemas or any other place which we desired. Several people visited the depot and left food, cigarettes, and clothing for us. But after the first day of excitedly sampling our freedom, we went to work writing letters to friends and acquaintances—seeking funds for buying passages on a friendly steamer to another port. Panama wrote to a friend in Colombia; Dadar, Bébert and Casquette hadn't any friends and expected nothing.

Chifflot, I discovered, had 4,000 francs in a suppository! He said he would buy a passage on a German ship and go to Europe to see his mother before she died. But to do that he needed a passport. We went to the Spanish quarter to see if we could get one. As usual in such matters, it proved to be simply a matter of price. A Venezuelan barber gave us the address of a former Venezuelan General, now in exile from his own country, but apparently still having some friends across the Gulf. The General had his headquarters over a drug store. He told us to come back in three days.

In three days Chifflot had a Venezuelan passport with all the necessary visas; he was now a Venezuelan citizen named Chifflara!

"My mother will be glad to see me—no matter what name I arrive under!" he said. "Better a live Venezuelan than a dead Frenchman!"

A week after our arrival he boarded a ship for Hamburg. I saw him off at the pier, hoping that I too would receive some money—from my cables and airmailed letters—and be able to embark like a human being and not a slinking beast.

I went to the bank every day. "Nothing, sorry!" said the teller each time. My companions begged me to stay with them and with them seek a better boat in which to continue our flight. I waited until June 6th and then went to the office of the Inspector General of Police. "My Friend," to whom I had talked, made the appointment and accompanied me.

The Inspector General, an elderly British Army Officer, who spoke beautiful French, talked with me for half an hour.

"Two things about the French I cannot understand —or stomach!" he said with a twist of his mustache. "One is their French Foreign Legion—and the other is Devil's Island!"

Then he asked me to wait in an antechamber while he talked with "My Friend." When he came out I stood stiffly at attention.

"We are going to give you a boat. Go through the harbor and see if you can find a boat, such as you will need, for sale." Then turning to "My Friend" he said: "There ought to be some fisherman's boat that would serve admirably."

At eleven o'clock the next day we had a boat. Casquette had spied it a few feet off the dock where several police launches were tied. It was a life-boat, rigged with a mast and sail. "With such a boat," Casquette laughed happily, "we can go to China!"

A naval officer inspected the boat with us. He authorized its purchase by the government from its owner, then ordered a government carpenter to be put at our disposal.

"Tell the carpenter what you want done with the boat and he will do it," he said. Then he asked me to make a list of materials and supplies which would be needed for the trip. A policeman would buy them for us from the wharf-front stores.

On a dining-room table at the Salvation Army depot I spread out a marine chart which a man had given us.

"We must not let ourselves be swept on a beach in either Venezuela or Columbia," I said. "We can reach the United States by skirting the West Indies, putting in now and then on a British island for rest and supplies, and continuing through the Caribbean until we reach Miami."

I picked out the islands on the chart—Tobago, 100 miles north of Trinidad, then Grenada, seventy-five miles farther, then Saint Vincent, then Saint Lucia, Saint Kitts. The Salvation Army Captain said that he would write the depots in these islands to be on the lookout for us—to help us.

253

"We'll have to keep clear of Martinique and Guadeloupe!" Casquette warned. "If we land in the French Islands we'll get a quick ticket back to Devil's Island."

"Puerto Rico is American!" I said. "Nothing to fear there. Haiti will be safe. Cuba we'd better skirt until, off Havana, we head north for Key West. All the journey," I said, "will be in frequent sight of land. When we lose sight of one island another will appear ahead of us! It's not too bad a road to freedom!"

In two days the boat was ready for sea. The bow had been decked over, the gunwales raised on both sides. Captain Heap had brought provisions. Compass, cookstove, charcoal, pots, hurricane lamp, had been donated by other well-wishers. We asked the Inspector General for a document stating that the boat and equipment had been given us, that it was ours and that we had not stolen it. The Inspector replied that he couldn't issue such a document.

"Many of you fugitives whom we help end up in Venezuela and we have received so many notes from Venezuela and Colombia, accusing us of aiding illegal entry into their countries, that we have to stop issuing papers of any kind. But the boat is yours—and good luck!"

On June 10th, a British navy launch towed us out to sea.

"Don't be afraid to steer for the east," the pilot said. "There are very strong currents. Pass to the east of the Antilles!"

He towed us for more than an hour, got us safely through the turbulent water of the Dragon's Mouth, took us ten miles off shore and then let go the tow line. The sea was rough, but we had a good boat. We hoisted the new sail.

"Due east!" I said to Casquette.

He looked at his compass. "But if I steer east I'm going to throw the boat ashore!" he said.

"Make it slightly north of east then," I suggested, "until we pass Trinidad."

"North of east steering, in these currents, will land us in Colombia," growled Bébert.

Casquette hesitated at the steering wheel. I looked at my four companions. Was the same thing going to happen, the same old controversy, anger, quarreling going to descend upon us again? Hadn't we quarrelled enough during the terrible voyage from Devil's Island to Trinidad? I felt suddenly very angry.

"Steer as I tell you to—or put me ashore and leave me behind!" I said.

Chapter XXXI

THE BRITISH people of Trinidad Island had been very kind to us. For the first time in fifteen terrible years I was treated as a man—an unfortunate man, perhaps—but not an animal. The sturdy life-boat with a stout mast and strong sail rode the Carribean waves easily. We were well stocked with food. Now there were only five of us—Chifflot was on his way to Germany. Casquette, Panama, Dadar, Bébert and I looked over our shoulders at the island that had given us sanctuary.

Ahead of us lay Grenada, Saint Vincent, Saint Lucia, Saint Kitts and the other islands of the British West Indies—stepping-stones to freedom as we headed northward for Miami. I'd have to watch only the winds and currents—and steer clear of Martinique and Guadeloupe, the French Islands.

The breeze from Trinidad and the Venezuelan coast blew us northward, the miles between Trinidad and Tobago passing uneventfully. We had finally agreed among ourselves that I was to steer for Grenada and pass by Tobago. At Grenada we would secure new supplies from the Salvation Army.

As the sun set we were at ease in the boat. Bébert and Casquette relieved me at the tiller. Under the stars

I curled up on a wad of canvas and went to sleep. "Steer due northwest," I told them. "It's only seventy-five miles before you'll see Grenada's light."

I slept the sleep of exhaustion. When I awoke, suddenly, four hours later the stars had disappeared, the sea around us was as black as ink. Here and there streaks of phosphorescent light cut the water and splashed green sparks over the sides of our boat. Two giant sharks were encircling us.

The sail hung listless, spasmodically flapped impotently this way and that as changing winds played with us. I hastened to the tiller, but we lay on the sea aimlessly in spite of all my exertions. When the day dawned at last, we could see no island, no land anywhere. At dawn a wind began blowing over us; the sail puffed out. I consulted the compass and the map. I steered in the direction I thought Grenada would be. But at the end of that day we still had not seen land.

The second night was windy, with a choppy sea. I did not sleep at all. At dawn there was still no sign of Grenada.

"We've surely passed that island!" said Casquette. "We passed it during the night."

That might have happened, I agreed, but Saint Vincent should have loomed up on the horizon. All day long we searched for it but saw no land. Another night passed, then another day. We seemed to be making good headway, before favoring winds, but mile after mile we searched the horizon and saw no island at all. Six days finally passed before we admitted we were lost upon a mystifying sea.

"I'll keep her going due north anyway!" I said. "That's where Puerto Rico, Haiti and Cuba lie." But my companions complained. They thought we were too far east of the British islands, that if we continued north we'd run into the French islands and be captured. They insisted on my heading west. I did not know whether they or I were right. I shifted the tiller, reset the sail. A gale started to blow, but in the boat which the British authorities had given us I feared nothing.

Six more days passed. Twelve days had come and gone, since leaving Trinidad, without sight of land.

Then at dawn Casquette suddenly cried, "A ship! There! A ship!" On the horizon smoke rose above the waves. Little by little a steamer was revealed. It was a tanker. I went to the bow and waved my pants. The ship changed her course and approached us. At her stern waved the German flag. A Jacob's ladder was lowered and we drew alongside. I climbed to the deck and faced the captain.

"Fugitives from Devil's Island, eh?" he said, rubbing his bearded chin. He took me to his chart room and showed me where we were—200 miles directly north of the Dutch Island of Curaçao!

"You'll never get to Miami from here!" the captain told me. Our boat, without an engine, would never be able to navigate the Gulf Stream's current. He offered to take us on board, for Curaçao, but I refused. My companions thought the Dutch on that island, like the Dutch in the colony next to French Guiana, would turn us over to a French consul for deportation.

Back in the sailboat again—with an armful of food and many packages of tobacco—my companions decided to head west for Panama. If we could reach the American zone, they said, we'd be safe. Panama took the tiller; we were fighting strong currents, but the wind held all night and all the next day. Sixteen days after leaving Trinidad we saw land. The sea calmed and we approached the coast, a long barren stretch of sand, slowly at first, and then with greater speed. Hastily we dropped the sail, but we were already being sucked into the rollers that were breaking over the shore. Before we could get out oars and try to pull away we were being carried with express-train speed through the surf. Five minutes later we lay bruised and water-soaked on the beach with our boat smashed and water-swamped fifteen yards from shore. We had worked furiously not only to save ourselves, but to rescue our remaining food and our knapsacks of personal effects.

We built a fire on the beach and prepared dinner.

Before we had time to eat it we saw that Indians were looking at us—wild-looking natives, naked and with big spears. They stuck their heads up over surrounding sand dunes. I called to them in Spanish, but they ducked back and disappeared. Half an hour later they returned with a savage assortment of spears, bows and arrows, and approached our camp fire. When only a few feet away they stopped and began talking to us. But none of us could understand a thing they said, and none of them could understand Spanish.

Then they began inspecting our kits and the rescued supplies. We tried to stop them, but they became so menacing that I cautioned my companions to go easy. One of the savages got hold of an oilcloth package containing my Devil's Island journals, my papers which I had written during fifteen years of imprisonment. I grabbed the package from him and opened it hastily to show him that it contained only papers; nothing which would be of any use to him. An Indian at his side gave me a painful jab with a spear that caused blood to spurt from my thigh, but the other Indian handed me back the package of papers with a humorous grimace. I suppose to him it was a joke that a white man should lug around such useless stuff.

These savages took our blankets, lamp, all personal effects, the cans of food that remained and all our clothing. They were, I found out later, the Cactus Eaters, wild savages of the La Guajira coastal desert of Colombia—we had been wrecked on Gallinas Point. They giggled among themselves as they suddenly turned and marched up the beach, soon disappearing behind the dunes.

"A fine lot of brave men we are!" I said as soon as they were out of sight.

"The devils!" Bébert exclaimed as soon as he caught his breath, from holding it so long in sheer fright, "I'll slit their throats!"

"With *what?*" I asked him. "They took your knife away from you."

Casquette suddenly turned and ran into the surf,

ploughed through the rollers and waves to the place where the ruined hull of our boat lay upside down. He began diving under the water, disappearing for a long time. Then with one hand he swam ashore—and held up a machete.

"I remembered that I stuck it in the boat ribs," he said gleefully.

So we five naked white men, with only a machete to protect us from whatever dangers we might walk into, started hurriedly over the hot sand. We discovered that the sand was a stretch of *playa* made by the currents, and now exposed by the Caribbean low tide. In two hours we had reached the narrower beach that skirted a desolate shore. At night we made a fire, after working for more than an hour rubbing two dried sticks. Any boy scout could have done it in a few seconds, but somehow we couldn't get the thing to work until all of us had blistered hands and aching arms and backs.

We had nothing to eat all night, but at dawn Casquette threw his machete at a big lizard and cut its head off. He shared it with us—two mouthsful for each. For a day and a half we had no water, crossed no rivers. We hunted for fresh water and at last found a stream and bathed in it to relieve the pain of many insect bites. Then the desert of sand dunes changed into jungle.

"What'll we do if we reach a town?" Dadar said. "We can't go into even an Indian village like this!"

For four days we saw no human being, as we kept skirting the jungle shore. We caught some fish by spearing them with sharply pointed sticks. We ate frogs which we killed with pointed bamboo spears. In a large sea shell we carried coals along with us from which, whenever we wanted, we easily started a new fire. We were all covered with festering insect bites. Our feet, softened by being so long at sea, were cut and very sore. But happily we had not, as I feared, started to quarrel among ourselves. Naked, we kept together out of pure fright and anxiety.

At sunset of the third day we came to a lone grass

hut, in front of which some very old nets, much patched, were drying. The fisherman was away, but we saw a large sea turtle and immediately began hacking it open with an ax which leaned against a corner of the hut. We cooked and ate chunks of fat meat and then climbed up into the rafters where we had seen a big tin canister. We opened the canister, eagerly hoping to find pants or shirts.

"Curses!" Panama exclaimed as he pulled some gaudy cloth out of the box. "There's only dresses—for women!" We pulled the garments out—seven old Mother Hubbards made of cheap printed calico. There was not a single pair of pants, or a shirt.

"Well! a dress is better than nothing!" Bébert said as he began to twist into one. Soon we all wore petticoats. With our bearded faces we were an astounding sight. But, clothed at last, we found that the insects didn't bother us so much.

Ten miles farther up the beach we came to a small hamlet. We hid in the jungle until it was dark and then went through the village at night, stopping frequently to hide until barking dogs quieted down, pausing often to look for clothing which some native, we hoped, might have left out all night. But we were not so lucky. We hastened on, once we passed through the town, and did not stop until dawn came. Then we curled up to sleep in what seemed to be a fisherman's deserted house.

"Why are you wearing women's clothes?"

Those were the words, spoken in angry Spanish, which I heard as I awoke. A man in the uniform of a soldier of some sort was speaking to Panama. Three other men, holding the reins of four nervous horses, outside the hut door, looked at us skeptically, but could not quite suppress their smiles.

I stood up. The soldiers outside the door burst out laughing. "We must take them to show the General!" one of them said. "Nothing so funny has happened for a long time."

We were told to come out and march ahead of the armed men. Their horses seemed also to think we were fantastic for they began prancing and shying, and balked at approaching too near our backs and flapping skirts.

In an hour we reached a little town—the Colombian coast town of Santa Marta. We were taken directly to the barracks which served both as police and army station. A great crowd of children, laughing women and joking men, to say nothing of several score barking dogs, followed us through the streets. The General didn't have his tunic on when we entered the barrack-room but an orderly hastily brought it, and soon, wearing epaulets, he gazed at us from across his wide mahogany desk. He asked for our passports. We had none.

"Profugos de Cayenne!" he said to the soldiers gathered about. "Fugitives from French Guiana!"

Casquette began shivering, not with fear, but with a sudden spasm of fever. His face was flushed. The General dug into his pocket, produced a wallet, took several one-peso bills from it. He gave them to an orderly. Soon a doctor arrived. We were all given quinine. Another orderly brought us some old uniforms and we got out of our dresses as quickly as possible. Food was brought to us by native women. The General picked up the telephone and asked to be put through to Barranquilla.

"Cinco profugos de Cayenne!" he said when the connection was completed. "You will notify the French Consul!"

Panama, Casquette, Dadar, Bébert and I looked at each other in disgust and sadness. At last, after two fearful experiences with the sea, we were going to be at the mercy of a far more dangerous foe—a French Consul!

"It is no pleasure for me," the General said. "But it is the law, and I must obey it. You will be sent to Barranquilla. There you will have a chance to talk your way out of deportation, if you can."

The next day we were behind the bars of the "Carcel

Naçional," the high-walled military and civil prison of eastern Colombia. The Warden, on receiving us, said that we were lucky. If we had arrived two days earlier we would have been put on board the French Mail steamer which had just sailed; there wouldn't be another French vessel for a month.

"But don't try to escape, gentlemen," he said, pointing to the rifle-armed guards who patrolled the wall of the *carcel*. "My men are crack shots—and the rifles are not the old blunderbusses they use in *Cayenne!* You wouldn't have a chance!"

But as I looked later in the afternoon out of the thick bars of my cell and saw the dense green jungle which was like a sea stretching to the north in mountainous waves, I told myself that indeed I would try to escape. In the month's wait for a French boat *I'd try every day to escape!* It would be better to be shot in Colombia than to return alive to Cayenne.

Chapter XXXII

LOOKING out from behind the heavy steel bars of the National prison at Barranquilla I could see twenty miles of jungle stretching into the north Colombian horizon. My fugitive companions sat in the damp cell and refused to look through the bars. They were worn out and pessimistic. They cursed their fate. In another month, they swore, we'd all be on board a French steamer en route to French Guiana—and to the dark-cell punishment which is the fate of all who attempt to escape.

But I knew something they didn't. The Colombians hate the French penal system and individually are often ready to help runaways. The day after our capture and imprisonment, under orders of the French Minister, a long article appeared in *La Prensa,* the Colombian paper, about our adventure—and misadventure. The editor himself came to the prison; if I would write a series of articles for him on the French penal colony, he said, he would pay me generously. He talked with Governor Blanco of the prison and things were immediately made more comfortable for us. He interceded with the French Minister in Bogotá, but the Minister was adamant. We were to be placed, he insisted, on the first French steamer. Two policemen from the Paris Sûreté, he advised, were catching the ship in order to take us into custody.

My four companions were very gloomy and quarrelsome, each finding some fault with the others, blaming the predicament on first one, then the other. They began swearing at me, and soon we were embroiled in a bloody fight. At first I thought I would surely succumb in that cell to their blows, but then Dadar took my part and with his strength we soon had the other three cowering in a far corner. He had broken a leg off the table and threatened to mash in the skull of any man who stepped from the shadows.

The noise of our combat brought guards. In a manner at first mysterious I was picked out, taken from the large cell and then locked up in a solitary cell. Then and this is hard to believe unless you know the South Americans, the prison Adjutant came to my cell with some paper and pencils and said: "Belbenoit, we are going to let you escape. Your friends are a different type of fugitive; they were convicted of far more serious crimes. We've checked up on you. Spend the day writing articles for *La Prensa*. The editor will pay you for them tomorrow afternoon. Tomorrow night you will find your cell door open. *Bon Voyage!*" He turned and left me before I had a chance to say a word.

All day long I wrote—seven articles altogether about different phases of the French penal administration. In the late afternoon, don Paez Reyna, the editor, came into my cell. He read the articles and handed me a roll of bills. Excitedly I ate the generous supper that was brought in to me. The key turned in the lock of my cell. I sat close to the bars of the window watching the moon come up from the eastern horizon. One hour, two hours, three hours, four hours I sat so and then I heard a key grating against the lock. I heard the lock snap. I heard the key being removed. Then nothing but silence. I stood up, went to the door and cautiously turned the door knob, pushed slightly—and the door opened. Not a soul was to be seen in the corridor. At the end of the building I saw that an outside gate was ajar—a door that would allow me to step right out into the open behind the prison's walled fortress.

Two minutes later I was in the side streets of Barranquilla. I twisted through the streets to the northern section of the town and then struck off hastily into the open country road that led to the sea coast. I knew that I was in danger as long as I stayed in Colombia, not from the Colombians but because of the hard-boiled French Minister at Bogotá, so I decided that I would try to reach the Panama Canal Zone as soon as possible. The Americans I knew would not deport me to French Guiana. Between Barranquilla and Panama, however, lay many tribes of very wild Indians, but I would take my chances with them—no matter what they did they would not turn me over to any French Consul!

The long night was fully moonlit. I stopped once at a shadowy little cross-road shop and bought a small machete, some food, some cigarettes and matches. I did not know one road or path from another, and there were no signposts. But I judged my direction by the stars and kept going until I reached the Caribbean shore. At dawn a small automobile came along the road behind me, a jitney bus, bound for Cartagena. Four hours later I was in Cartegena. I had heard that there were many smugglers working out of the Colombian city, and I went to the waterfront to find some of them. But after two hours investigation I found that each one wanted forty *pesos* ($20.00) to take me to the islands of San Andres and Providencia, belonging to Colombia but lying only a short swimming distance off the coast of the Republic of Panama. I had only forty-three pesos in my pocket—so I decided to hurry on out of the Colombian town and try to make the journey on foot. Between Cartagena and the Panamanian frontier I knew that there was another fugitive from French Guiana, Charlot Gautier, who has escaped in a boat with nine companions, eight of whom had been caught and sent back. An ex-Ensign in the French Navy, he had received a large amount of money from relatives, and, so I understood, had built a lonely retreat in the jungles, and was spending his time catching butterflies.

Gautier was very surprised when I knocked on his door; the last thing he expected was a visiting Frenchman. *"Je viens de là-bas!"* I said the password and only introduction needed between évadés, "I come from over there!" I explained my situation and he invited me to become his guest. "Where there is enough food for one," he said, "there's enough for two!"

In the forest surrounding his home there were hundreds of Blue Morpho butterflies, and with a homemade net I succeeded in getting several beautiful collections which Gautier sent to Cartagena and had sold to tourists. They brought me a total of one hundred dollars—for four months' work. I obtained a good map of the Colombian coast and Panamanian frontier, and began studying it.

To reach Panama would require walking some four hundred miles along the uninhabited coast around the Gulf of Darien, but I decided to push on. I purchased the bare necessities of life, made them up in a back pack into which I stuck my butterfly net, and said goodbye to Gautier. But before I had left the clearing in which his home was situated a native arrived with his mail. In the copy of *La Prensa* I read that my four companions had been shipped on the *S. S. De La Salle* for Martinique—and thence to Devil's Island. One fugitive the paper said has mysteriously escaped! Also, in a copy of the French newspaper, *Excelsior,* which had been sent to him from Paris, I read that my fifth companion, Chifflot, who had obtained money and secured a forged passport and passage from Trinidad to Europe on a German boat, had tried to re-enter France, and had been arrested and sent to the prison depot at La Rochelle to await the next convict ship back to French Guiana.

So, as I struck off alone through the Colombian shore jungles and swamps I knew that all of the men who had escaped with me were en route back to the Dry Guillotine; I alone was free! I made up my mind more firmly than ever to guard this freedom and not allow myself to be caught, no matter what the odds might be against me. At my back now was civilization—and the long arm of French injustice. Ahead of me lay a territory inhabited only by savages.

For five days I walked uneventfully except for having to find my way through a number of swamps. Then the ground became higher and firmer—and suddenly I came to a clearing full of neat thatched huts. Indians, clad only in loin clothes, saw me and hastily grabbed spears and bows. Five men came to meet me as I continued walking. Their faces were spotted with bright red paint and their hands and legs were painted black. One of them spoke Spanish—and with relief I asked to be taken to their chief.

Through the interpreter the chief questioned me. I told him that I was trying to go to Colon, on the Panama Canal. But the chief said that I could not continue. I would have to turn back. The territory ahead of me, he said, was "closed country"—no white man could enter it.

Indians had gathered around my pack, and were examining my butterfly net with special interest. I caught sight of a dazzling blue Morpho and took the net quickly from them and chased it until I caught the beautiful insect. The Indians laughed and thought it was very funny. Then I explained that I wanted butterflies—that I was on an expedition hunting them, and would pay as much as two *pesos* apiece for any which the tribesmen caught. The chief's eyes lighted up, and suddenly he announced that I could stay in the village all night—that in the morning some of the children might catch plenty of butterflies for me. He had a hut set aside for me. Alone I cooked a chunk of wild pig meat which he sent me, brewed some coffee. After night fell I strolled down to the beach—where I had seen many canoes—and then went back to my hut and lay in a hammock which he had loaned me.

I lay silently until almost midnight. Not an Indian stirred. The fires had gone out. Quietly I crept out of my hut and went to the beach. I selected a sixteen-foot canoe which had a sail wrapped around a small mast, and putting several paddles into the hull I noise-lessly slid the boat down the sand and into the water. When the water reached my waist I pulled myself into the boat and started paddling as hard as I could. I knew nothing about paddling a canoe at sea all by myself, and found it very difficult to get the boat away from shore but at last I managed to get one hundred fifty yards or so between me and the shadowy coast. I then kept paddling for almost three hours. I tried once to untie and raise the sail but couldn't make it; the boat was too small for me, inexperienced as I was, to move about in it without capsizing. So at last I determined to land for a few minutes and put the sail up. There was a cross-yard on the mast which I did not know how to use, and it was an hour before I had the sail properly set and the canoe out again in the open water. One thing I knew quite definitely. I certainly was not a sailor!

My hands were blistered from paddling, and now I had all I could do to hold the helm and guide the narrow craft safely over the waves. The wind seemed to play tricks on me and there wasn't a moment that didn't seem to challenge all my strength and ingenuity. I covered only about thirty miles during the night, and when the sun came up I put in to shore. I was afraid to travel during the day for fear that the Indians who by this time had undoubtedly discovered that I, as well as their canoe, was missing, would sight me. The shore was lined with coconut trees and with my machete I opened ten big nuts, drank the juice.

I scanned the horizon continually and stayed in hiding all day. Ahead of me I saw many off-shore islands —the San Blas Keys—and at night when I took to the water again I found that I had to negotiate many shoals and reefs over which heavy rollers rushed. Waves roaring over boulders warned me to keep farther and farther out, and a shark that started to follow and encircle me didn't add anything to my comfort or ease of mind. After an all-night struggle I decided to give up and beach the canoe. I was so tired I fell asleep in the vine-matted jungle and did not wake up until noon. The water along the shore was now full of massive boulders and dashing waves. I knew I could never negotiate the stretch of sea ahead of me. I hid the canoe in the bushes and started along on foot.

I walked for three hours and then saw two Indians on the beach. They came at me the instant they saw that I was a white man, and with many scowls began questioning me. But I understood nothing of their jargon. Again I opened my butterfly net. The butterfly net had acted as a passport for me on the previous occasion. I'd try it again. I showed them the blue Morpho butterfly. They stopped scowling and murmured the word "momorro" several times. They waved me to get into their canoe and I was taken in state to a primitive village—a big settlement at the mouth of a coastal creek. Several hundred Indians, seeing that a stranger was arriving in the canoe, came down to the water's edge to look at me. Many children came, touched me as I stepped ashore, and then fled howling to their mothers.

The chief's hut was immense, 130 feet long by 100 wide. I opened my pack and showed everything to him. Through another Indian who spoke Spanish I said that I was a butterfly collector. Again I spoke of being willing to pay two pesos for any blue Morphos the villagers would care to catch. Women at the chief's command brought me big gourds of food and fruit.

They were the handsomest primitive women I'd ever seen. The men dressed in loin cloths only, but the women wore a nose ring and all had earrings of pure gold in various sizes. About fifty men gathered around me in the chief's house, many of them talking to me in Spanish. They seemed greatly interested in my statement that butterflies were valuable—could be caught and traded for two pesos each.

Toward midnight, when all was quiet in the village I again went down to the waterside, selected a good boat and pushed off. I followed the coastline all night and landed next morning on a strip of land that jutted far out into the sea. I hadn't the strength to paddle far out to sea and go around it—I'd leave the canoe and cut across the peninsula on foot. The going was very difficult, wading creeks and swamps, cutting myself constantly free of vines and thorns. I had to stop frequently and sharpen my machete on a rock. When night came and it was too dark to see I camped. All the next day I cut through the jungle. I saw three jaguars and over fifty wild boars, but didn't dare get in their way with only my machete for a weapon. I listened constantly for sound of the sea surf, but could hear nothing. Again at night I camped. I killed a large land turtle and ate it with the last of my hoarded coconut meat.

On the fifth day of cutting through the forest I again heard the sound of the surf, and an hour later I came out into the sunlight on a broad sandy beach. Several hundred yards out in the blue water there was a large island full of Indian huts. The San Blas Indians were watchful guardians of their coastal domain; as soon as I stepped out of the jungle they saw me, set up a great amount of shouting and running about —and within two minutes five large canoes loaded with furiously paddling men and with other men standing in the bow, with spears and guns, were on the water and coming rapidly toward me.

Again I was taken to the chief's house. Again I showed my butterfly net and my blue Morpho. The big insect now was almost useless as a specimen for it had been handled so much by previous Indians. Again my butterfly net gained me freedom and a place to sleep—and plenty of food. If I had not had it I know that I never would have gained a mile of the San Blas coast, for over a period of many years the San Blas Indians have learned to hate the Spaniards—both the Panamanians and the Colombians. My net set me apart from all white men they had ever known. I was, clearly, not a gold prospector or a slave hunter.

In the next six days I stole six more Indian canoes. It seems almost as if some protecting hand of Fate watched over me and made that feat possible. I know that I could never repeat it. I kept paddling all day, struggling with currents and waves. Then at night I would land on the coast, hide the canoe and walk until I encountered some more Indians. The Indians habitually worked during the day in their coconut, banana, and potato plantations on the coast where the land was fertile, and my technique was always the same. I'd land about two hours before sunset and start walking. In an hour or so I'd encounter some Indians of another island. They would take me to the chief. I would explain that I was hunting butterflies—on my way to the Panama Canal. I would again offer two pesos for insects which the village would catch for me in the coastal jungles the next day—and then at night I would sneak to the canoes, select one and paddle off into the darkness. I had but one single thought the whole time: Colon. Behind me, I knew, I was building up an accumulating number of hostile villagers. Whether they were now combining and coming along behind me to capture me I did not know, but, as though they were right at my heels, I never wasted a moment.

For twenty days I worked along the Panama coast, being challenged each night and having to explain my presence to an island chief. Twenty canoes I had stolen —and then, on the morning of the twenty-first day, I reached the coast opposite the island of Porvenir. On that island there was a garrison of Panamanian soldiers.

I dared not be seen by any of them, for as I was without a passport they would have been certain to send me back to Colombia. I cut into the forest and walked all day, screened from the sea, until I came to a small village of Panamanian natives engaged in fishing and in cutting mahogany. A woodcutter gave me some food and was amazed when I told him I had come through from Colombia. He said that no other man ever accomplished that before. Colon, he said, was seventy-five miles away. But the currents and tides, he warned, were very bad. A lone canoeist would have a very dangerous time.

I continued on a trail which he said would take me to a village of half-caste Indians. I needed another boat. If I were lucky it would be my last night of toil. I did not enter the Indian village but stopped in the forest. After dark I walked along the beach, selected a canoe with sail, pushed it down into the waves and after much struggling managed to get into the hull. I untied the sail and began making good speed over waves bigger than those I had to fight before. Water splashed over me, and I had to bail almost constantly to keep the frail craft from being swamped. After several hours I saw the flash of a lighthouse, and then in a little while the lights of several steamers gleamed on the horizon. On my left the sky glowed as though lit up by a multitude of searchlights. My heart throbbed with excitement. Those would be the lights of the Panama Canal.

Night passed and day came, and still I sat struggling with tiller, sail, and gourd-bailer far out at sea. The wind died and left me to the mercy of currents. All day long I tried to get the canoe under steady headway but it was not until night that the little sail puffed out again and the canoe's bow began cutting the waves. The lights grew brighter, the guardian city of the Canal Zone appeared above the horizon, steamers passed me, several times almost capsizing me in their wake. Cautiously I drew nearer and nearer the shore. I did not want to be stopped or questioned. I headed for a piece of beach some little distance from the town, but the waves and currents were too strong.

One hundred hards from shore I saw that the canoe would be dashed bodily into a jetty. I made up my mind in an instant. Leaning over the side I swamped the canoe with inrushing water and as it went down under me I began swimming, saving only my bundle of manuscript in oil cloth. I had had a terrible adventure. I was famished and my throat and mouth were aching from thirst. But as I gained the jetty and climbed out of the water I saw silhouetted against the sky the fortresses of the United States Government. When the sun rose again I would be able to look up and see— at last—the Stars and Stripes!

Chapter XXXIII

MIND often wins over matter. As I climbed out of the salt water, pulled myself up the slippery steps of the jetty, and slumped in the dawn shadows of a new day, I knew that only one thing had brought me through the terrible adventure. It was not my muscles, for I am very weak. It was not my knowledge of the jungle, or of the sea, for I had none. It was not my experience in dealing with primitive, possibly savage, natives, for they were as strange to me as they would have been to you. The one thing which had brought me through was just this: I kept repeating over and over to myself the sentence "I *will* reach the Panama Canal! I *will* reach the Panama Canal!"

Food hadn't mattered. My days of struggle with the coastal waves hadn't mattered. Nothing had mattered en route—but now that I was, at last, under the big American guns, could look up and see the flag mast on which, at dawn, the Stars and Stripes would unfurl, I gave way completely. I shook as though a terrible physical convulsion had overtaken me. My mind seemed to swim. I remembered looking up at the morning stars and saying a prayer of thanks—and then I remember nothing.

How long I lay there, huddled under the eaves of the wharf storehouse, I do not know. Groggily I awoke in the broad sunlight. A man in uniform was jabbing his toe against my hip.

"Come, Buddy!" he kept repeating. "Come, Buddy. You can't sleep it off here. Get a move on!"

I got to my feet. I swayed as though, as he thought, I had spent the night in a grog-shop. Dizzily I began finding my way through the tin warehouses past many Zone policemen who looked at me and smiled knowingly. Gradually I realized, by the lack of laborers, that it must be Sunday morning—that all the American police thought I was just coming out of a big Saturday payday celebration. I made my way to the French quarter of Colon.

The French quarter of Colon harbors many outcasts of the world. I was fed hot stew and hot coffee as soon as I spoke a few words. A woman took up a collection of clothing from near-by houses and soon I had changed from the sea-ruined pants and shirt, had shaved, and made myself presentable. The Canal train for Panama City left at seven o'clock. Many times during the afternoon I repeated my story to Frenchmen and obtained a few more coins. It was the first time in my life that I had ever begged, but there is no way to get from one side of the Canal to the other save by riding on the American train. I was warned against trying, as I planned, to walk the tracks and bridges. I would be arrested for trespassing on government property.

When I reached Panama City, on the Pacific side, I went to the address of a Frenchman whose name I had memorized—who was a writer and surely would befriend me. But I found that he was away. His servant let me sleep in the storeroom of his house, and fed me generously. I learned that it would be dangerous, if not impossible, for me to continue my way north through Central America immediately. The Costa Rica border, and the western portion of Panama, was being very closely watched due to the fear of an uprising in that part of the Republic over the coming Presidential election. The servant, who was from a western state of the Republic, warned me against trying to go on until the elections were over.

"The Boss," he said, "has a banana plantation in the jungles of Darien. Why don't you go on the boat which leaves tomorrow and rest up there for a while. It's well stocked with food and I'll give you a letter to the foreman."

Thus it was that with only two days of rest in civilization I was again in the jungle. The boat was a shallow-draft bargelike vessel that went out into the Pacific and then up the Yape River, twisting deeper and deeper into the jungle. In the bow a man began blowing on a giant sea shell. I asked why he did so, and was told that he was notifying all the Indians in the villages back from the river that the monthly banana boat had arrived—warning them to have their bananas cut and at the waterside when the vessel came back down the river.

Here and there a painted brown face looked out at us from the jungle foliage, as a primitive Indian waved to the captain in the pilot house and signalled, by raised fingers, the number of bunches of fruit he had ready for market. In the late afternoon I transferred to a canoe with outboard motor attached and, amidst a great noise, we skimmed the twisting river. At sunset we turned in a high jungle bank and after walking through jungles for ten minutes came to a clearing. Three small houses stood on stilts in the fading sunlight. In back of them were acre after acre of banana palms.

This secluded banana grove was just such a place as I might, at other times, have liked very much. It seemed far away from trouble, and the foreman made things comfortable for me. But at sunset many fruit cutters came in and, resting up from their all-day labors, began drinking raw alcohol made from distilled sugar cane. They argued wildly, fought among themselves, gambled—and, as I sat over in my dim corner, I couldn't help but feel that here, far away from Devil's Island, I was in the midst, again, of uncongenial people . . . of riff-raff, of the dregs of human society. The banana workers and the prisoners of French Guiana might have been interchanged and no one would have known the difference. Two men were badly cut in knife fights over the cards, just as they often were in French Guiana. In the early morning I realized that I had come a long way only to get out of a kettle into a frying pan.

But the Indians who came to the clearing were soft-voiced. They smiled when I talked with them and seemed very much interested in my butterfly net. Three of them accompanied me on a hunt in the jungles, and when I caught a giant Morpho they told me, in Spanish, that in their country—in their mountain villages—there were butterflies of even larger size.

They were very primitive, clad only in loin cloth and paint but suddenly I decided that I would much rather stay with them than in the camp of the noisy, foul-mouthed banana cutters. I just kept on walking with them until, on reaching the river, they agreed to take me in their long canoe to the Indian village at the headwaters of a shallow creek.

Thus began for me a seven-month adventure of sheer tranquility, peace, and I suppose you could even call it happiness. The Kuna and Chakoi Indians are called savages. They have killed many white men. They hate the Spaniards, because of their early cruelties and gold thefts. But I passed from one village deeper and deeper into the Indian country and no one raised a hand against me. The fact that I chased butterflies, that I cared nothing for their gold ornaments, that I was not a *patrone* accompanied by an armed band looking for slave labor, gave me, uniquely, an open path into the wild Kuna country. Each village became more primitive-looking as I drew deeper and deeper away from the civilized fringe. Finally after six days of following Kuna trails, being escorted from one village to the other by a dozen or more men, I arrived at the biggest village of the tribe, the village wherein lived the chief. Here every man, and many women, wore heavy gold ornaments, many of them shaped like small human skeletons.

Many of the Indians talked to me in Spanish, but among themselves they spoke in a guttural tongue of which I knew no word.

The *cacique,* or chief, was a very large, tremendously muscular savage who eyed me coldly when I held out my hand. I had been told that if I wanted to live in any Kuna village I would have to get his permission. "Are you willing that I live in your city?" I asked. "I would like to do so."

The Indians who accompanied me began talking, and from the expressions of their faces I knew that they were giving a friendly report of my behavior in the earlier villages. The chief listened to them, then asked me to show him my *momorros*—my butterflies. I opened up the package of dried wings and he gazed at them with long interest and amazement. Then he looked up at me and frowned.

"Why do you kill the *momorros?*" he asked. He said something to a small boy who ran off and returned with a tiny cage made of palm ribs. The chief held up the cage and showed me the little bird held captive behind the woven palm. It was brilliantly feathered, almost as iridescent as a Morpho's wing. "See!" the chief said. "We catch pretty things too. But we put them in cages. Why don't you catch butterflies alive and put them in cages also?"

I explained to him that Morphos had no value alive. It was only after their blue wings were carefully dried that they became valuable for ornamental purposes. This seemed to amaze him at first. Then he shrugged, talked with many of the village Indians for a few moments and said that I could settle down in the Kuna country as long as my behavior was satisfactory. He itemized the things I could not do; I couldn't walk in the forest alone, I must always be accompanied by some man or a youth on my butterfly hunts; I could not dig anywhere for gold; I could not possess gold in any form—or take any kind of gold out of the jungle when I left; I could not bathe in the river naked at the same time that the villagers did. I would have to keep away from the river then and take my bath alone before or afterwards. If I stayed in the village longer than two moons, he said, I must have an Indian wife.

"But a wife is a thing of permanence," I said. "I cannot do that."

"Then you can stay less than two months. A man without a wife is always looking at other men's wives," the *cacique* grunted. "Do you want to stay home all day and do your own work? Without a good wife how will you have time for catching butterflies?"

A soft-eyed woman, barely out of her teens, came up and quite coyly gazed at me. She left the group for a moment and then returned with a gourd of rice and a bunch of bananas. When she held them out to me all the Indians began laughing. Children ran up and began laughing also.

"Yes," the *cacique* said. "This one would be a good woman for you. She's an excellent worker."

The girl was attractive. In that tribe, where women wore only narrow strips of cloth wrapped tightly about their hips, it was not hard to pick out many young women who would be able to chop plenty of wood to keep the home fires burning. But there was no sense in my continuing to quibble. I would very probably need someone to keep house for me, to help me in my new use of purely primitive things.

"By giving you food she agrees to become your wife," the chief said impatiently. "What is your decision?"

"I will take her," I said.

"Good!" the *cacique* grunted. *"Bueno! Bueno!"* many of the other natives chimed in.

"Eat some of the food the woman has brought you,"

the chief directed me. "That is according to custom. That is the public sign that you take her for your wife." I peeled a banana and ate it, much to the amusement of the villagers. Then the chief spoke to the girl in his own language. She stood very straight and respectfully while she listened. Then when he was finished she said a few words, turned and started through the crowd of natives who immediately made room for her.

"Follow the woman," the chief said. "She will take you to the house which we give you for a home."

I caught up with her. She walked through the entire village to a large thatch dwelling raised above the ground on eight-foot posts—with a notched log stairway leading up to the flooring from the ground. The ground under the house was neatly swept. A small dog that stood looking down at us appeared to be well cared for and unusually clean. The girl stopped and stood away from the steps. I stopped also. She shook her head, as though I had done the wrong thing. She pointed to the raised floor and motioned me to climb up ahead of her. I was, I must admit, somewhat a creature of confusion—because of this sudden and unexpected wife-taking—and I didn't watch where I put my foot. I slipped, fell to the ground. With a merry little laugh she began helping me up.

It may well be, for all I know, the first time in the history of the world that a husband was assisted over the doorsill of a new home by the bride!

But that incongruity was to continue for hours and, as I found out, for days and weeks and months. Whose house it had been I did not know. I could not speak a word with her. She blew on the embers that lay on flat slabs of rock until they caught fire again and then started cooking. She had plenty of wild rice. A leg of venison hung from a rafter. In baskets there were *casava* roots, sweet potatoes, squash, corn. There was a big gourd of thick sugar syrup. Several bunches of bananas hung under the eaves. It was apparent that I was going to have plenty to eat. But, only as I saw in a moment, if I did the cooking myself. She seemed to think that the way to prepare dinner was just to toss everything she could get her hands on into a big pot and throw water on top. I reached her before she could drop five big red hot peppers into the concoction. I emptied out the pot and decided to cook the dinner myself. The sweet potatoes I put beside some coals to roast. The venison I cut into two steaks and stretching them over forked sticks, set them against the coals to broil. The rice I put in a small pot to boil.

"You go cut some more wood!" I said with pantomime accomplishment. "I'll do the cooking!"

Many of the village women came up and peeked at me and began giggling. It was a strange sight, to them, to see a man doing his own cooking. I could tell that they were making a big joke of it. They set up so much noise that finally the chief and a dozen or more Kuna hunters came over to see what was going on. The *cacique,* on finding me bent over the fire, seemed very much disturbed.

"What is this?" he said. "Won't the woman work?"

"Very eagerly!" I said. "But she doesn't know much about cooking!"

The chief and his men discussed this with apparent amazement. It was a week later that I learned that she was considered the best cook in the entire village; at all the great feasts, when hunters and chiefs came from outlying villages, she had cooked the ceremonial banquet!

The Kuna Indians are one of the few primitive tribes left in Central America. Although their villages were pillaged repeatedly by the early Spaniards they never bowed under the yoke of the conqueror. Many of them, in order to revenge the wrecking of their settlements by Balboa and Pizarro, the Kunas, as well as the San Blas Indians, joined many later English privateer expeditions, notably those of Morgan against the Caribbean colonies of Spain. And even today, had I been a Spaniard, or a Latin-American, I never could have won their permission to live in Kuna country.

"*Nikat-chipu!*" a woman's voice called shrilly from

the jungle in back of my new home. *"Nikat-chipu!"* So busy had I been with my cooking that I did not notice my "wife's" disappearance.

"It's your woman!" the chief said. "She is calling for you!"

I left the fire and went toward the calling voice. Twenty paces in the forest I found the girl. She was sitting on the ground holding a bleeding foot in her hands—gripping it with all her might to keep the blood from spurting from an ugly wound. A blood-smeared cutlass lay beside her. Splitting firewood by holding it on end with her toe, as most Indians do, the cutlass had glanced off a hardwood knot and sliced her foot. Hastily I tore a limber vine from nearby bushes and made a tourniquet. Then I picked her up in my arms and staggered back through the forest to my jungle home. The *cacique* and the other villagers had gone back to their thatched homes. *"Nikat-chipu!"* the girl whimpered, nestling her head against my neck. *"Nikat-chipu!"*

I had no idea what *Nikat-chipu* meant. But evidently it was the name the Kunas had given me. I suddenly realized, as I carried the wounded girl up the steps of our home, that here I was, far, very far from Devil's Island—far from all civilization, far from all worries, punishments, and the need for escape, with a primitive wife with whom I couldn't exchange a single word—whose name I didn't even know!

Chapter XXXIV

THE white man who takes up his life, suddenly, among primitive people—who goes the whole way, lives as they do, sits at their tribal ceremonials, hunts in the forest with bow and arrow, shares a home with a tribal daughter—comes to feel very quickly that life when undressed of all unessentials becomes exceptionally peaceful. Not in fifteen long years had my days dawned so pleasantly or ended so satisfactorily. The Kuna River was full of fish. In the forest there was an abundance of game. The small burnt clearings produced a large variety of vegetable sustenance. Cotton grew sufficient for all cloth requirements. Tobacco hung drying from the rafters.

Days dawned and came to a close in almost unbelievable peace. It was the first time in my life that I had been really free. I feared nothing. I needed nothing. At last I was a man engaged in merely the pleasure of living. The first week flowed evenly into the second, the second into the third.

At the end of the first week I knew my wife's name. It was *Rachi-ti*. In the Kuna language I learned that it meant "The-Flower-that-Sleeps." Word after word I learned by pointing to some object about our home and then listening to her repeat its Kuna name until I could master it. By the end of the first month we could talk together quite a little. I added to my vocabulary by sitting for hours with some of the Kuna men who knew Spanish.

Rachi-ti cut the firewood, kept the house neat, washed my few clothes, brought in food from the plantations. I fished and hunted, did the cooking, and sewed some new clothes out of the cloth which she wove. I spent many hours in the forest with my butterfly net and my collection of rare wings grew larger each day. One month flowed into another, and Morpho wings mounted up to a fortune of several hundred dollars—if there had been a market available in which to sell them. I was invited to the tribal conferences and ceremonials and sat next to the *cacique*. Like them I painted my face, my chest, and my arms. I wore, as the only sign of my civilization, a pair of pants, the legs of which I had chopped off short above the worn-out knees. I wore a necklace of wild boar's teeth which *Rachi-ti* made for me. The chief's ruling that I could possess no gold evidently did not apply to silver, and many of the tribesmen presented me with silver ornaments, silver wrist bands, rings, and hair ornaments. With my flesh deeply sunburned it would have been difficult for a stranger to recognize me as a white man.

But as the months passed I began to get restless again. I had made a calendar. The elections for the new President of the Republic of Panama were drawing near. As soon as things quieted down it would be safe for me to continue my flight to the United States.

For hours I debated whether or not to continue. What more peace would I ever find than I had now in this primitive sanctuary? What more freedom would I ever have than to live without fear or worry day after day? If I continued I would take on again the trials and tribulations of a life-long struggle with civilization—and against the long arm of French injustice. Thus day after day I debated giving up the thought of trying to reach the United States. But on my thirty-eighth birthday I realized that life in a primitive doldrum was not what I wanted. My past life had been ruined. There was no doubt about that. But ahead of me lay, perhaps, thirty-eight more years. If I could reach the United States I felt that I would be safe. It was the land of the free. They would not send me, who had so much overpaid any debt I owed society, back to Devil's Island. Free of the fear of arrest and deportation I might plead my cause effectively, get back my French citizenship or at least papers that would permit me to live freely and in peace somewhere else. Then I could start building a life for myself—the kind of a life I would like to have.

Between my jungle refuge and the borders of the United States lay thousands of miles of jungles and mountains, and many Central American frontiers. I had no passport of any kind. I would have only the money I could get for my butterfly collection. But one night, as we sat swinging in the firelight in our hammocks, I turned to *Rachi-ti* and told her that when the moon became full again I was going away.

"Do you go far?" she asked.

"Very far," I said. "I may return—and I may not."

"Do you go so that you can catch many more butterflies?" she asked. "There are plenty of butterflies in the mountains near by—and I will go there with you and help you catch them if you like."

"It is not butterflies," I said after a long silence. "I am not a Kuna, *Rachi-ti*, I am of another country."

That was all that was said. She didn't question me further. The next morning I talked with the chief, told him that I'd like some men to paddle me down the river to the trading station on the Paya. He said he would arrange it. There was no word of regret at my going, nor was there any sign that the tribe was upset about the future of *Rachi-ti*. I had nothing to leave behind as a present for her except the household things which I had made with my own hands. I packed my manuscript and a small bale of Morpho wings carefully.

Rachi-ti told me that she would wait twelve moons, to see if I came back. If I did not return by the thirteenth moon she would become the wife of another husband, she said. Sentiment, I had often seen, was not a part of Kuna temperament—and I was happy now that there would be no tears to bring me dark hours of regret later on.

The entire village gathered on the river bank to see me depart. The water was very swift. Five muscular paddlers sat in the slender dugout canoe. I took my place amidships.

"*Ati Nikat-chipu!*" the natives called and waved at me. "*Ati Nikat-chipu!*—Good-bye, White Man!"

Swiftly the current sucked us downstream. The Indians paddled hard to set the bow straight in the middle current. Then we turned a sharp bend and *Rachi-ti,* the *cacique* and all my primitive hosts were shut from view. The river twisted like a great serpent. We shot small waterfalls, negotiated many rapids. Five times we had to portage the canoe over rocks. We camped at night under tremendous trees. The next afternoon we reached the Yape River and found that, luckily, the monthly fruit boat was there, waiting to start down stream ladened with green bananas for the Canal Zone.

Four days later I arrived in Panama City. There I found a curio shop run by an American. He bought my butterflies. On May second, exactly two years from the day of my escape from French Guiana, I left Panama City in an automobile truck which distributes newspapers throughout the interior province of Chiriqui. I slept that night at David, the capital of the gold mining territory, only a few miles from the border of Costa Rica. In the morning I took a train to Potrero, the border town. Unobtrusively I embarked with other passengers. I singled out a native who looked hungry and made a deal with him. For five dollars he would guide me, over infrequently used trails, across the border to the Costa Rican town of Buenos Aires. We started walking. But passing through an outpost settlement we were stopped by two mounted policemen on guard against smugglers. They noted the pack on my back and asked for my identification papers. I had none, so they took me to jail at La Cuesta. The next morning they escorted me back across the Panama border and turned me over to the Panama police who arrested me and took me to the jail at David. The next morning I was brought before the Governor of the province.

I was very frightened. It might be that I would be sent back to Panama City, and turned over to the French Minister. Like the five companions who escaped with me I might quickly find myself back in French Guiana again. I decided to take a chance. I spoke frankly of my desire to reach the United States. The Governor after a while signed a release.

"I don't see how you can get across the border again after having been arrested," he said, "but if you can, good luck!"

His assistant pulled me aside and advised me to go to the port of Armuelles where I would find some Costa Rican smugglers who, for a small sum, would take me on one of their nightly trips up the coast. Before nightfall I was in a dingy café on the Pacific coast, talking with three contrabandists who were about to leave to smuggle into Costa Rica a quantity of Japanese silk shirts. For ten dollars they said they would include me in their illicit cargo. By nine o'clock I was at sea and going along the Costa Rican coast, bound for Punta Arenas, a hundred miles to the north.

Some ten miles south of the port the little boat put in to a sandy beach and the merchandise was hastily unloaded before dawn. En route I had talked with the smugglers, asked their advice about the best way to cross the Nicaraguan border. They told me to engage a horse and attendant and ride four days to the north through the province of Guanacaste, crossing the border at the San Juan del Sur River. It was the first time in my life I was ever on a horse. I rode for four days and then my guide collected his thirty *colones,* approximately six dollars, and told me I would have to go the rest of the way on foot. He pointed out a mountain. "Nicaragua," he said, "is all the other side of that hill."

All the next day I walked without seeing a soul. Looking for a place to sleep, I continued until sunset and walked right into a camp of frontier bandits. They were uncouth-looking creatures, armed to the teeth. I raised my hands as soon as I saw they had so many guns pointed at me. They began frisking my clothes, looking for money. They took every cent I had and then waved me to go on. I went a little ways along the trail and then stopped. For an hour in the darkness I debated the idea of sneaking back over the trail and trying to get my money back. But I had no weapon of any kind so I curled up between the great buttressed roots of a jungle tree and went to sleep.

All the next day and the next I walked, and at sunset came into the town of Managua, the capital of Nicaragua. I sent some collect telegrams from there to Panama City: I explained to the curio dealer that bandits had stolen all my money and asked him to send me fifty dollars against butterflies which I would collect and send to him. Happily within four hours I had money again in my pocket. I bought a few yards of mosquito netting and then started for Corinto by narrow-gauge railroad. Between Corinto and the Honduran border there were many little towns. I got off the back platform of the train, as at each stop police boarded it at the front car on a tour of passport and identification inspection. Then I walked through the station crowd up to the first car and took a seat there. This I repeated eight times before reaching Honduras. Thus I crossed another frontier. Now I was in Spanish Honduras. For eighteen days I walked, over steep mule roads, climbed mountains, went down into deep ravines, passed interminable banana plantations. Everywhere I stopped and asked for a place to sleep, such hospitality as the poor people had was generously given me. Crossing from Honduras into Salvador was easy. I spent practically nothing. A few cents for native cigars. I stopped and picked bananas whenever I felt hungry. But I was continually warned not to try to cross the Guatemalan border. The new regime in that country, under a very strict Dictator, had tightened up on both the entry and exit of strangers. Many passports and special permits were necessary both to enter and to leave that country. Policemen stopped all strangers, even in the city, and asked to see their papers.

A Frenchman with whom I talked advised me to go to La Libertad. He was sending some merchandise there by truck and offered to give me a ride all the way to the Pacific coast. My shoes were beginning to pull apart at the seams. The soles were already worn through. The long ride through the mountains and the frequent stops to let the old engine cool off were no luxury, but I was deeply grateful that, at least, I did not have to walk. I arrived at the port of La Libertad on June 4th.

How was I going to get, by way of the sea, around Guatemala? If I could get past Guatemala, the Mexican authorities, I heard, were lenient. I could go the whole length of Mexico without worrying. I spoke Spanish fluently, and very few Mexicans had any identification papers. I went down to the waterfront to look for smugglers, but found none. There was a freighter, though, at one of the docks loading cargo. It was bound, I was told, for Canada. I decided to attempt to stow away. I went to a native restaurant and ate all the food I could hold. I bought a few cans of sardines. As soon as it was dark I went on board and joined the men who, returning from dinner, were loading the ship. When I thought it was safe I left the group of laborers and walked all the way aft. Back of the room which contained the steering engine I saw a trap door. I raised it and saw below a lighted room packed with coils of hawsers and wire cables. I climbed down into the room and hid behind a big coil of rope. Two hours later some sailors entered the room to coil additional rope which was being lowered to them through the trap door. Then they put out the light, climbed the ladder and shut the door over my head. I was in absolute darkness. The ship's engines started turning and soon I felt the sea-sickish motion of the iron hull as it went up over the waves.

In the darkness I carefully took off my clothes. I knew that if I kept them on I would be filthy later on and that my dirty appearance might give me away. Naked, I spent hour after hour in the black hold until I thought at least two days must have passed. My sardines were finished. I was very thirsty. I decided to go on deck, if it were night, and look for food and water. I climbed the ladder and raised the trap door. It *was* night. Only two yards in front of me was a big dish of food—collected and left for a dog. Beside it was a tin pan of water. The dog was playing with a ball which a sailor tossed him far down the deck. I crept out, drank the water and took the pan of food back into the hawser room.

I did not know how many days went by, for I lived

in complete darkness. Twice I was hungry enough to sneak up to the deck and steal the dog's food and water. Then I heard the ship's whistle blow. We were arriving somewhere—but where? I felt my way to the place where I had hidden my clothes. I took my razor out of my coat and began shaving off my beard. The ship stopped. I heard the sound of winches. I dressed carefully and ascended the ladder. I pushed up the trap-door and climbed out into broad daylight. We were alongside a dock. The landscape against the horizon was marvelous. Great rocky mountains of a yellowish color were piled up into magnificent shapes. I thought we must be at some small Mexican port. I crept to the rail and looked down. At the foot of the gangplank two men in uniform stopped each sailor who left the ship. I couldn't tell what kind of uniforms they were but the men were too big and light-skinned for Guatemalans. I felt certain that I was either at a Mexican or American port. I noticed that the guards only questioned the sailors and frisked them. They didn't ask anyone for identifying papers.

I decided to risk everything on one play. An officer was going ashore. Two sailors were on the bottom of the gangplank. I hurried along the deck and started down the steps. The uniformed men greeted the officer cordially—in English, much to my happiness. I stepped down, opened my only possession, the bundle of papers, and manuscript, as a signal for them to freely search me. One of them mechanically frisked me, felt my pockets and motioned me to pass on without saying a single word. With my heart in my throat, I walked a few hundred yards up the wharf and then came to a grilled gate. On the other side there was another man in uniform. I passed through the gate and again I had my clothes rapidly searched. Then I walked on, free at last on the soil and under the clear blue sky of the United States.

In what state I was, what was the nearest city, how many days I had been at sea, I did not know. I came to railroad tracks. Every now and then an electric car passed me. I kept on walking. A group of laborers were working to put up a telegraph pole. I stopped for a moment. I wanted to ask them where I was but I realized that such an inquiry would sound very silly. Finally I said, "Will you tell me where the car tracks go?"

"What?" one of them said, and all the others put down their tools and looked at me. "What you want?"

"Where do these tracks go?" I repeated.

"To Los Angeles!" the man nearest me said, "To Los Angeles, you dope!"

To Los Angeles! Then I was in California! With a song in my heart I started down the tracks as fast as I could. Two workmen were walking toward me. I decided to ask another question. When they drew abreast I stopped. "Can you tell me what day this is?" I asked them.

"Tuesday!" one of them said. "Tuesday, you dope!"

Tuesday! Then I had been in that hawser room seven whole days and nights! But they had ushered me far up the latitudes—and right into the open air of the land of proverbial freedom. I didn't mind that the workmen called me a dope! I guess the questions I asked did seem, to them, those of a lunatic. But now after twenty-two months of almost unbelievable trials as a fugitive I had come from Devil's Island up through the length of Central America into the United States, alone, and travelling always under my own name. Down through the history of the French penal settlement thousands of men had dreamed of being able to accomplish that feat. *In over seventy-five years not one man had been able to do it!* Some had died in the South American jungles. Some had died in the shark-infested sea. Some took root, perforce, in a Central American Republic and changed their names. Not one other man had made good an escape through the whole of northern South America and the Central American isthmus.

I walked with a springing step. I was terribly emaciated. I had no teeth. I had one pair of cotton pants. One cotton shirt. One handmade cotton coat. A pair of ragged shoes. That was all I possessed. But I was no longer afraid. I entered the outskirts of Los Angeles—the City of the Angels—as happy as a lark.

Appendix

(French original of song on pages 51-52)

Le bronze a retentit. Debout! il est cinq heures;
Les voiles de la nuit couvrent encore l'Oraput,
Les vampires affreux regagnent leurs demeures
Ivres de sang humain dont ils sont repus.
Pour beaucoup d'entre nous réveil épouvantable;
Notre esprit vagabond plane sous d'autres cieux,
Mais la cloche a sonné l'appel impitoyable
Pour nous dire à nouveau de souffrir en ces lieux!

Chacun pour le travail s'arme d'une bricole
Et dans le forêt sombre avance en trébuchant;
L'on dirait des démons, la sarabande folle,
Car l'enfer est au bagne, et non pas chez Satan!
On passe les rouleaux, on tombe, on se relève;
La vase et les chicots, rien ne peut nous lasser;
On ne connait pour nous que ces mots: Marche ou
    crève,
Le bateau mènera de quoi vous remplacer!

Le soleil cherche en vain à montrer son visage,
Mais un nuage épais le cache à nos yeux;
Il pleut, il pleut toujours dans ce pays sauvage,
France, en ces instants nous regrettons tes cieux!
Allons vite au biseau, que la corde se place,
Et chantez, malheureux, pour réchauffer vos coeurs:
Hourrah! hourrah! garçons, la pièce se déplace,
Et glisse sous les yeux des surveillants moqueurs!

Enfin vers le dégrad l'on arrive, et sans trêve
Ils nous faut retourner au second numero
De douleur, de dégoût notre coeur se soulève,
Car la voix d'un arabe a crié: *Roumi ro!**

Derogatory Arab word meaning: "Get moving, white man!"

Ce supplice sans nom chaque jour se repète:
Enfants des vieux gaulois, qu'êtes vous donc devenus?
Les plus forts d'entre nous marchent en courbant la tête,
Pleurez, pleurez forçats, vos coeurs ne battent plus!

And After? . . .

In 1939 René Belbenoit was ordered to leave the United States. Although friends urged him to conceal his identity and remain, he said: "I will not do this thing. This country has been good to me and I will not be dishonest with it." But after wandering through Central America he was so anxious to return to the United States that he attempted to do so in 1941. He was arrested and served a fifteen-month sentence for illegal entry.

After his release he was permitted to remain because deportation to Occupied France was then impossible. He tried to enlist in the U. S. Army but was rejected because of his age and physical condition. He settled down in Los Angeles, married a widow with a twelve-year-old son and went to work for the Santa Fe Railroad. But the shadow of deportation hung constantly over his head. Sympathetic immigration officials tried to delay action on his case, but he once again faced banishment in 1947.

However Congress would not let the matter rest. On the first day of its session that year, a bill (H. R. 4485) was introduced—a matter of six lines entitled: "A Bill for the relief of René Belbenoit." Its text: "Be it enacted by the Senate and House of Representatives of the United States of America in Congress assembled, that notwithstanding any provision of the immigration laws to the contrary, the alien René Belbenoit . . . shall be permitted to remain in the United States in permanent residence."

The reason for Congress's interest? On Isle St. Joseph, the Island of Hell, the roofless punishment pens were being demolished; Isle Royale was to be converted into a deep-water port; more than one thousand *libérés* had been shipped home from French Guiana. The hellish Devil's Island tradition had been broken. For this, René Belbenoit—and his book—could take some of the credit.

BANTAM BESTSELLERS

OUTSTANDING BOOKS NOW AVAILABLE
AT A FRACTION
OF THEIR ORIGINAL COST!

Contemporary Literature

- [ ] BARABBAS *Par Lagerkvist* — NY5671 — 95¢
- [ ] V *Thomas Pynchon* — QY4203 — $1.25
- [ ] DEMIAN *Hermann Hesse* — Q5544 — $1.25
- [ ] NOTES OF A NATIVE SON *James Baldwin* — NY5259 — 95¢
- [ ] THE LAST TEMPTATION OF CHRIST
  Nikos Kazantzakis — RY5716 — $1.45
- [ ] MY LIFE AND HARD TIMES *James Thurber* — SY4091 — 75¢
- [ ] THE IMMORALIST *Andre Gide* — Q5571 — $1.25
- [ ] MAGISTER LUDI *Hermann Hesse* — T5555 — $1.50
- [ ] LOOK HOMEWARD, ANGEL *Thomas Wolfe* — T5860 — $1.50
- [ ] ONE DAY IN THE LIFE OF IVAN DENISOVICH
  Alexander Solzhenitsyn — N4639 — 95¢
- [ ] ALL THE KING'S MEN *Robert Penn Warren* — QY5249 — $1.25
- [ ] STEPPENWOLF *Hermann Hesse* — Q4789 — $1.25

By Aldous Huxley

- [ ] APE AND ESSENCE — NY5468 — 95¢
- [ ] CROME YELLOW — NY4157 — 95¢
- [ ] EYELESS IN GAZA — QY5940 — $1.25

- [ ] LADY CHATTERLEY'S LOVER *D. H. Lawrence* — NY4089 — 95¢
- [ ] OUR LADY OF THE FLOWERS *Jean Genet* — T5606 — $1.50
- [ ] DARKNESS AT NOON *Arthur Koestler* — Q5779 — $1.25

By Jean Paul Sartre

- [ ] AGE OF REASON — QY5301 — $1.25
- [ ] REPRIEVE — QY5791 — $1.25
- [ ] TROUBLED SLEEP — QY5665 — $1.25

- [ ] MAN'S HOPE *André Malraux* — QY4013 — $1.25
- [ ] THE MAGICIAN OF LUBLIN
  Isaac Bashevis Singer — N5930 — 95¢
- [ ] A SPY IN THE HOUSE OF LOVE *Anais Nin* — SY4098 — 75¢
- [ ] THE BALLAD OF THE SAD CAFE AND
  OTHER STORIES *Carson McCullers* — NY4216 — 95¢

Ask for them at your local bookseller or use this handy coupon: